THE ENLIGHTENMENT STORIES REPRESENTED IN THE *SAMGOOK YUSA* AND THE *PRINCESS BARI*

TERRI KIM

Order this book online at www.trafford.com
or email orders@trafford.com

Most Trafford titles are also available at major online book retailers.

© Copyright 2022 Terri Kim.
All rights reserved. No part of this publication may be reproduced, stored in a retrieval system, or transmitted, in any form or by any means, electronic, mechanical, photocopying, recording, or otherwise, without the written prior permission of the author.

Print information available on the last page.

ISBN: 978-1-6987-1140-9 (sc)
ISBN: 978-1-6987-1142-3 (hc)

Library of Congress Control Number: 2022904871

Because of the dynamic nature of the Internet, any web addresses or links contained in this book may have changed since publication and may no longer be valid. The views expressed in this work are solely those of the author and do not necessarily reflect the views of the publisher, and the publisher hereby disclaims any responsibility for them.

Any people depicted in stock imagery provided by Getty Images are models, and such images are being used for illustrative purposes only.
Certain stock imagery © Getty Images.

Trafford rev. 07/19/2023

 www.trafford.com
North America & international
toll-free: 844-688-6899 (USA & Canada)
fax: 812 355 4082

CONTENTS

Chapter 1 Introduction 1

    1.1. The Purpose of the Research 1
    1.2. The Examination of Previous Research 8
        1.2.1 Previous Research of the *Samgook Yusa* 8
        1.2.2 Previous Research of "Princess Bari" 22
    1.3. The Methodology of the Research 47
    1.4. The Sources of the Research 54

Chapter 2 The Meaning of Enlightenment
             Represented in the Stories 59

    2.1. The Meaning of Enlightenment 61
    2.2. The Meaning of *Nirvana* Enlightenment 64
        2.2.1 Comparative Research on the
             Extrovertive Mystical Experience of
             Eckhart and Jitong 76
        2.2.2 Comparative Research on the
             Introvertive Mystical Experiences of
             Eckhart, Ruysbroeck, Jinjeong, and
             Princess Bari 81

Chapter 3   The Enlightenment Methodologies Represented in the *Samgook Yusa* and "Princess Bari" 109

    3.1. The Enlightenment Methodology Represented in the *Samgook Yusa* *114*
    3.2. The Enlightenment Methodology Represented in "Princess Bari" 132

Chapter 4   The Necessity in Gaining Enlightenment Suggested in the *Samgook Yusa* and "Princess Bari" Stories 193

    4.1. Communicating with a Divinity Is Possible ... 195
    4.2. Gaining Spiritual Power Is Possible by Having the Union with the Universal Self or a God 202
    4.3. Offering Salvation Is Possible by Transporting the Deceased Souls to a Higher Realm 216

Chapter 5   Conclusion 245

Bibliography 259

For my mom and grandpa

CHAPTER 1

INTRODUCTION

1.1 The Purpose of the Research

For mankind, gaining enlightenment is like gaining the highest goal in life. For so long, countless religious practitioners, philosophers, literati, artists, etc., have been pursuing ceaselessly on the goal, as many texts suggest. Literature especially expresses mankind's long-cherished desire to obtain enlightenment, among which myths contain stories of figures who could have existed in history and illustrated their enlightenment experiences figuratively; in this treatise, I shall examine seven enlightenment related stories recorded in the *Samgook Yusa* (Three kingdoms anthology of myths)[1] and an orally transmitted shamanic song, "Princess Bari,"[2] to compare their enlightenment experiences' attributes represented in the stories. By comparing enlightenment experiences represented in both recorded text and an orally transmitted source, we can understand the nature of enlightenment in-depth. While studying the above text, I shall introduce other countries' texts, which express the same enlightenment pursuits; thus, I can not only compare

---
[1] Ilyeon, comp., *Samgook Yusa*, trans. Won-joong Kim (Seoul: Eulyu Moonhwasa, 2003).

[2] *Bari Gongjoo Jeonjib* (The complete collection of "Princess Bari"), 2 vols., ed. Jin-young Kim and Tae-hwan Hong (Seoul: Minsokwon, 1997).

cross-genre Korean sources but also can compare cross-culture enlightenment experiences to find unique and universal elements in Korean enlightenment experience stories.

The enlightenment stories recorded in the *Samgook Yusa*, many allude to encountering gods or goddesses, the differences being which god or goddess and what kind of mystical experience[3] one is having with that particular god or goddess. "Princess Bari," a shamanic song, also alludes to having the sacred marriage to the shaman god Musang. The Indian Hindu text (i.e., the *Upanishads*) suggests to have the union with one's Self (*Atman*, true ego) and the Universal Self[4] (*Brahman*), whereas Western Christian texts express to have the union with God, although there are figures who voice different aspects of the union. These distinctions arise due to different religious beliefs; depending upon the type of religion, the god's or goddess's attribute is different. In some, the god is in the shape of mankind; in others, nature, the universe, or the universal energy.

In the enlightenment stories in the *Samgook Yusa*, mostly Buddhist stories are represented, and they are symbolically or metaphorically indicated that the true meaning of the stories is difficult to understand. Moreover, the enlightenment stories

---

[3] Mystical experience is referring to one who is experiencing a god or a goddess or divine elements.

[4] Swami Paramananda, who translated and commented *The Upanishads*, said that *Brahman* equated to the Ultimate Reality and *Atman* the Soul or the Self. *The Upanishads* (San Bernardino, CA: Pantianos Classics, 2017). In this research, I will use the Universal Self for *Brahman*, and the Self for *Atman*.

are mostly about Buddhist monks' enlightenment experiences, and nuns' or women's enlightenment stories are rare, and they are mostly represented as the helpers of men's enlightenment. The book includes stories on women who already became goddesses, but hardly represent stories about how women become enlightened and thus become goddesses. In this respect, "Princess Bari" is a good example, in which the story voices how a woman gained enlightenment and became the Goddess of Necromancer.

"Princess Bari" is a shamanic song, but Shakyamuni, who is a Buddhist god, helps Princess Bari survive in this world when her parents abandon her in the sea because she was born as the seventh girl. Then Shakyamuni aids her in entering the other world or the nether world,[5] where she gains *nirvana* enlightenment. In this aspect, the *Samgook Yusa*, which mostly records Buddhist enlightenment stories, can be studied together with "Princess Bari." Princess Bari was born as the seventh daughter, in which the seven signifies wisdom;[6] in other words, she can be deemed to have gained wisdom or enlightenment from the story's onset. However, fully matured or advanced enlightenment is *nirvana* enlightenment, which I shall discuss the meaning in detail in chapter 2. Princess Bari, having the

---

[5] In my research, "the other world" or "the nether world" means the world after death, not inferno or hell. Refer to the *Webster's New Universal Unabridged Dictionary*, 2d ed. (New York: Barnes and Noble Books, 2003), 1290 and 1372.

[6] "The Myth of Er" in *The Republic* refers to number seven as the sun. Plato, "The Republic," in *Six Great Dialogues*, trans. Benjamin Jowett (Mineola, New York: Dover Publications, Inc., 2007), 456. The sun symbolizes brightness; thus, it is deemed to represent wisdom.

resolution to find the water of life for her dying parents, travels to the other world, gains the *nirvana* enlightenment by having the sacred marriage to the shaman god Musang, and returns to this world, revives her parents, and becomes the Goddess of Necromancer.

However, the way Princess Bari gains the *nirvana* enlightenment is not only by utilizing shamanism but also by adopting different religious elements, such as the Buddhist ritual of transporting decedent souls, gaining immortality, scholastic cultivation of Confucianism, the *kundalini* awakening and the activation of *chackras* practiced by Indian Hindu Brahmin, and the ritual of expelling evils performed by the ancient Mesopotamian priests as well as heroism. Therefore, I deem Princess Bari gained the *nirvana* enlightenment through the influence of *poongrhudo*,[7] which has existed since ancient Korea, which accepted and tolerated different religious elements to make society a harmonious living environment.

There are Korean scholars who perceive *poongrhudo* as the way of aesthetic value, but there seems to be consensus among Korean scholars who find the origin of *poongrhudo* to be the ancient Korean national level of rituals performed at the national

---

[7] *Poongrhudo* nowadays literally means "the way of elegance," but its original meaning held more of a religious connotation than an aesthetic value. For example, in the *Samgook Saki* (Three kingdoms historical records) mentions that the way of *Poongrhu* in the Silla Kingdom period was known "to contain three religious elements—Confucianism, Buddhism, Immortality—and which was to edify people." Bu-shik Kim, "Silla Bonki," *Samgook Saki*, commentary by Jong-sung Kim, vol. 4 (Seoul: Janglark, 2004), 73.

holidays by shamans and shamanesses. Based on *poongrhudo*'s origin in the ancient shamanic rituals, we can perceive *poongrhudo* originally embraced mystical elements as well as aesthetic elements. However, as time passed on, *poongrhudo* might have developed more aesthetically than before. The trend of *poongrhudo*'s aesthetic change can also be found in the story variations of "Princess Bari." The first recorded aesthetic version of "Princess Bari" represents sublimeness; but in later periods, it depended on the regions' variations; it changed to humor. A total of fifty-three variations of "Princess Bari" exist all over Korea. The first recorded version is Seoul's Gyung-jae Bae's. There are a total of seven variations of Seoul's version. For this research, I have selected two of Seoul's variations, the Gyung-jae Bae's and Deok-soon Moon's, to examine; both stories' background periods are of the Joseon Dynasty. However, their stories allude to some ancient Korean historical elements. One Korean scholar who contends for such a view is Cheol-su Cho, who claims the archetype story of "Princess Bari" might have formed in the ancient Silla Kingdom period.[8] The reason for his contention is that the main figures of the story, Princess Bari and the shaman god Musang she married to, seem to signify the actual historical figures existed in Silla: Princess Bari, as a woman going to the other world, covertly suggests Queen Seondeok, who enthroned the kingship as a woman; the shaman god Musang alludes to King Talhae, who enthroned the kingship as a son-in-law.[9] If we hypothesize that

---

[8] Cheol-su Cho, *Godae Mesopotamia-e Saegyeojin Hangook Shinhwa-ui Beemil* (Seoul: Kimyoungsa, 2003).

[9] Ibid. Cheol-su Cho alleges the shaman god Musang might be

the archetype story of "Princess Bari" was formed in the Silla period, then the story background period could be similar to the *Samgook Yusa*; even if the Princess Bari story was formed in the latter period, in the Joseon Dynasty, the main theme of this research is examining enlightenment experience represented in different genre's stories. Therefore, comparing recorded text in the *Samgook Yusa* with an orally transmitted source, "Princess Bari," could still be meaningful. In addition, the Princess Bari story is composed of ancient cultural elements; thus, comparing both stories of the *Samgook Yusa* and "Princess Bari" would not be too unreasonable. Dong-il Cho also asserts the importance of comparing both recorded myths in the *Samgook Yusa* and orally transmitted stories that he published comparative research.[10]

Moreover, for the purpose of understanding enlightenment experience stories in-depth, I shall bring other countries'

---

alluding to a historical figure, Talhae, who might have come from the *Seoyuck* (Western region), which figuratively means any regions west of Korea to the Near East. There are two routes to the *Seoyuck*, the northern route and southern route: the northern route refers to any area starting from the far west border of China, which used to be known as the Silkroad. Thus, any country located along the west of the Chinese border was known as the northern route of the *Seoyuck*. The southern route of the *Seoyuck* was the sea trade route starting from any western region of ancient Korea. Therefore, starting from the Southeast Asia to the Near East was considered to be the southern route of the *Seoyuck*. Based on the story of the Seoul's versions of "Princess Bari," it refers to changing the sea into land by shaking an implement given by Shakyamuni, when she walks to the *Seoyuck*; thus, it seems to be referring to the southern route she is taking. Hence, my view of the *Seoyuck* concurs with Cho's opinion.

[10] Dong-il Cho, *Samgook Sidae Seolhwa-ui Theut Pullyi* (Seoul: Jibmoondang, 1990), 229–33.

enlightenment experience sources, which express obtaining the *nirvana* enlightenment or the introvertive mystical experience,[11] as their highest goal; thus, they share similar aspirations to the enlightenment experience stories in the *Samgook Yusa* and "Princess Bari." In this way, I can compare Korean enlightenment stories with other countries' sources and probe into their unique and universal attributes.

Among Western philosophers of mysticism, based upon how they interpret mystical experience, they are divided into several schools. In this treatise, I shall examine two main opposite schools' views: Perennialist and Constructivist. The Perennialist claims all mystical or enlightenment experiences are the same; only their interpretations differ based on country, language, period, culture, religion, etc.[12] The other school, which opposes the Perennialist, is the Constructivist, who argues there is no same mystical or enlightenment experience, and they are all different.[13] Therefore, in my research, I will probe which school's Korean enlightenment experience stories coincide with.

---

[11] Walter T. Stace perceived the *nirvana* enlightenment as the introvertive mystical experience. *The Teachings of the Mystics*, ed. Walter T. Stace (New York, NY: A Mentor Book, 1960), 17–22, 83.

[12] Jerome Gellman, "Mysticism," *The Stanford Encyclopedia of Philosophy* (Summer 2019 Edition), ed. Edward N. Zalta https://plato.stanford.edu/archives/sum2019/entries/mysticism, 4–8.

[13] Ibid.

1.2 The Examination of Previous Research

1.2.1 Previous Research of the *Samgook Yusa*

Previous research of the *Samgook Yusa* have been accumulated enormously in various subject matters. However, the topic related with the enlightenment experience has not been accumulated enough, still less comparing the enlightenment experience with other countries' texts and women's enlightenment experience stories. Therefore, in this treatise, I will examine previous research done upon enlightenment experience in general.

Moon-tae Kim compares several stories in the *Samgook Yusa* for the way Buddhist monks, in pairs, adopt different cultivation methods—Mahayana Buddhism (the Greater Vehicle Buddhism) cultivation method and Hinayana Buddhism (the Lesser Vehicle Buddhism) cultivation method—to obtain their enlightenment.[14] To be more specific, it is about how Nohill-Boodeuk and Daldal-Barkbark, Guangdeok and Umjang, and Wonhyo and Uisang obtain enlightenment by employing different cultivation methods, and how the Bodhisattva, Avalokitesvara, grants them the enlightenment experiences.[15] Kim claims that for mythical figures (i.e., Nohill-Boodeuk and Daldal-Barkbark, Guangdeok and Umjang), Avalokitesvara grants enlightenment experience to the ones who adopted the Mahayana method; but for the

---

[14] Moon-tae Kim, "Samgook Yusa Sojae Daebijeok Inmool-ui Deukdo Yangsang," *Gojeon Moonhark Yeongoo* (Gojeon Moonharkhui) 41 (2012): 294–316.

[15] Ibid.

historical figures (i.e., Wonhyo and Uisang), the story does not express which cultivation method is a superior way in obtaining enlightenment, but it only introduces a variety of ways to acquire enlightenment. Therefore, he concludes that Ilyeon, who was the compiler and the commentator of the *Samgook Yusa*, did not prefer either the Mahayana or Hinayana cultivation method to gain enlightenment, but he only introduced different ways of obtaining enlightenment.[16]

However, I do not completely agree with Kim's view. Yes, Ilyeon introduced stories that symbolized various ways in obtaining enlightenment, but he also covertly conveyed what was his preferred cultivation method in getting enlightenment. This is more apparent when we examine enlightenment seekers not in a pair's structure but in a single person's structure. Moreover, if we consider why Ilyeon chose to conclude the *Samgook Yusa* with stories representing filial piety, such as the Jinjeong's and Daesung's stories, which symbolize Mahayana Buddhism Bodhisattva's ideal, we can be certain Ilyeon preferred the Mahayana cultivation method in obtaining enlightenment. In the Jinjeong story, by utilizing his ability to fall into deep meditation, he understands what decedent souls go through in the other world, especially in the case of his deceased mother's soul. Thus, he helps his mother's soul to be transported to the heavenly realm with help from his teacher, Uisang. Then, in the Daesung story, Daesung is a servant of a rich person, and he hears what Jeomgae, a famous Buddhist monk well-known for his virtue, says about donating to a Buddhist ritual called

---

[16] Ibid., 306, 314–5.

yooklunhui[17] and becomes awakened by it; thus, he donates everything he possesses, and afterward, he dies and reincarnates as Silla's prime minister's son. Then he ends up living together with his present-life parents and his past-life mother; when he grows up, he becomes Silla's prime minister and builds a famous Buddhist temple and stone grotto, the Boolgooksa and Seokgoolarm, for his present-life parents and the past-life parents, respectively.

Both Jinjeong's and Daesung's stories represent what Ilyeon deemed an ideal of Mahayana Buddhism Bodhisattva; in other words, Ilyeon wanted to send the message that a Mahayana Buddhist monk should obtain the *nirvana* enlightenment and endeavor to bring mankind to salvation by transporting their souls to higher realm, just like in the Jinjeong story, and make others perform filial piety to their parents, as in the Daesung story. Ilyeon probably deemed fulfilling filial piety was one of the most important aspects of Mahayana Buddhism Bodhisattva's ideals. Both the Jinjeong and Daesung stories illustrate sons fulfilling filial piety to their parents. Therefore, Ilyeon tacitly conveyed what he deemed the ideal of a Mahayana Buddhism monk representing a Bodhisattva by listing filial piety stories at the end of the *Samgook Yusa*; to put it another way, he is emphasizing that the Mahayana Buddhism monk as a Bodhisattva should gain the *nirvana* enlightenment, should be able to transport the deceased souls to the higher realm, thus bringing them to salvation, and should be able to make others

---

[17] *Yooklunhui* is a Buddhist ritual held to prevent the deceased souls from falling below the human stage.

perform filial piety to their parents. These ideals seem to be what Ilyeon pursued.

Next is Seung-chan Kim's article, which examines the Silla period's most cherished Buddhist belief: "the earthly paradise in Western Pure Land" and *hyangga*,[18] which contains that belief: "Wonwang Sengga" and "Jaemang Maega."[19] According to Kim, there were three kinds of pure lands in the Silla period: Tabang Pure Land, Yongjang Pure Land, and Youngsan Pure Land; of those, Dosol Pure Land (the heavenly paradise), which was the belief in Mireuk Bodhisattva, and Seobang Jeongto (the earthly paradise in Western Pure Land), which was the belief in Mita Buddha, fall under Tabang Pure Land belief.[20] He claims that in the Silla period, belief in Dosol Pure Land, which was the heavenly realm, where Mireuk Bodhisattva was known to live, was hardly accepted, and only belief in Seobang Jeongto, which was the earthly paradise in Western Pure Land, where Mita Buddha was known to reside, was accepted.[21] He contends that this "earthly paradise in Western Pure Land" was combined with the *hwarang* system[22] and evolved into setting up the foundation for the unification of the three kingdoms: Silla, Baekjae, and Goguryeo; then, in Silla, they eventually

---

[18] *Hyangga* are the Silla songs, and they were written in regulated poetry forms by literati in the Silla dialect during the Silla Kingdom period.

[19] Seung-chan Kim, "Silla Jeongto Wangseng Sasang-gua Hyangga," *Inmoon Nonchong* (Busan University) 28, no. 1 (1985): 1–19.

[20] Ibid., 1–2.

[21] Ibid., 2.

[22] The *hwarang* system is like the present-day military.

ended up worshiping Shakyamuni Buddha, Mireuk Bodhisattva, Avalokitesvara Bodhisattva, Four Directions' Heavenly Emperors, and Diamond God.[23] However, Kim argues that right before and right after the three kingdoms' unification, the earthly paradise in Western Pure Land, Mita Buddha worship, was greatly prospered due to the collapse of the Silla's class system and the people's suffering, which was caused by long years of wars among the three kingdoms; hence, Buddhist belief is said to have changed the people seeking salvation not for the present life but for the afterlife.[24] In addition, says he that there were a group of monks who criticized the strict class system of Silla and tried to propagate the royal and aristocrat-centered Buddhist worship of Dosolcheon or the heavenly paradise in Dosol Pure Land belief to the commoner-centered Buddhist worship of Seobang Jeongto, or the earthly paradise in Western Pure Land; the most active figure was Wonhyo, who was an apostate bonze and spoke freely negating Dosolcheon and showing approval of Seobang Jeongto.[25] The following is his reason for negating Dosolcheon:

> There are seven reasons why it is difficult to be reborn in Dosolcheon, and easy to be reborn in Seobang Jeongto. That is, Seobang Jeongto is the earthly realm, and Dosolcheon is the heavenly realm. If one upholds five Buddhist precepts,

---

[23] Seung-chan Kim, op. cit., 2.

[24] Ki-baek Lee, *Silla Sidae-ui Gooksa Boolkyo-wa Yookyo* (Seoul: Hangook Yeongoowon, 1978), 28–54. As referred to by Seung-chan Kim, loc. cit.

[25] Seung-chan Kim, op. cit., 3.

then one can be reborn in Seobang Jeongto; but to be reborn in Dosolcheon, one has to uphold ten goodnesses.

By calling ten of Buddhas or Bodhisattvas, one can go to Seobang Jeongto, but to go to Dosolcheon, one has to commit a whole life of devotion to religious austerities...[26]

Therefore, Wonhyo claimed that to go to Dosolcheon or the heavenly paradise in Dosol Pure Land, one had to live in religious austerities one's whole life, like Buddhist monks; but to be able to go to Seobang Jeongto or the earthly paradise in Western Pure Land, one just needs belief in Buddha or Bodhisattva. In this instance, Wonhyo was trying to propagate Buddhism to common people, so he made it easy to accept Buddhism by making its threshold of the earthly paradise in Western Pure Land to be suitable for everyone so that people could believe anyone could go there if they had firm faith in Buddhism. However, it is conspicuous that being able to go to the heavenly paradise, Dosolcheon, is the result of a higher level of religious devotion.

Seung-chan Kim's article reviews different types of Buddhism worshiped in the Silla period. Before Silla unified the three kingdoms, Buddhist belief that Mireuk descended to the earth was upheld, and its belief contributed to Silla unifying the three kingdoms. After Silla unified the three kingdoms,

---

[26] Wonhyo's "Yooshim Anlarkdo," as quoted by Seung-chan Kim, op. cit., 4. (The translation is mine.)

people worshiped Mita Buddha's earthly paradise in Western Pure Land, which pursued salvation in the afterlife rather than the present life; *hyangga,* which he examines in the article, well reflected these changes in Buddhist belief accordingly.

The following article is "Women's Images Denoted in the *Samgook Yusa*" by Seon-gyung Choi. She reviews six pieces of *hyangga* and their related stories by dividing them into two types: one type of *hyangga* consists of "Seodongyo," "Heonhwaga," and "Cheoyongga," which denote women's perfection symbolized by beauty; and the other type of *hyangga,* "Jaemang Maega," "Wonwang Sengga," and "Docheonsu Daebiga," in which perfection is symbolized by goodness.[27] In her article, I shall examine only the latter type of woman, whose goodness symbolizes Bodhisattvas, who help others to achieve enlightenment or help others to fulfill their wishes. Choi also perceives in the *Samgook Yusa,* there is not much story about women obtaining enlightenment themselves but effectuating the role of helping men achieve enlightenment.[28] However, she claims that women playing the role of Bodhisattvas, helping men to achieve their enlightenment, have much progress in women's status in Silla society compared to the early period of Indian Buddhism; and she views this as the unique feature of Silla Buddhism.[29] Dae-hyung Lee also asserts that unlike other countries' Buddhist tales, the Silla Buddhist stories

---

[27] Seon-gyung Choi, "Women's Images Denoted in the *Samgook Yusa,*" *Hangook Gojeon Yeosung Moonhark Yeongoo* (Hangook Gojeon Yeosung Moonharkhui) 16 (2008): 351–78.

[28] Ibid., 367.

[29] Ibid.

represent women conducting as a symbol of Avalokitesvara and, as mothers of well-known Buddhist monks, are quite a positive aspect of Silla Buddhism.[30] I agree with both Choi's and Lee's opinions. For sure in Silla Buddhism, the role of women effecting as Bodhisattvas was highly promoted in comparison to the early period of Indian Buddhism, which was the Hinayana (the Lesser Vehicle Buddhism) tradition that their practices were mainly based on meditation; thus, the Indian Buddhists viewed women were biologically different from men because their function in society was to produce their progeny, and they thought the women's main function brought about obstacles in pursuing their enlightenment. However, Silla Buddhism was the Mahayana (the Greater Vehicle Buddhism) tradition, in which Bodhisattvas (i.e., Avalokitesvara) achieved the major role in helping men to obtain enlightenment. Therefore, women being perceived as the avatars of Avalokitesvara were of a highly promoted status in Silla society. This was due to the arrival of Bodhisattva belief in Silla Buddhism. In other words, Mahayana Buddhism, which upholds Bodhisattvas as the ideal figures to look upon as a role model of greatly enlightened beings, and also who can grant the others to achieve enlightenment, played a major role in promoting the women's status in the Silla period. As in the stories of Nohill and Daldal, Gwangdeok and Umjang, Wonhyo and Uisang, they all denote women as the avatars of Avalokitesvara or as Bodhisattva herself, who helps men obtain enlightenment. This was only possible because the Bodhisattva

---

[30] Dae-hyung Lee, "Samgook Yusa-ae Natanan Mosung-ui Hyungsanghwa," *Hangook Gojeon Yeosung Moonhark Yeongoo* (Hangook Gojeon Yeosung Moonharkhui) 14 (2007): 86.

belief existed in Silla Buddhism. In early Indian Buddhism, there was no Bodhisattva belief; thus, women's status in society was not as promoted as in Silla Buddhist society.

Choi also argues that in "Jaemang Maega," which connotes Wolmyung's deceased sister's soul transported to the earthly paradise in Western Pure Land, while her brother, Wolmyung, was performing a Buddhist ritual for her, it was a very rare phenomenon for a woman's soul to go to paradise in Silla society.[31] The reason for her point of view is based on the opinion of other scholars who perceive Wolmyung's deceased sister's soul being transported to paradise is mostly credited to Wolmyung's efficacy in performing the Buddhist ritual done for her, and credited not to his deceased sister's soul being cultivated in Buddhism while alive; thus, Choi questions if Wolmyung's deceased sister did not cultivate Buddhism while alive, whether Wolmyung would still be able to transport her soul to paradise in Western Pure Land.[32] Choi contends that no matter how powerful Wolmyung's efficacy was in the Buddhist ritual, if Wolmyung's deceased sister did not cultivate Buddhism while she was alive, it would be impossible for Wolmyung to make her soul be transported to paradise in Western Pure Land.[33]

Then there are many other scholars who argue different viewpoints on Wolmyung's deceased sister's soul being transported to the earthly paradise in Western Pure Land. For

---

[31] Seon-gyung Choi, op. cit., 367.

[32] Ibid., 368.

[33] Ibid.

example, Ho-gyung Sung analyzes "Jaemang Maega" with a new interpretation and speculates that Wolmyung's deceased sister seemed to be "merely a confused being who could not shake off the fear of death and reincarnation" and "could not accept her facing death and left this world without even saying farewell to her brother, Wolmyung"; but her soul was transported to a good place because Wolmyung performed a painstaking Buddhist ritual for her.[34] Thus, he gives all credit to Wolmyung's efficacy in performing the Buddhist ritual of transporting her soul to paradise. Another scholar, Pyung-hwan Cho, has a similar view but with a little different nuance. He perceives what Wolmyung's sister feared on her death does not particularly pertain to her alone, but it pertains to all other mankind who have not gained the *nirvana* enlightenment; they would face the same fear on death; therefore, the fear she faced on her death was due to her not yet reaching the *nirvana* enlightenment.[35] The different views about the issue of how Wolmyung's deceased sister could have been able to go to paradise in Western Pure Land can be argued in two aspects: the one is Wolmyung's efficacy in performing the Buddhist ritual to transport the deceased soul is the most crucial, regardless of Wolmyung's deceased sister's Buddhist virtue was cultivated while she was alive. The other is that both Wolmyung's efficacy as well as his sister's Buddhist virtue cultivation are equally

---

[34] Ho-gyung Sung, "Jaemang Maega-ui Shi Saegae," *Googer Gookmoonhark* (Googer Gookmoonharkhui) no. 143 (2006): 274–75, 284–85.

[35] Pyung-hwan Cho, "Mita Sasang-gua Hyangga," *Gyeorae Ermoonhark* (Geongookdae Googer Gookmoonhark Yeongoohui) 19 (1995): 365.

important. Hence, Korean scholars are divided in these two aspects.

The Jinjeong story shares a similar issue as "Jaemang Maega." In the story, Jinjeong's deceased mother's soul is said to be transported to the heavenly realm. Choi asserts it was possible because of not only Jinjeong's efficacy in Buddhist rituals but also because his mother lived a virtuous life and made her son a Buddhist monk.[36] I agree with her point of view that both Jinjeong's efficacy in the ritual and Jinjeong's mother's pious living, with combined efforts, resulted in her soul being transported to the heavenly realm, which was not just a one-sided effort. However, in "Jaemang Maega," Wolmyung's deceased sister is connoted to be transported to the earthly paradise in Western Pure Land, and in the Jinjeong story, his mother to the heavenly realm. As aforementioned, says Choi that as a woman, Wolmyung's deceased sister being transported to the earthly paradise in Western Pure Land is very rare,[37] still less for Jinjeong's deceased mother to the heavenly realm. In a previous example of what Wonhyo mentioned about how difficult it would be to go to Dosolcheon, the heavenly realm, from which it is said that one had to cultivate one's whole life as a Buddhist monk, devoting oneself to religious austerities was needed. Nevertheless, in the Jinjeong story, his mother, a secular Buddhist devotee, is said to be reborn in the heavenly realm. I deem this has to do with what Jinjeong and his teacher Uisang pursued. So to speak, it can be perceived that Jinjeong's

---

[36] Seon-gyung Choi, op. cit., 368 and footnote 26.
[37] Ibid., 367.

deceased mother's soul transportation to the heavenly realm symbolized what Jinjeong endeavored to achieve. Wonhyo's pursuit of paradise in Western Pure Land, which is the earthly realm, was rather an exception to a religious figure who devoted a whole life to pious living. It seems natural for other religious devotees (i.e., Buddhist monks and nuns) to pursue Dosolcheon or paradise in the heavenly realm.

The other reason how Jinjeong's deceased mother was transported to the heavenly realm had to do with Ilyeon's pursuit. Ilyeon deemed carrying out filial piety to parents as a necessary duty and viewed motherhood as the same as Bodhisattva having compassion for mankind. There are also other scholars who perceived motherhood as the ideal world pursued by Ilyeon.[38] In the Jinjeong story, he endeavored to transport his deceased mother to the heavenly realm. He accomplished his duty of filial piety to his deceased mother with the help of his teacher, Uisang.[39] Jinjeong's mother was a devout Buddhist who had awakened his son that his attainment of enlightenment was better than fulfilling filial piety at home and had hastened his departure to make him a disciple of Uisang;

---

[38] Gyung-hee Seo, "Samgook Yusa-ae Natanan Hwaumseon-ui Moonharkjeok Hyungsanghwa" (Ph.D. diss., Seogang University, 2004). As referred to by Dae-hyung Lee, op. cit., 84.

[39] Cheol-won Seo, "Hyangga geurigo *Samgook Yusa*-reul Tonghae Bon Sillayin-ui Naesae Guannyum," *Hangook Shiga Yeongoo* (Hangook Shiga Harkhui) 37 (2014): 117; Gang-ok Lee, "Choolga Deukdodam mit Choolga Sungbooldam-ui Chosesok Jihyang Yangsang," *Gojeon Moonhark Yeongoo* (Hangook Gojeon Moonharkhui) 30 (2006): 219. Both Seo and Lee perceive Jinjeong's teacher, Uisang, helped his deceased mother's soul to be transported to the heavenly realm.

thus, she could represent ideal motherhood, symbolizing an ideal Bodhisattva who helped others gain enlightenment. Moreover, Ilyeon might have sympathized with Jinjeong because he was in a similar situation, in which he had to take care of his mother all his life.[40] It is possible he even identified with Jinjeong and himself, and Jinjeong's mother with his mother. Hence, Jinjeong's deceased mother being transported to the heavenly realm could mean for him his mother also was transported to the heavenly realm.

Choi's article is meaningful in focusing on women's abilities to surface when their abilities were hidden and did not receive much attention in Silla society by analyzing *hyangga* and *hyangga's* related stories (i.e., "Jaemang Maega"). Moreover, Choi's contention in giving credit to both Wolmyung's efficacy in the Buddhist ritual for his sister and his sister's virtue cultivated while alive for her to be transported to paradise in Western Pure Land is an important issue to address. I will analyze further in detail the issue in chapter 4 with Henry More's theory on the nature of decedent souls. The next article to review is by Hae-choon Rhu, who suggests an interesting view on Wolmyung.

According to Rhu, Wolmyung, who composed "Jaemang Maega" for his deceased sister on her memorial ritual, seemed to have worshiped Mita Buddha at that time; and when he composed "Dosolga" for King Gyungdeok, he seemed to have

---

[40] Woon-gi Go, *Ilyeon* (Seoul: Hangilsa, 1997); Gang-ok Lee, op. cit., 220.

worshiped Mireuk Bodhisattva.[41] The reason Rhu claims this is because in "Jaemang Maega," Mita Buddha is suggested at the end, whereas in "Dosolga," Mireuk Bodhisattva is mentioned. But I do not agree with his view because it is difficult to know whether Wolmyung actually worshiped different Buddhas, Mita or Mireuk, so he composed the above *hyangga* with different Buddhas, or he composed with different Buddhas because the subjects of the above *hyangga* worshiped different Buddhas. Properly speaking, Wolmyung mentioned Mireuk in "Dosolga," whose object of the *hyangga* was aristocrats, who worshiped Mireuk; and in "Jaemang Maega," Mita because Wolmyung's deceased sister might have worshiped Mita Buddha. It seems that Wolmyung composed *hyangga* with different Buddhas based on who were the subject of the *hyangga*. Rhu mentions that in the Silla period, aristocrats and intellectuals worshiped Mireuk, who was supposed to reside in the heavenly realm, and commoners worshiped Mita, who stayed in paradise in Western Pure Land, which is the earthly realm.[42] It seems that Wolmyung's *hyangga*'s composition well reflected the Silla period's social, religious, and political environments accordingly. Rhu's article, suggesting several interesting views about Silla's different Buddhist beliefs, is meaningful.

---

[41] Hae-choon Rhu, "Wolmyungsa-ui Hyangga Moonhark-gua Geu Baegyung Seolhwa-ui Yeongoo," *Ermoon Nonchong* (Gyungbook Ermoonharkhui) 31, no. 1 (1997): 426.

[42] Ibid.

1.2.2 Previous Research of "Princess Bari"

A considerable amount of previous research has been accumulated on an orally transmitted shamanic song, "Princess Bari." Most of the research are done with focus on shamanism. However, its story embraces several religious elements besides shamanism (i.e., Buddhism, immortality, Confucianism, Hinduism, and the ancient Mesopotamian purification ceremony) as well as heroism. Therefore, I deem "Princess Bari" has been influenced by *poongrhudo*, which has existed since ancient Korea; moreover, the way Princess Bari gains the *nirvana* enlightenment, thus she becomes the Goddess of Necromancer, is deemed to be by adopting *poongrhudo*. Nevertheless, not much research has been done with the perspective of her getting the *nirvana* enlightenment compared with other enlightenment texts, nor in the aspect of *poongrhudo*. Hence this research could serve a new outlook on the way we understand "Princess Bari."

In 1937, the first recorded version of "Princess Bari," the Seoul Gyung-jae Bae's, was recorded in the *Joseon Moosok-ui Yeongoo* (The research of Joseon's shamanism) by Japanese scholars Jeoksong Jisung and Chu Yeopgang; in 1966, Tae-gon Kim published research on collected "Princess Bari" in the *Hwangcheon Mooga Yeongoo* (The research of Hwangcheon's shamanic song), after which it attracted many Korean scholars' interests on the source.[43] In the 1980s, Hangook Jeongshin Moonhark Yeongoowon published the *Hangook Goobi Moonhark*

---

[43] *Bari Gongjoo Jeonjib* (The complete collection of "Princess Bari"), 2 vols., ed. Jin-young Kim and Tae-hwan Hong (Seoul: Minsokwon, 1997), 1: 11.

Daegae (The compendium of Korean orally transmitted literature), which listed "Princess Bari" variations from all over Korea; in 1997, when the *Bari Gongjoo Jeonjib* (The complete collection of "Princess Bari") was published, the editors Jin-young Kim and Tae-hwan Hong suggested that "Princess Bari" needs to be researched within the context of the actual shamanic ritual called "Ogoo Goot" to understand it in-depth; so Princess Bari's role could be understood in more context of a whole ritual performance.[44] In 2004, Heon-seon Kim published an article about a close relationship between "Princess Bari" and the actual shamanic ritual called "Jin Ogui Goot"; hence, it became possible to understand the role Princess Bari plays in the actual ritual.[45]

Moreover, another Korean literature scholar, Dae-seok Seo, examined literary aspects of "Princess Bari" (i.e., literariness of the shamanic song, historical aspects of orally transmitted literature, etc.) by studying all different variations, then by analyzing their distinctions, he divided the songs into their constructive aspects and the aesthetic categories.[46] In his examination on constructive aspects, he claims that the Seoul versions are based on consistent logic, constructed with the cause-and-effect, and between plots, a taboo and prepared subplot exist; thus, they articulate a carefully planned

---

[44] Ibid., 52.

[45] Heon-seon Kim, "Bari Gongjoo-ui Yeosung Shinhwajeok Sunggyuck Yeongoo," *Jonggyo-wa Moonhwa* (Jonggyo Moonjae Yeongooso, Seoul University) no. 1 (2004): 21–84.

[46] Dae-seok Seo, "Bari Gongjoo Yeongoo," *Hangook Mooga-ui Yeongoo* (Seoul: Moonhark Sasangsa, 1997), 200, 219.

construction.[47] For example, when Princess Bari's parents ask a diviner when would be a good day to get married,

> If you marry this year
> you will have seven princesses.
> If you marry next year
> you will have three princes.[48]

The diviner tells them this year is not a good year to get married because they will have seven daughters instead of sons; but they could not wait till the following year, so they get married, not listening to the diviner's advice. Seo claims that Princess Bari's parents committed a taboo by getting married in a prohibited year, thus, they have seven daughters; then, says he that there are prepared subplots to overcome taboo.[49] When Princess Bari's mother is pregnant with the princess, she has an auspicious dream, which signifies the baby in her womb could be a prince; hence, her parents ignore completely what the diviner had said before and try to pray for a prince by committing good deeds for people.[50] However, they have the seventh daughter; but the daughter appears to be extraordinary, perhaps due to good deeds and prayers performed on behalf of her thinking she was a prince before she was born. Seo contends that Princess Bari, born as an extraordinary figure,

---

[47] Ibid., 220.

[48] Jin-young Kim and Tae-hwan Hong, ed., "Seoul, Gyung-jae Bae's," *Bari Gongjoo Jeonjib*, 2 vols. (Seoul: Minsokwon, 1997), 1: 118.

[49] Dae-seok Seo, op. cit., 220.

[50] Kim and Hong, "Seoul, Gyung-jae Bae's," 129.

is the prepared subplot to overcome taboo.⁵¹ Nevertheless, Princess Bari's father could not control his rage for having the seventh daughter, so he abandoned her. Here again Seo asserts that Princess Bari's father commits another taboo because the princess's apparent extraordinariness could be the sign of her having a streak of god's touch, yet he ignores that element and throws her away in the sea.⁵² Subsequently, the princess's parents' committing taboos to cause them to get to deathbeds, and the only way to regain life is by finding the abandoned princess and letting her find the water of life for them. Seo perceives that this is another prepared subplot to overcome their taboos.⁵³ Therefore, he contends that the Seoul variations of "Princess Bari" are constructed repeatedly with "taboo given—taboo committed—result—prepared subplots to overcome result"; hence, he finds in the Princess Bari story, some common constructive elements with the North American Indian folktales.⁵⁴

Next, Seo examines the aesthetic category of "Princess Bari." He argues that the Seoul variations are expressed in part heroic aesthetic but, on the whole, sublime aesthetic: the dream of which her parents have in conception of the princess symbolizes her extraordinariness; regardless of that, the king first abandoned her in the palace back garden, then birds fly over

---

⁵¹ Dae-seok Seo, op. cit., 221.

⁵² Ibid.

⁵³ Ibid., 222.

⁵⁴ Alan Dundes, "Structural Typology in North American Indian Folktales," *The Study of Folklore* (Englewood Cliffs: Prentice Hall, 1965), 206-65. As referred to by Dae-seok Seo, op. cit., 222.

to her and protect her with their wings, which signifies her life would be heroic and mythical, yet she is thrown into the sea, which is tragic.[55] Then Seo views Princess Bari going to the other world to find the water of life to resuscitate her parents and ends up marrying the shaman god Musang and bears seven sons as something tragic; however, says he that she finds the water of life, returns to this world and revives her parents; such motives denote the whole story as a sublime aesthetic.[56] Moreover, he claims that the Seoul and Jeonnam variations articulate sublime aesthetic, and the east coast Gyungbook variations include both sublime and humor.[57]

Next Seo scrutinizes the literary-historical aspect of "Princess Bari" with Saint King Dongmyung, who was a mythical hero, and Choong-ryul Yu, who was a novel hero; Seo finds "Princess Bari" stands in the middle of these figures.[58] However, he contends that when he compares Princess Bari with Saint King Dongmyung, she can be seen as a subordinate heroine because her struggle began due to her parents' need, not hers, whereas Saint King Dongmyung's struggle arose due to his power increase, which signified he was the main hero of

---

[55] Dae-seok Seo, op. cit., 227-8; the reason birds were protecting the baby princess Bari with their wings is considered heroic because the motif is similar to the myth of the Goguryeo Kingdom founder, the Saint King, Dongmyung.

[56] Ibid., 228.

[57] Ibid., 228-36.

[58] Ibid., 244; Hwa-gyung Kim perceives the Princess Bari story as an adopted heroic story construction. *Saegae Shinhwa sokui Yeosungdeul* (Seoul: Dowon Media, 2003), 295.

the story; furthermore, Princess Bari's struggle was based on filial piety, and at the end of the story, she receiving the goddess gratuity from her parents for her deed of reviving them, which was a similar motif to a hero accepting a political position for his deed performed.[59] I do not agree with Seo's point of view on this matter. Princess Bari began her struggle for filial piety, but she gained the *nirvana* enlightenment while getting the water of life, and she became the Goddess of Necromancer. So the beginning of her struggle started for her parents, but after she acquired the *nirvana* enlightenment, she changed from a subordinate heroine to the main heroine. Especially, at the end of the story, when her father asks her how to repay her deed, he suggests very secular payments.

> Do you want half of the country?
> Do you want all textiles coming from the whole country?
> I can not hold the country, so what is the meaning?
> I can not hold the textiles, so what is the meaning?
> I was not brought up under your protection.
> And I did not have a good life.
> I would rather become the king of shamanesses.[60]

Princess Bari now gained sacredness and became the goddess, so secular richness has no meaning. She completely emancipated from secular glory that the meaning of "subordinate heroine" has no place in her stage. She is at the

---

[59] Dae-seok Seo, op. cit., 244, 247.

[60] Kim and Hong, "Seoul, Gyung-jae Bae's," 145-6.

stage where she transcended everything, so what is the meaning of secular limitation (i.e., richness, political power, etc.)? These have no place in her stage.

Thereafter, Seo analyzes Princess Bari's transcendental ability by comparing her with Saint King Dongmyung. He contends that Princess Bari can wield metal batons for space contraction even without learning how to use it; and this was the same instance of Saint King Dongmyung, who became a figure like the God of Archery even without learning the art of archery.[61] In the story, Princess Bari having a superior ability is suggested when it says that she knows how to read even without learning at the age of eight or nine. But I wonder if she did not learn anything while she was growing up with her foster parents. Most of all, where she lived with her foster parents was a deep mountain, where ordinary people could not find them.

> Chanting Amita Buddha, entered the Daesang area.
> Biri Gongdeok Grandpa and Grandma say,
> Are you human beings or ghosts?
> Even bugs and birds cannot enter here.
> Why did you come?[62]

In a place like this, deep in the mountain, most living beings, even bugs, cannot enter where she grew up. People who live in a deep mountain are usually into spiritual cultivation, like Buddhist monks and nuns. Biri Gongdeok grandpa and

---

[61] Dae-seok Seo, op. cit., 246.

[62] Kim and Hong, "Seoul, Gyung-jae Bae's," 138.

grandma are a couple, so definitely they are not a Buddhist monk and nun. But considering they live in a deep mountain without possessing anything, which suggests they might have been a shaman and a shamaness or into some kind of spiritual cultivation.[63] When Princess Bari asks them about her natural parents, they tell her that her father is the king bamboo tree in Jeollado, and her mother is the quince tree in the backyard.[64] I wonder why they said that her parents were trees. Princess Bari did not believe their answer completely, but she visited the quince tree in the backyard three times a day, and she could not visit the king bamboo tree because it was located too far away.[65] This story element reminds me of worshiping trees as a god in ancient shamanism; hence, I wonder whether this refers to Princess Bari receiving some kind of shamanism training while she was growing up there. Moreover, when she leaves to the other world, she carries metal implements (i.e., metal baton, metal backpack) and wears metal shoes.[66] According to Heon-seon Kim, carrying these metal implements suggests she is the one who could visit the other world.[67] Examining this part of the story, when Princess Bari goes to the other world looking for the water of life, she already had some kind of

---

[63] Hwa-gyung Kim, op. cit., 295. Kim perceives where Princess Bari lived with her foster parents was like *Seongyung* (paradise in Daoist terms).

[64] Kim and Hong, "Seoul, Gyung-jae Bae's," 135.

[65] Ibid.

[66] Jin-young Kim and Tae-hwan Hong, ed., "Seoul, Deok-soon Moon's," *Bari Gongjoo Jeonjib*, 2 vols. (Seoul: Minsokwon, 1997), 1: 167.

[67] Heon-seon Kim, op. cit., 31.

transcendental ability and was ready because she had some sort of shamanism training; thus, she was fully equipped to go to the other world, just like Inanna in ancient Mesopotamia said that she descended to the nether world although she was the queen of heaven.[68] Inanna, being the queen of heaven, which suggested she possessed supernatural power, went down to the nether world with confidence. In the same way, we can perceive Princess Bari could have left to the other world fully equipped with metal paraphernalia, or as a general with metal armor on, which alluded mental readiness; furthermore, it is possible to view she was prepared because she had shamanism training or some other kind of spiritual cultivation.

Seo claims that the shamanic song "Princess Bari," as an orally transmitted epic, has not been long since it was recorded; therefore, while it has been orally transmitted, several different elements have been incorporated into the song: when we examine it in a literary-historical aspect, considering the song as an epic means, says he, it is "generally known to be positioned in the middle of myth and novel"; and in the case of "Princess Bari," it also falls into the same position; hence, this Korean source deems to coincide with other general views.[69] However, I perceive "Princess Bari" is syncretized with several religious elements, which was possible due to the influence of *poongrhudo* that has existed since ancient Korea. This is one unique characteristic of Korean literature since such complex

---

[68] Samuel Noah Kramer, *Sumerian Mythology: A Study of Spiritual and Literary Achievement in the Third Millennium B.C.*, rev. ed. (Philadelphia: University of Pennsylvania Press, 1972), 83–96.

[69] Dae-seok Seo, op. cit., 247.

mixtures of different religious elements cannot be found in other countries' sources. There has been so much research accumulated on the Princess Bari story, but I have yet to find any research focused on *poongrhudo*.

Moreover, Princess Bari becoming the Goddess of Necromancer by marrying the shaman god Musang is well-known; nevertheless, how her sacred marriage to the god is related to her gaining sacredness is not much discussed in previous research. For example, says Cheol-su Cho, Princess Bari's story can be regarded in the category of a human being becoming a god, yet he does not explain in detail how she transforms, but he just mentions that by marrying the god and bearing seven sons.[70] This is the general explanation of how other shamanic myths explain how a shamaness gains sacredness. Therefore, in my research, I shall analyze how Princess Bari marrying the god Musang is related to her gaining sacredness.

Another Korean scholar who inquires into how Princess Bari becomes sacred by marrying the god Musang in detail is Hwan-hee Kim.[71] He analyzes it with Jung's theory of Individuation, which signifies the process of a person becoming sacred; in other words, in the theory, Jung perceived the mind of masculine element and feminine element united to become a whole and complete condition.[72] However, Kim focuses on

---

[70] Cheol-su Cho, op. cit.

[71] Hwan-hee Kim, "The Shamanist Myth of 'Princess Bari' and Its Western Counterparts: A Comparative Study of the Tales of the Water of Life," *Comparative Korean Studies* 10, no. 1 (2002).

[72] C. G. Jung, *The Redbook*, ed. Sonu Shamdasani (New York: W. W.

"the sacred marriage" in more of a physiological condition than a psychological condition and perceives the condition as having physically both maleness and femaleness, but Jung focused upon the psychological aspect of femininity and masculinity having the union to become a whole person. This approach is more appropriate because when a person gains sacredness, the maleness and femaleness of physical sexuality disappears and only the sacred mentality remains. If I interpret the mind of maleness and femaleness as being united to become a whole person from an Indian Hinduism perspective, it is like the god Shiva and goddess Shakti having the union to make the complete condition.

I deem Princess Bari gained sacredness by marrying the shaman god Musang. Still she achieves sacredness by utilizing how Indian Hindu Brahmins gain sacredness by having the union in their s*ahasrara chakra* (the crown of the head) with a god or a goddess (i.e., the union between Shiva and Shakti);[73] and she

---

Norton and Company, 2009).

[73] The Shiva and Shakti's union is recorded in an ancient Yoga-related treatise: Yogi's consciousness (known as Shiva), residing in the crown of the head (s*ahasrara chakra*), meets Yogi's life energy (known as Shakti), existing at the end of his spinal cord (known as the k*undalini*), in the crown of the head. This phenomenon is figuratively known as "God Shiva's and Goddess Shakti's union." When the Yogi's meditation practice awakens the k*undalini*, the life energy (Shakti), full of light, residing there arises through his spinal cord and activates six *chakras* along the way to the seventh *chakra* (s*ahasrara chakra*), where Shiva resides, and Shiva and Shakti have the union; in the moment of their union, the Yogi is known to see a bright light that appears to be like a fully blown flower and experiences utmost bliss. Moreover, from the union, the Yogi is known to realize his true Self. Gopi Krishna, *Kundalini*, trans. Ki-cheon Yu (Seoul: Goryeowon Media, 1991), 169–70.

having seven sons symbolizes activation of her seven *chakras* in her body. When seven *chakras* are activated, they could provide some power of energy and efficacies associated with *chakras*,[74] so they could be signifying as having progenies. Therefore, it all depends upon how we perceive one can become a whole, the complete person, by uniting the mind of maleness and femaleness, whether to apply Jung's theory of Individuation or Indian Hindu meditation philosophy; they seem to be different, but they are referring to the same matter. The next article is Heon-seon Kim's comparison of different shamanism-related stories.

Heon-seon Kim compares the Princess Bari story with the Manchurian "Nishan Shamaness Song" and the Japanese "Isanagi Simon" and contends that these stories include a similar journey to the nether world or the other world, which seems to indicate the stories are based on the northeast Asian shamanism.[75] I agree that "Nishan Shamaness Song" articulates typical northeast Asian shamanism. According to Mircea Eliade, shamans have an ability to fall into trance at their will, and their spirits can take magical flight to heaven or to the nether world to get the soul they want.[76] Not only this, said Eliade,

---

[74] There are seven *chakras* in the body. Once their function is activated, they provide some efficacies: for example, *anahata chakra* is located in the heart. Once it is activated, he or she becomes "universal and transparent which causes his or her consciousness to be uplifted even more that all conflicts and contentions disappear"; moreover, this *chakra* is related with love and where the union with a god or goddess takes place. Gopi Krishna, op. cit., 170.

[75] Heon-seon Kim, op. cit., 83.

[76] Mircea Eliade, "Shamanism: An Overview," *Encyclopedia of Religion*

typical northeast Asian shamans can control their protective souls, which usually appear in animal forms; if they cannot control their protective souls, they become possessed by them and become the medium of the souls, thereby they cannot be called true shamans.[77]

In the Nishan Shamaness Song story, the definition of the northeast Asian shamanism is well reflected. She brings Seregudai Pianggo's soul, whose father requested, successfully from the nether world, and it illustrates her control of the protective animal; in this case, a crane is summoned to throw away her deceased husband's soul when he tries to kill her in revenge for not saving him.[78] However, the Princess Bari story does not clearly mention her flight to the other world, although it is possible. It directly tells that she walks to the other world by crossing land and sea. Moreover, Princess Bari is not going to the other world to find a soul requested by a third party. She goes there to find the water of life to revive her dying parents; in addition, there is no mention about controlling her protective animal. Shamans are known to take flight professionally to find a soul requested by another person.[79] "Princess Bari" is about how she gains sacredness or the *nirvana* enlightenment, which is also symbolized as gaining the water of life. Therefore, the Princess Bari story does not seem to fall under the category

---

13 (1987): 201–8.

[77] Mircea Eliade, *Shamanism: Archaic Techniques of Ecstasy*, trans. Willard R. Trask, 2d ed. (Princeton: Bollingen Paperback Printing, 1974), 450.

[78] Heon-seon Kim, op. cit., 77.

[79] Eliade, "Shamanism: An Overview," op. cit., 202–5.

of typical northeast Asian shamanism although there are some common elements: for example, when they return to this world from the nether world, Nishan shamaness learns how a Bodhisattva designates people with different grades based on their *karma*, and how they get to be reincarnated to this world.[80] This element is very similar to what Princess Bari learns on the way back to this world from the other world. She sees several kinds of boats, full of decedent souls, divided by different *karma*; some go to heaven, others to hell, so she learns about the philosophy of cause-and-effect. Another similarity is that both stories have the element of reviving people in this world: Nishan Shamaness revives Seregudai Pianggo, and Princess Bari her parents with the water of life.

In the Isanagi Simon story, Tenchuwoo travels to the other world, where it seems to be India, to find the way to a perfect prayer method, and she accomplishes her mission by meeting Simon there and by exchanging knowledge needed by each other; then she returns to Japan and becomes the goddess of perfecting prayer method and being worshiped for her accomplishment.[81] It is difficult to perceive this story is based upon the northeast Asian shamanism because the story does not connote magical flight to the nether world. It denotes that she travels to the other world with appropriate paraphernalia, just like the way Princess Bari travels to the other world fully equipped with metal paraphernalia.

---

[80] Heon-seon Kim, op. cit., 82.
[81] Ibid., 78.

The Princess Bari story has some unique elements that the other two stories do not have. Princess Bari marries the god Musang in the other world and bears seven sons, whereas the other two stories do not have the motif of a woman uniting with a god. In "Isanagi Simon," Tenchuwoo meets Simon and exchanges knowledge needed by each other;[82] thus, it reflects that they are in equal status. In "Nishan Shamaness Song," Nishan Shamaness throws away her husband's soul when he tries to kill her in the nether world, which alludes to her control over her husband's soul.[83] Heon-seon Kim contends that Princess Bari getting married in the other world signifies how she gains the role of mediating this world and the nether world.[84] I agree that her sacred marriage to the god Musang enables her to go back and forth from this world to the nether world. Nevertheless, I perceive Princess Bari marrying the god Musang and bearing seven sons seem overtly reflective of the Korean traditional ideal that women should get married and bear many sons, although the marriage theme symbolizes how she obtains sacredness. Examining both stories of Nishan Shamaness Song and Isanagi Simon, women do not illustrate having the union with a god in order to be a mediator of this world and the other world. Another excellent example in which a woman does not have the union with a god to be a mediator of different realms is the Sumerian myth "Inanna and Enki: The Transfer of the Arts of Civilization from Eridu to Erect."[85] According

---

[82] Ibid., 82.
[83] Ibid., 77.
[84] Ibid., 71.
[85] Samuel Noah Kramer, op. cit., 65–66.

to the story, Inanna goes down to the underworld to see Enki, who is the god of subterranean water, to make her city prosper, whereupon she impresses him so much while drinking together and enjoying their conversation that he hands over to her over one hundred divine decrees to make her city prosper.[86] In the story, Inanna does not unite with Enki but impresses him with her appearance as well as with her art of conversation. There is also a possibility of exchanging some information upon issues related to different realms. This is rather similar to Tenchuwoo exchanging needed information with Simon to perfect the prayer method in the Isanagi Simon story.

Therefore, the sacred marriage theme in "Princess Bari" is very unique, and it symbolizes the way she gains sacredness or the *nirvana* enlightenment because she gets married in the other world. This sacred marriage is rather similar to the Nohill and Daldal story in the *Samgook Yusa*. In the story, Nohill spiritually uniting with Avalokitesvara is symbolically expressed as taking the bath together. In both Nohill's and Princess Bari's sacred unions, the different element is the name of the god or goddess accordingly to their relevant religions; nevertheless, by getting sacred marriage or united spiritually with the god or the goddess, in order to gain sacredness or the *nirvana* enlightenment, is the same. Once he or she obtains sacredness or the *nirvana* enlightenment, he or she can transport the deceased souls to the other world. Therefore, as aforementioned, Heonseon Kim's claim, of which Princess Bari's marriage to the

---

[86] Ibid.

god Musang in the other world enables her to gain the role of mediating this world and the other world, is convincing.

The next article to examine is Seon-young Yu's research of the Korean view on death represented in "Princess Bari" and other sources.[87] Yu contends that the Korean view on death has existed before Buddhism, Confucianism, and Christianity were transmitted to Korea, and she hypothesizes the Korean shamanist's view on death would reflect the Korean traditional view on death.[88] Thus, in order to compare the shamanist's view on death before and after Buddhism transmitted to Korea, she selected "Princess Bari" to examine the issue because its variations exist all over Korea.[89] Out of fifty-three total variations, she selected the Seoul and Gyunggido regions' variations, which contain the most Buddhist elements, and the Jeollado region's variations, which do not embrace much Buddhist element to compare the Korean view on death.[90] From the comparison, the following are what she finds out about the traditional Korean view on death before Buddhism transmitted to Korea: (1) Although the physical body dies in this world, its

---

[87] Seon-young Yu, "Bari Gongjoo-reul Tonghaeseo Bon Hangookyin-ui Joogeumguan," *Hangook-ui Minsok-gua Moonhwa* (Minsokhark Yeongooso, Gyunghee University) 13 (December 2008): 141–69.

[88] Seok-su Kim, "Cheolharkjeok Guanjeom-aeso Bon Hangookyin-ui Jugeumguan: Seoyang Cheolhark-ui Jugeumguan-gua Guanlyeonhayeo," *Hangookyin-ui Jugeum-gua Salm* (Seoul: Cheolhark-gua Hyunsilsa, 2001): 106–7. As referred to by Seon-young Yu, op. cit., 143.

[89] Seon-young Yu, loc. cit.

[90] Ibid., 149.

soul will transport to the nether world; thus, Koreans believe in immortality. (2) The boundaries of this world and the nether world are not clearly distinguished, so decedent souls can come and go easily. (3) The nether world is not vertically structured, which is impossible to visit, but horizontally structured somewhere in the western region and thus can be visited easily. And (4) death is considered a natural process of going back to nature.[91]

Based on the above findings, says Yu that in the traditional Korean view on death, she hypothesizes the same as the Korean shamanist's view—unlike foreign religions, such as Buddhism and Christianity transmitted to Korea, which emphasize the afterlife through religious salvation—decedent souls guaranteed to have the afterlife without any religious influence are accepted as a natural process of nature.[92] Furthermore, the designation of the nether world or the other world is naturally accepted as the place of decedent souls' afterlife in the Korean shamanist's view on death, although where the nether world exists is not specifically mentioned.[93] Then in the Korean shamanist's point of view, regardless of how one faced death—unlike the Confucian, when natural death is met, could only be transported to the nether world by Confucian ritual—decedent souls can

---

[91] Ibid., 151–4, 156–7.

[92] Tae-gon Kim, "Hangook Moosok-ui Naesaeguan," *Hangook Jonggyosa Yeongoo* (Hangook Jonggyosa Harkhui) 1 (1972): 14; Jong-ui Kim, *Minsok Harksool Jaryo Chongseo Moosok* 8 (Seoul: Doseo Choolpan Woori Madang Ter, 2005), 14. As referred to by Seon-young Yu, op. cit., 157.

[93] Seon-young Yu, loc. cit.

be transported to the nether world by a ritual performed by a shamaness.[94]

Thereafter, she probes into the Korean view on death after Buddhism has been transmitted to Korea as the following: (1) names of gods mentioned in different variations, (2) names of the nether world designated in different variations, and (3) viewpoints of their afterlife. Yu claims that in the Seoul and Gyunggido regions' variations of "Princess Bari," from which they display the most Buddhist influence, the gods that appear in the nether world are Buddhist gods (i.e., Shakyamuni and Jijang Bodhisattva) who help Princess Bari; in the Jeollado regions' variations, with the least Buddhist influence, cranes, angels, old men, and a magpie are the ones that help her.[95] Even with the designation of the nether world, definite distinctions exist between the regions' variations with Buddhist influence existing or not: for example, says Yu, the Seoul and Gyunggido regions' variations, which Buddhist influence exists the most, designate the nether world with Buddhist terms, such as, Western Pure Land, Seocheon Country in western region, *Nirvana*, hell, etc.; in the Jeollado regions' variations, which have the least Buddhist influence, they designate the nether world with traditional Korean terms, such as, Siyang Mountain, Suyang Mountain, Bookmang Sancheon, etc.; furthermore, based on whether the Buddhist influence exists or not, their views on the afterlife also differ by the regions; in the Seoul and Gyunggido regions' variations, which denote the Buddhist influence exists the most,

---

[94] Ibid., 157–8.
[95] Ibid., 159.

people believe in the logic of cause-and-effect (i.e., if one lives a virtuous life, one would go to *Nirvana*); on the contrary, in the Jeollado regions' variations, which have the least Buddhist influence, theirs do not express the logic of cause-and-effect.[96] Then Yu concludes that the Buddhist view of the afterlife has not replaced the traditional Korean view of the afterlife, but rather both have been existing side by side.[97]

Based on these examinations, Yu claims that stories of Princess Bari variations are difficult to clearly distinguish between the time before and after Buddhism transmitted; moreover, to make more specific distinctions between the traditional Korean and Buddhist points of view on death and the afterlife, a good understanding of how "Princess Bari" is performed in a ritual is necessary because its variations have been changing continuously with different influences.[98] This is an important indication because whether the variations have the Buddhist influence or not, where Princess Bari takes decedent souls is different: for example, says Heon-seon Kim, in the Seoul and Gyunggido regions' variations, which have the most Buddhist influence, Princess Bari is known to take decedent souls to the Lotus region, *Nirvana*; thus, Buddhism must have been incorporated on their death or the afterlife views.[99]

---

[96] Ibid., 161–3.
[97] Ibid., 165.
[98] Loc. cit.
[99] Heon-seon Kim, "Jeoseung-ul Yeohenghaneun Yeoshin-ui Bigyo Yeongoo: Bari Gongjoo, Cheon Choong-hee, Inanna," *Bigyo Minsokhark* (Bigyo Minsokharkhui) 33 (2007): 166.

Yu's article is a good source for understanding the difference between the Korean traditional and Buddhist views on death and the afterlife. I also agree with her viewpoint that the variations of "Princess Bari" have been changing continuously with different influences. I deem the Seoul's variations have not only Buddhism influence on the view of death but also other religious influences (i.e., immortality and the ancient Mesopotamian purification ceremony). For this reason, I contend that the research on Princess Bari needs reconsideration. Hence, in this research, I shall examine "Princess Bari" with *poongrhudo*'s influence, which embraces several religious elements in one source.

The next previous research I will examine is that of Cheol-su Cho, who claims that the archetype of Korean mythology is related with the ancient Mesopotamian culture, especially in finding the archetype of the water of life and the herbs of life in the Princess Bari story, comparing it to the Sumerian mythology, "Inanna Travels to the Nether World," which contains a similar motif, is very intriguing.[100] Moreover, says he that a mythical element of "Princess Bari" reviving her parents with the water of life is similar to priests in ancient Mesopotamia performing a purification ritual; and after Princess Bari revives her parents, her parents accept Princess Bari's husband, the god Musang, as their son-in-law, and celebrating them is like other stories, which existed from the ancient Silla Kingdom period with the theme of *"Byucksa Jingyung"* (expelling

---

[100] Cheol-su Cho, op. cit.; for the example text of "Inanna Descent to the Nether World," refer to Kramer's *Sumerian Mythology*, 83-96.

the evils and celebrating the effects).[101] Furthermore, he perceives the archetype story element in "Princess Bari" might have been formed from the actual historical figures (i.e., King Talhae, who was enthroned after King Yuri, as a son-in-law of King Namhae in ancient Silla; and Queen Seondeok, who was enthroned after King Jinpyung, as his daughter in the Silla period).[102] His supposition is very appealing, and the archetype element of "Princess Bari" as the theme of "expelling the evils and celebrating the effects" existed in the ancient Silla Kingdom is very amusing. His research upon finding the archetype element in "Princess Bari" with various cultures' literature sources is very thought-provoking. Hence, I can hypothesize all the more the possibility of "Princess Bari" being orally transmitted with the influence of *poongrhudo*, which accepts different religious elements, and it has been known to exist since ancient Korea.

The next analysis on previous research is about *poongrhudo* specialist Dong-shik Yu's claim of "If one understands *poongrhudo*, then one can understand all three [Confucianism, Buddhism, and Daoism] religions."[103] This claim he based on the record of "Nanrangbi," which was written in the Silla period by Chi-won Choi, who said, "In our country, there is the Way of Mysterious Idea, which is called '*poongrhu*' . . . which includes three religions, Confucianism, Buddhism, and Immortality, to

---

[101] Cheol-su Cho, op. cit.

[102] Ibid.; Ilyeon, "Wang-lyeok," *Samgook Yusa*.

[103] Dong-shik Yu, *Poongrhudo-wa Hangook-ui Jonggyo Sasang* (Seoul: Yeonsae University Press, 1997), 59.

edify people."[104] Yu explains the way of *poongrhu* used to refer to having a mysterious union with a god and a shamaness who performed a dance during the national founding day celebration ritual in ancient Korea; by experiencing the union with the god, she can gain enlightenment, which awakens her mind to have a nature similar to the god; hence, this enlightenment experience can be considered the goal of the three religions aspired to.[105] So to speak, by having the union with the god, one can gain the nature of the god, and thus one becomes sacred; the sacred person behaves with proper courtesy and righteousness, which are common characteristics gained from enlightenment in all three religions.[106] Therefore, says Yu, if one gets enlightened in *poongrhudo*, one can also get enlightened in all three religions, because in religious practice, having the union with the god is the highest stage, and it is enlightenment, which is the same in other religions; in mythology, it is denoted as having the sacred marriage between the heavenly god and a woman who represents the earthly goddess.[107] This is a very similar concept of the sacred marriage Princess Bari has with the god Musang. She gains sacredness by having the union with the god, and afterward she becomes the Goddess of Necromancer. The difference is Princess Bari does not have the union with the god by performing a dance in the ritual, but by gaining the water of life with motivation to revive her dying parents, so she pays the price with physical labor (i.e., getting water for

---

[104] Bu-shik Kim, "Silla Bonki," *Samgook Saki*, 73.

[105] Dong-shik Yu, op. cit., 60.

[106] Yu, loc. cit.

[107] Ibid.

three years, making fire for three years, and cutting wood for three years). Her physical labor could symbolize the purification process of her body being prepared to have the union with the god Musang, or it might be alluding to merits and virtue she needed to accumulate to have the sacred marriage.

The next examination is Sung-arm Hong's article about *poongrhudo*.[108] Hong also refers to Chi-won Choi's remark on "Nanrangbi," in which says, "In our country, there is the Way of Mysterious Idea [*hyunmyo jido*], which is called '*poongrhu*.'"[109] Hong says, "'*Hyunmyo*' is very deep and abstruse," and he explains the meaning of *hyun*, which is the keyword in *hyunmyo jido* (the way of mysterious idea), as signifying "heaven and the main body of the universe; all creatures in the universe's creation, growth, and destruction by fire begin from true nature of heaven, which is '*hyun*'"; therefore, he says that "grasping '*hyun*' is the way of understanding human and the original nature of the universe."[110]

Based on Hong's view, when I apply it to the Princess Bari story, *hyun* can be understood as the Seocheon Flower Field, where Princess Bari goes to get the water of life and the herbs of life and is also the other world. The logic of *hyunmyo jido* can be understood as the way Princess Bari takes decedent souls to the other world and brings other decedent souls to this world and

---

[108] Sung-arm Hong, "Poongrhudo-ui Yinyum-gua Moonharkae-ui Sooyong Yangsang," *Hanminjok Moonhwa Yeongoo* (Hanminjok Moonhwaharkhui) 1 (1996): 229.

[109] Bu-shik Kim, op. cit., 73.

[110] Hong, loc. cit.

revives them. In other words, the logic of Princess Bari bringing the water of life and the herbs of life from the other world is *hyunmyo*. The logic of reviving her parents with the water of life and the herbs of life she got in the other world is *hyunmyo jido*. *Hyunmyo* also can be understood as how Princess Bari goes through the process of having the sacred marriage with the god Musang in the other world and gains sacredness. After she gains sacredness and becomes the goddess, thus enabling her to go back and forth with decedent souls, is *hyunmyo jido*. The thought of *poongrhudo* is well reflected with the way Princess Bari gains sacredness and the function she carries out afterward. Therefore, I contend that *poongrhudo* played a major role in orally transmitted "Princess Bari" from long ago, and how she gained enlightenment.

Furthermore, says Hong, "*Poongrhudo* is a religion that refines within the social system's framework to know the proper way to behave as mankind. It is a religion with a flexible framework, which is undogmatic, and when necessary, it seeks the wisest alternative; then, it transforms pertinently when needed."[111] Thus, it came to be possible in "Princess Bari" to embrace a variety of religious elements (i.e., Buddhism, Confucianism, immortality, Hinduism, the ancient Mesopotamian purification ceremony) as well as heroism besides shamanism in the story. In other words, the foundation story of "Princess Bari" is shamanism, which has existed since ancient Korea; then with the influence of *poongrhudo*, it embraced all other religious elements transmitted to Korea as time passed and

---

[111] Ibid., 227.

tried to construct social harmony to have a peaceful life. When foreign religions (i.e., Buddhism and Confucianism) became the national religion during the Silla, Goryeo, and Joseon periods, respectively, they wielded enormous power upon politics and society. During those periods, shamanism infiltrated into the masses; by tolerating *poongrhudo*, they tried to sustain their unconscious values (i.e., the Princess Bari story). By doing so, they were able to distribute "Princess Bari" all over the country and have been able to sustain the rituals even up to the present; thus, "Princess Bari" became one of the oldest shamanic songs to exist in Korea.

1.3 The Methodology of the Research

For the research, I have selected seven enlightenment related stories in the *Samgook Yusa* and a shamanic song, "Princess Bari," to examine their unique and common enlightenment experiences represented in the stories. Moreover, I will compare the Korean enlightenment sources with other countries' mystical experience sources since mystics are the ones who consider enlightenment experiences as the most cherished aspiration; therefore, there is a common ground to be examined. By comparing the Korean sources with other countries' sources, I could probe into the Korean enlightenment sources' unique and universal attributes. In order to examine other countries' enlightenment sources, I shall briefly explain different opinions on philosophy of mysticism being discussed in different schools of philosophy.

In the 1960s, Walter T. Stace, a philosopher, claimed that all mystical experiences were the same, but based on different religions, periods, languages, cultures, and society's influences, the way mystics interpreted their mystical experiences were different; this was called "the common core theory," and philosophers who espoused the theory were called the Perennialist.[112] In the 1970s, Steven T. Katz, a philosopher, gainsaid "the common core theory" and argued that there was no common mystical experience and that they were all different; the claim was called "the diverse theory," and philosophers who supported the theory were called the Constructivist.[113] In the 1980s, Robert K. C. Forman, a scholar of religion, argued for the existence of pure consciousness, which alluded that similar mystical experiences among mankind were possible; thus, the common core theory became more relevant.[114] Then in the 1990s, Ralph W. Hood Jr., a psychologist, developed a survey to research a mystical experience; it was called the Mystical Scale and was based on the Stace's theory of mysticism; in 2010, several scholars who experimented with the survey of the Mystical Scale published an article on the result of their research at a university in Tamil Nadu, India, among the Christian,

---

[112] Gellman, op. cit.

[113] Steven T. Katz, "Language, Epistemology, and Mysticism," in *Mysticism and Philosophical Analysis*, ed. Steven T. Katz (New York: Oxford University Press, 1978), 22-74.

[114] Robert K. C. Forman, "Introduction: Mysticism, Constructivism, and Forgetting," in *The Problem of Pure Consciousness: Mysticism and Philosophy*, ed. Robert K. C. Forman (Oxford: Oxford University Press, 1997), 3–49.

Muslim, Hindu, and Buddhist students.[115] According to their article, the goal of the research survey was to verify whether the students experience "the common core theory" or "the diverse theory" when they encountered mystical experiences; moreover, if students experience the common core theory, whether their mystical experience was the extrovertive mystical experience or the introvertive mystical experience.[116] However, the results from the survey illustrated students who believed in Western religions (i.e., Christianity, Judaism, and Islam) had vertical mystical experience, and students who believed in Eastern religions (i.e., Hinduism and Buddhism) had horizontal mystical experience; in these instances, vertical mystical experience means "the divine Reality transcends or is beyond the world as we experience it. Therefore a loss of self is implied because the truth of the self is in God."[117] And the horizontal mystical experience is "the divine Reality is immanent, so to speak, within everything we experience. Therefore, the self should be transformed in conformity with this all pervading divine Reality, or brought to God-realization."[118] The result of the students' survey was not what they expected. It conveyed that students of the Eastern and Western religions have different mystical experiences; furthermore, researchers realized that researching Stace's extrovertive and introvertive mystical experiences in terms of

---

[115] Francis-Vincent Anthony, et al., "A Comparative Study of Mystical Experience Among Christian, Muslim, and Hindu Students in Tamil Nadu, India," *Journal for the Scientific Study of Religion* 49, no. 2 (June 2010): 264–77.

[116] Ibid.

[117] Ibid., 275.

[118] Loc. cit.

vertical or horizontal mystical experience would not be effective for future comparative research because Stace's extrovertive and introvertive mystical experiences are about "type of search one engages in rather than to the experience of the reality/Reality as such"; therefore, they concluded that they would need more comparative research in the future with a more diverse age group.[119]

In my opinion, it seems unreasonable to perceive college students who answered the survey were the ones who had a lot of mystical experiences because mystical experience is not something that can be experienced easily at an early age, and even if they experienced it, it would be difficult for them to realize that was a mystical experience at that age. Especially, Stace's extrovertive and introvertive mystical experiences were for the people who had enlightenment experience at least once. Stace's mystical experience measures the degree of enlightenment; in other words, to measure whether one had the enlightenment experience (the extrovertive mystical experience) or the *nirvana* enlightenment experience (the introvertive mystical experience). Therefore, surveying college students with Stace's mystical experience theory might not have been effective.

In 2011, the next group of researchers, including Hood, published an article about a mystical experience research they had done on 139 Buddhist monks and nuns in a Buddhist temple in China, who cultivated their seeking in Pure Land and

---

[119] Ibid.

practiced meditation.[120] The researchers expected they could get more advanced results since Buddhist monks and nuns had a lot of mystical experiences; however, they faced other kinds of problems (i.e., Buddhist monks and nuns did not want to reveal their mystical experiences, and they could not express their experiences because they were ineffable).[121] Hence they realized some limitations in researching mystical experiences with the survey alone, and some even suggested researching stories written about mystical experiences could be more effective.[122] Thus, based on their previous research, I have decided to research the enlightenment stories recorded in the *Samgook Yusa* and the shamanic song "Princess Bari."

The *Samgook Yusa* was compiled and commentated by Ilyeon, the Most Reverend Buddhist Priest at the Goryeo Dynasty in the thirteenth century; according to sources, Ilyeon selected and compiled stories that existed in the *Hyangjeon* (The records of the local people), the *Goki* (The old records), the *Beemoon* (The esoteric records), historical records, some Chinese records, etc.[123] There are different scholars' points of view on whether we could treat stories in the *Samgook Yusa* as an actual historical record. However, nowadays, more scholars give credit for its significance in the actual records of people

---

[120] Zhuo Chen, et al., "Common Core Thesis and Qualitative and Quantitative Analysis of Mysticism in Chinese Buddhist Monks and Nuns," *Journal for the Scientific Study of Religion* 50, no. 4 (December 2011): 654–70.

[121] Ibid., 667, 669.

[122] Ibid., 669. As they refer to Wildman and McNamara, 2010.

[123] Ilyeon, *Samgook Yusa*, 9, 14.

and historical events; thus, they have probed into stories in the *Samgook Yusa* as an additional reference to the actual historical records, i.e., the *Samgook Saki* (Three kingdoms historical records). Ilyeon recorded anecdotes about historical people figuratively: as Moon-tae Kim suggests, for historically well-known people, he used their actual names in their anecdotes; but for historically unknown people, he used names that symbolized their attributes.[124] Especially seven enlightenment stories in the *Samgook Yusa*, which will be examined in this treatise; whether the names of the monks involved refer to historical figures is difficult to know; however, their names signified their special talents, and they were either disciples of a historically well-known, eminent monk, Uisang, or known historically because of their contribution (i.e., for building famous architecture and for composing famous *hyangga* during the Silla Kingdom period). Therefore, researching their enlightenment experiences based on their records would not be too far-fetched an investigation in my research because they were the actual historical figures that existed in the Silla period.

For the enlightenment experience of Princess Bari, it is actually recited in shamanic rituals even nowadays; thus, it can be deemed that the story is still effective and can be a valuable source to investigate as a representative of an actual figure's enlightenment experience especially, considering the scarcity of women's enlightenment stories to probe in the *Samgook Yusa* and any other Korean texts. Hence the story of Princess Bari

---

[124] Moon-tae Kim, op. cit.

obtaining enlightenment could provide useful insight to women aspiring to acquire the enlightenment experience.

With the *Samgook Yusa* and "Princess Bari" enlightenment stories, I shall examine the following enlightenment aspects:

1. The meaning of enlightenment represented in the stories: does the story represent enlightenment or *nirvana* enlightenment? I shall compare the sources with other countries' appropriate mystical experiences.
2. The enlightenment methodology represented in the stories: does the story represent the Mahayana Buddhism cultivation method or Hinayana Buddhism cultivation method? Or does it represent any other cultivation method?
3. The necessity of gaining enlightenment represented in the stories, I shall examine the enlightenment stories in three aspects.

    a. One can possibly communicate with gods; therefore, one can effectuate the role of an intermediary between a god and mankind.
    b. One can achieve the union with the Self (*Atman*, true ego) and the Universal Self (*Brahman*, Ultimate Reality) or with a god or with nothingness; thus, one can gain spiritual power to achieve one's aspiration as well as to help others.
    c. One can make others gain salvation by performing rituals of transporting decedent souls to a higher realm.

1.4 The Sources of the Research

In the research, I shall examine the following seven stories recorded in the *Samgook Yusa* and an orally transmitted shamanic song, "Princess Bari," to examine the enlightenment attributes represented in the stories.

The *Samgook Yusa*

1. Book 2, Giyi, volume 2, the article "King Gyungdeok, Choongdamsa, Pyohoon-Daedeok" (in short, the Pyohoon story).
2. Book 3, Tarpsang, volume 4, the article "Samso-Guaneum-gua Joongsengsa" (in short, the Samso-Guaneum story).
3. Book 3, Tarpsang, volume 4, the article "Nambackwol-ui Doo Sungyin Nohill-Budeuk-gua Daldal-Barkbark" (in short, the Nohill and Daldal story).
4. Book 5, Gamtong, volume 7, the article "Wolmyungsa-ui Dosolga" (in short, the Wolmyung story).
5. Book 5, Pieun, volume 8, the article "Nangji-ui Gooreumtagi-wa Bohyun-Bosal Namoo" (in short, the Jitong story).
6. Book 5, Hyoseon, volume 9, the article "Jinjeong-Bubsa-ui Hyodo-wa Seonheng-yi Modoo Areumdabda" (in short, the Jinjeong story).
7. Book 5, Hyoseon, volume 9, the article "Daesung-yi Doo Saesang-ui Boomo-aegae Hyodohada" (in short, the Daesung story).

Furthermore, I shall compare the enlightenment experiences mentioned in the Jitong story and Jinjeong story with Western mystical experience sources, such as *The Teachings of the Mystics,* and the *Mysticism East and West*. I will also refer to the Indian Hindu philosophy text, *The Upanishards*, and some articles in the *Understanding Mysticism* to grasp the nature of mysticism, which is similar to enlightenment experiences mentioned in the Korean sources.

"Princess Bari"

1. The Seoul Gyung-jae Bae's version (first recorded 1937).
2. The Seoul Deok-soon Moon's version (recorded 1966).

In examining "Princess Bari," I shall use the first recorded text of the orally transmitted version, the Seoul Gyung-jae Bae's, because in analyzing the basic construction of the story, the first recorded version has less variation; therefore, it seems more pertinent to my topic of the research. Then I will also refer to another Seoul version, the Deok-soon Moon's, since the logic of the story is more consistent that it seems to be a good additional text to the first recorded version when investigating the construction of the story. Thereafter, I will compare the enlightenment aspect of "Princess Bari" with the *Cinderella* by referring to *The Myth of the Goddess*, *The Lost Language of Symbolism*, and the *Three Hundred and Forty-Five Variants of Cinderella, Catskin, and Capo'Rushes*.

In the research of the enlightenment stories in the *Samgook Yusa* and "Princess Bari," I will examine the meaning of enlightenment first in two stages: the first stage is enlightenment, which is similar to obtaining wisdom, and it is also the extrovertive mystical experience in Western mysticism.

I will compare the Jitong story and Eckhart's extrovertive mystical experience, which illustrate similar attributes. Then the second stage is *nirvana* enlightenment, which is the same as the introvertive mystical experience in Western mysticism.[125] For this experience, I shall compare the Jinjeong story, Eckhart's and Ruysbroeck's introvertive mystical experiences, with *The Upanishads*, and the Jinjeong story with "Princess Bari."

To investigate the enlightenment methodologies represented in the stories of the *Samgook Yusa* and "Princess Bari," I will probe into the Nohill and Daldal story, the Jitong story, and "Princess Bari." To examine the necessity of gaining enlightenment suggested in the stories, I will study the Pyohoon story for carrying out an intermediary role between the god and King Gyungdeok. For stories displaying the union with the Self and the Universal Self, thus gaining spiritual power, I will analyze the Samso-Guaneum story and the Wolmyung story. Thereafter, for stories that illustrate transporting the deceased souls to the higher realm of the other world, I will examine the Jinjeong story, the Daesung story, and "Princess Bari."

In the above enlightenment stories, some express the actual enlightenment experiences and conclude when they obtain enlightenment (i.e., the Nohill and Daldal story and the Jitong story). However, there are other types of enlightenment stories that illustrate how they carry out their efficacies of acquired enlightenment (i.e., the Pyohoon story, Samso-Guaneum story, Wolmyung story, Jinjeong story, and Daesung story). "Princess

---

[125] Stace, *Teachings of the Mystics*, 17-22, 83.

Bari," unlike aforementioned enlightenment stories, embraces both how she gains enlightenment and what kind of efficacy she effectuates after she obtains enlightenment. Hence, in the enlightenment stories, two types of the enlightenment aspects can be researched.

CHAPTER 2

THE MEANING OF ENLIGHTENMENT REPRESENTED IN THE STORIES

Moon-tae Kim perceives the meaning of enlightenment in Buddhism as "one who renounces worldly desire, and free from any bindingness, or emancipated, thus gains Buddhahood, and enters *Nirvana*; however, the meaning could be used in a comprehensive term, unrelated to Buddhism, to mean as 'awakened to truth or mysterious way' in other Korean literature or as used in the volume 1 and 2 of *Giyi* (records of unusual events) in the *Samgook Yusa*."[126] Thus, enlightenment means, on the one hand, in the Buddhist point of view, having entered *Nirvana* by renouncing worldly desires or becoming free from any worldly bindings; on the other hand, with more inclusive term unrelated to Buddhism, it means to be awakened to truth by realizing the law of nature or human life. I shall use both terms when I examine the sources in my research. So to speak, in the research of discussing Korean literature, gaining enlightenment means either one is free from any bindingness in the world and enters *Nirvana* or one is awakened to the truth in an inclusive term. However, the higher stage of enlightenment is when one can enter *Nirvana* at one's will. Hence, in the process of examining the enlightenment aspects in the Korean sources, to understand the meaning of enlightenment in-depth,

---

[126] Moon-tae Kim, "Deukdo Yangsang," 295.

I will study other countries' sources that define the meaning of enlightenment and its experience, to compare with the Korean sources.

Presently, in the Western philosophy school of mysticism, one of the topics hotly debated among them is about the experience of *Nirvana*. This *Nirvana* mystical experience in this research is the *nirvana* enlightenment, which is a higher stage than enlightenment. I will discuss their different meanings in detail in the upcoming sections. The *nirvana* enlightenment is also called "the introvertive mystical experience" in Western mysticism; and the lower level of experience is "the extrovertive mystical experience," which is equivalent to enlightenment.[127] Based on these distinctions, the corresponding examples of the Korean sources for the *nirvana* enlightenment or the introvertive mystical experience are the Jinjeong story, in which Jinjeong falls into seven days of meditation, and "Princess Bari," which illustrates she has the sacred marriage in the other world. For comparative Western sources in the *nirvana* enlightenment or the introvertive mystical experience are Eckhart and Ruysbroeck mystical experiences, which I will probe into. For the Korean source in enlightenment or the extrovertive mystical experience, I will examine the Jitong story; and for the Western source, Eckhart's extrovertive mystical experience. When I study the above enlightenment experience sources in two different stages—the *nirvana* enlightenment and enlightenment—I will begin with the lower stage, enlightenment or the extrovertive mystical experience. Then, I shall probe into the higher

---

[127] Stace, *Teachings of the Mystics*, 15-16, 17-22, 83.

stage, the *nirvana* enlightenment or the introvertive mystical experience.

2.1 The Meaning of Enlightenment

The meaning of enlightenment in an inclusive term is obtaining wisdom, which enables one to awaken to the truth of nature or the world; thus, there is no obstacle in knowing the matter of nature or the world. However, in Buddhism, enlightenment can be perceived in two stages: the first stage is obtaining wisdom, which is enlightenment; and the second stage is acquiring *nirvana* enlightenment, which is a more complete stage than enlightenment. In general, if one obtains wisdom, then it is considered one gained enlightenment; nevertheless, in Buddhism, it is considered the first stage of enlightenment, although there is an exception (i.e., in the Jitong story, from which a source says, his wisdom obtained is high enough to enter *Nirvana*).[128] D. T. Suzuki also perceived enlightenment as wisdom, which eventually guided one to *Nirvana*; however, in his text, he alluded to two different stages. He first explained wisdom as "it is the seeing by means of a *prajna*-eye which is a special kind of intuition enabling us to penetrate right into the bedrock of Reality itself."[129] Hence, Suzuki was referring to wisdom that eventually would lead one to the procurement

---

[128] Ilyeon, comp., "The Jitong Story," *Samgook Yusa*, trans. Won-joong Kim (Seoul: Eulyu Moonhwasa, 2003), 548.

[129] D. T. Suzuki, "The Basics of Buddhist Philosophy," in *Understanding Mysticism*, ed. Richard Woods (Garden City, NY: Image Books, 1980), 128.

of Reality. Then he analyzed Buddha's enlightenment with the role of wisdom (*prajna*-eye) by examining metaphysical and existential aspects, in which, said he, the existential was psychological; however, in the metaphysical, he analyzed the doctrine as non-ego, which meant that "there is nothing permanent," hence "nothing worth clinging to in this world."[130] He asserted that Buddha's claim of non-ego rejected the psychological view of ego because mankind needed to go out to "a broader field of Reality where *prajna*-intuition comes into play."[131] In other words, the psychological view of ego mainly dealt with the senses and intellect; thus, Suzuki interpreted it as not the true ego but "the shadow of the ego"; hence, he claimed that the true ego must be caught within himself with *prajna* (wisdom), which meant *prajna* played the role of a catcher.[132] Then, in his point of view, there was another reason the psychological view of ego did not work with Buddha's view of non-ego, which, said he, "psychological ego fails to see into the egolessness of all things (*Dharma*), which appears to the eye of *prajna*-intuition not as something sheerly of private value but as something filled with infinite possibilities."[133] Therefore, Suzuki argued that only when one saw the world with the *prajna*-eye (wisdom), one could discover non-ego, which in turn helped to break the illusion built on *maya* and created a new world based on wisdom and love; and this process he called enlightenment.[134]

---

[130] Ibid., 127.

[131] Ibid., 128.

[132] Ibid., 128–9.

[133] Ibid., 129.

[134] Ibid., 129–30.

However, in the next example text, he demonstrated how enlightenment progresses into *nirvana* enlightenment.

> 1) The enlightenment-experience therefore means going beyond the world of psychology, the opening of the *prajna*-eye, and seeing into the realm of Ultimate Reality, and 2) landing on the other shore of the stream of *samsara*, where all things are viewed in their state of suchness, in the way of purity. This is when a man finds his mind freed from everything (*sabbattha vimuttamanasa*), not confounded by the notions of birth-and-death, of constant change, of before, behind, and middle...[135]

In this example, Suzuki stated two different stages of enlightenment: (1) referring to enlightenment, which is the stage of obtaining wisdom and realizing Reality through it; and (2) about entering *Nirvana*, which one is freed from all bindingness as well as reincarnation and death, thus joining *Nirvana* for good. However, if this *Nirvana* can be experienced while one is alive, then it can be understood as acquiring the *nirvana* enlightenment. Afterward, Suzuki stated that one who had entered *Nirvana* as "conqueror" by referring to *The Dhammapada*:[136] "Such an awakened one is an absolute conqueror and nobody can follow his tracks as he leaves none";

---

[135] Ibid., 130; *sabbattha vimuttamanasa*, Suzuki's footnote 4, which says from *The Dhammapada*, verse 348, p. 167. (The number 1, 2 is mine.)

[136] *The Dhammapada*, trans. S. Radhakrishnan (Oxford: Oxford University Press, 1951), as referred to by Suzuki, op. cit., 130.

then he described the nature of *Nirvana* as "like a circle whose circumference is infinite, therefore with no center to which a path can lead."[137] In the following section, I shall discuss the meaning of *nirvana* enlightenment in more detail.

2.2 The Meaning of *Nirvana* Enlightenment

The meaning of *nirvana* enlightenment could be used in two different ways. In the above remark by Suzuki on enlightenment, the beginning stage is obtaining wisdom, which is awakening to the truth or Reality, then one progresses into the stage of *nirvana* enlightenment by cultivating one's religious practice in-depth; when one enters *nirvana* enlightenment, which connotes one being free from any restraint in the world, one's soul is completely ready to join the state of *Nirvana*, and one never falls back into the *karma* of reincarnation. This nature of *Nirvana* is called *tatha-ta*[138] (suchness, as Suzuki stated in the above); it means one's soul permanently entering *Nirvana*. Buddha is known to have joined *Nirvana* like this. However, in the school of philosophy of mysticism, the state of *nirvana* enlightenment varies in several ways. They are arguing that the enlightened one or a mystic[139] can enter the state of *nirvana* while

---

[137] Suzuki, op. cit., 130.

[138] Heinrich Zimmer, *Myths and Symbols in Indian Art and Civilization*, ed. Joseph Campbell (Princeton, NJ: Princeton University Press, 2017), 145.

[139] A mystic is one who has an enlightenment experience. Gellman, op. cit.

alive.¹⁴⁰ Buddhists claim Buddha entered *Nirvana* not only the postmortem but also while alive in this world; also, Catholics perceive entering the heavenly realm while alive as the state of deification, which symbolizes being married to Jesus (i.e., St. Teresa of Avila or other Catholic mystics who claim to be in the union with Jesus, Virgin Mary, or God or the Godhead).¹⁴¹ Therefore, the meaning of the *nirvana* enlightenment is not only the decedent soul entering *Nirvana* but it also refers to the enlightened one's Self (*Atman*, true ego) having the union with the Universal Self (*Brahman*, Ultimate Reality) or the One or God or the emptiness while alive. "Katha Upanishad" explains the state of union with one's Self with the Universal Self as the following:

> There is one ruler, the Self of all living beings, who makes the one form manifold; the wise who perceive Him seated within their Self, to them belongs eternal bliss, not to others.¹⁴²

In the example, the Universal Self is equated with the Self, or claiming the state of being in the union with themselves. Thus, it says that the one who perceives them being in the union

---

[140] In my treatise, I will distinguish *Nirvana* to mean permanently entering a state after death, and the *nirvana* enlightenment is used to refer to a similar state while alive. Also refer to *The Teachings of the Mystics*.

[141] This state is referred to as the introvertive mystical experience or the *nirvana* enlightenment. Stace, *Teachings of the Mystics*, 17–22, 83.

[142] Swami Paramananda, trans., "Katha Upanishad," part 5, section 12, in *The Upanishads* (San Bernardino, CA: Pantianos Classics, 2017), 54.

is the enlightened one. The next example describes knowing the Universal Self being in the union with the Self as Truth.

> If one knows It here, that is Truth; if one knows It not here, then great is his loss. The wise seeing the same Self in all beings, being liberated from this world, become immortal.[143]

It says that the Universal Self being in the union with the Self is Truth, and the same Truth exists in all beings, and one who realizes that will be liberated from this world and becomes immortal. This remark connotes one gaining the *nirvana* enlightenment because it refers to one who is awakened by wisdom, which enables one to realize one and all the others in the world being united with the Universal Self and the Self, then one is liberated from this world, which means entering the *nirvana* enlightenment. Hence the meaning of *nirvana* enlightenment could be Buddha entered *Nirvana* permanently, or a mystic could have entered it for a few minutes, hours, or for several days while alive by uniting one's Self (true-ego, pure consciousness) with the Universal Self. A good example is the Jinjeong story, in which Jinjeong entered seven days of meditation when he heard the news of his mother deceased.[144] His state in deep meditation is like being in the *nirvana* enlightenment while alive. There are also other countries' mystics who illustrated that they had entered the *nirvana*

---

[143] Swami Paramananda, trans., "Kena Upanishad," part 2, section 5, in *The Upanishads* (San Bernardino, CA: Pantianos Classics, 2017), 70.

[144] Ilyeon, comp., "The Jinjeong Story," *Samgook Yusa*, trans. Won-joong Kim (Seoul: Eulyu Moonhwasa, 2003), 573.

enlightenment or the introvertive mystical experience, such as Eckhart and Ruysbroeck.

In the *Samgook Yusa*, besides Jinjeong entering the *nirvana* enlightenment for seven days, there are other stories that connote people seeking the heavenly realm, Dosolcheon, where Mireuk Buddha is known to reside. In the Silla period, there existed mostly Mahayana Buddhism, in which Bodhisattvas effected a major role in helping others gain enlightenment; hence, their seeking the heavenly realm did not mean permanently entering *Nirvana* and never reincarnating in this world, but it rather meant decedent souls ascending to the heavenly realm paradise, Dosolcheon, or entering the earthly realm paradise in Western Pure Land, where Mita Buddha was known to reside. According to Hae-choon Rhu, in the Silla period, the ones who pursued the heavenly paradise, Dosolcheon, where Mireuk Buddha existed, were aristocrats and intellects who followed religious practice of their salvation on their own efforts; but the ones who pursued the earthly paradise in Western Pure Land, where Mita Buddha resided, were commoners who believed their salvation depend on others' help, such as Bodhisattvas.[145]

In the *Samgook Yusa*, there are several stories about entering the earthly paradise in Western Pure Land, Seobang Jeongto, and also a few stories going up to the heavenly paradise, Dosolcheon, unlike Seung-chan Kim's claim, in which he says that in the Silla period, people hardly accepted the heavenly

---

[145] Hae-choon Rhu, "Wolmyungsa-ui Hyangga," 434.

realm, Dosolcheon; thus, there was no story about the heavenly realm in the *Samgook Yusa*.[146] The example stories about ascending to the heavenly realm are the Pyohoon story and the Jinjeong story. In the Pyohoon story, he goes up to the heavenly realm where the heavenly emperor stays and conveys King Gyungdeok's wish to have a male heir to his throne. Ilyeon referred Pyohoon as a saint in the story, which makes it possible to suppose Pyohoon had acquired the *nirvana* enlightenment; hence, he was able to visit the heavenly realm at his will. In the Jinjeong story, Jinjeong's deceased mother's soul was known to be born again in heaven. Both Pyohoon and Jinjeong were two of the ten disciples of Uisang. It was known that Uisang's ten disciples had some kind of religious skills: Pyohoon was known to have a skill to go up to the heavenly realm.[147] Then Jinjeong, based on the meaning of his name, seemed to be skilled at entering deep meditation. Uisang also was known to walk up Buddha's pagoda on air, and his disciples followed him behind four feet away also walking on air.[148] The allusion of the story is that Uisang and his disciples pursued Dosolcheon, the heavenly realm. Wonhyo criticized the Silla's class system and strived to propagate aristocrat-centered Buddhism to commoners; thus, he accepted the earthly paradise in Western Pure Land favorably. However, Uisang was known to be "an incarnate of Buddha,"[149] and Buddha was known to have entered *Nirvana*; hence, would

---

[146] Seung-chan Kim, "Wangseng Sasang," 2.

[147] Ilyeon, comp., "Uisang-yi Hwaumjong-eul Jeonhada," *Samgook Yusa*, trans. Won-joong Kim (Seoul: Eulyu Moonhwasa, 2003), 466.

[148] Ilyeon, loc. cit.

[149] Ibid., and footnote 16.

it not be natural for Uisang to pursue either permanently joining *Nirvana* or ascending to the heavenly realm? These stories in the *Samgook Yusa* illustrate that during the Silla period, based on their political and social status, people pursued either the earthly paradise in Western Pure Land or the heavenly paradise in Dosolcheon. Next, I will inquire into how enlightenment and *nirvana* enlightenment are denoted in other countries' mystic sources. Firstly, I will explain how their points of view on mysticism are divided into two main schools of thought; thereafter, I will compare their sources with the Korean sources.

In the school of Western philosophy of mysticism, based on the contention of what *nirvana* enlightenment experience is like, they are divided into several schools. In my treatise, I will study two main opposite viewpoints about *nirvana* enlightenment and compare those sources with the Korean sources. They are the schools of the Perennialist and the Constructivist. From the 1950s to the 1960s, a philosopher representing one of the Perennialist, Walter T. Stace, developed a theoretical way to investigate mysticism in philosophy and claimed that the people who experienced mysticism might interpret their experiences differently based on their countries, religions, periods, languages, societies, cultures, etc., but their actual mystical experiences might be the same; and he argued for the common core theory.[150] In the 1970s, a philosopher representing the Constructivist, Steven T. Katz, criticized the Perennialist and contended that based on different backgrounds of mystical experiencers, their mystical experiences were all different; and

---

[150] Stace, *Teachings of the Mystics*, 14, 24; Gellman, "Mysticism."

he asserted the diverse theory.[151] Then in the 1980s, a scholar of religion, Robert K. C. Forman argued for the existence of pure consciousness based on his brief moments of the *nirvana* enlightenment experience and other mystics' experiences.[152] What Forman claimed, the existence of pure consciousness, means *when* a mystic is in the state of *nirvana* enlightenment can experience it. In other words, when the mystic empties all contents in the soul, pure consciousness appears; and Forman called this state Pure Consciousness Event (PCE);[153] and Stace called this state "the introvertive mystical experience," which is the same as the *nirvana* enlightenment.[154] Based on Forman's contention, what the Perennialist claimed became more relevant because all mankind can have pure consciousness if they cultivate their consciousness regardless of their different backgrounds.

Then the next contention between the Perennialist (i.e., Walter T. Stace, William James, Evelyn Underhill, R. M. Bucks, R. C. Zaehner, Rudolf Otto,[155] etc.) and the Constructivist is

---

[151] Katz, "Language, Epistemology, and Mysticism"; Gellman, op. cit.

[152] Forman, "Introduction: Mysticism."

[153] Ibid.

[154] Stace, *Teachings of the Mystics*, 17–22, 83.

[155] Rudolf Otto, *Mysticism East and West: A Comparative Analysis of the Nature of Mysticism*, trans. Bertha L. Bracey and Richenda C. Payne (Eugene, OR: Wipf and Stock Publishers, 2016). In his book, Otto claimed that he perceived only a few exceptional mystics (i.e., Meister Eckhart of Germany, Shankara of India, Plotinus of Greece, and mystics of Mahayana Buddhism) who seemed to share similar mystical experiences. Hence, Otto seems to be rather the Centrist than the Perennialist. Katz perceives him as the Perennialist (Katz,

when the mystic is in the state of *nirvana* enlightenment, or in the introvertive mystical experience, whether the mystic is in the union with God (theistic) or in the union with the Universal Self or the One (monistic). The mystics who claim to have the union with God are those who follow Western religions (i.e., Catholic, Protestant, etc.); they insist that they still feel a separate entity when they are in the union with Jesus or God, which means they have not achieved the same identity with God (dualism).[156] The mystics who claim to have the union with the Universal Self or the emptiness are those who follow Eastern religions (i.e, Hinduism, Buddhism, etc.), and the mystics who have the union with the One are Neo-Platonists; then they assert that when they are in the union with the Universal Self or the One, they feel identical to them (monism).[157] This is the same theory aforementioned in *The Upanishads*, in which the Universal Self (*Brahman*, Ultimate Reality) and the Self (*Atman*, true ego) are identical.[158] However, when a Christian mystic claims to have achieved the same identity as God, the mystic can be accused of being a heretic. A good example is Eckhart, who claimed in some of his sermons he was identical to God; thus, he sometimes expressed monism, which caused him posthumously to be assigned as a heretic by the Church.[159] Stace stated that besides

---

op. cit.), but Forman does not include him under his Perennialist list (Forman, op. cit.). Thus, it seems it all depends on the criteria of a scholar; members of the Perennialist could be different.

[156] Stace, *Teachings of the Mystics*; Gellman, "Mysticism."

[157] Ibid.

[158] Paramananda, "Katha Upanishad," part 5, section 12, p. 54.

[159] Stace, *Teachings of the Mystics*, sermon 22, 23, pp. 155,157, respectively.

Eckhart, some other Christian mystics also expressed having mystical experiences of the same identity with God, monism, during their union with God; however, due to pressure of being assigned them as heretics from the Church, they interpreted their mystical experiences more suitable to their doctrine; hence, Stace argued that there was no absolute boundary of mystical experiences, that the Christians only experience dualism and no monism, and the Hindus and Buddhists only experience monism and no dualism, and there were some exceptions to general boundary of their religions in mystical experience.[160]

Subsequently, Stace perceived that the same mystical experiences were possible among people of different periods, cultures, and traditions and examined their mystical experiences into two groups, the extrovertive mystical experience and the introvertive mystical experience; however, he considered the introvertive mystical experience as more advanced and thus a more important form of mystical experience than the extrovertive mystical experience.[161] This introvertive mystical

---

[160] Ibid., 161.

[161] Stace, *Teachings of the Mystics,* 15–16; Some scholars criticize Stace's viewpoint on the introvertive mystical experience as a more advanced form of mystical experience. See Robert M. Gimello, "Mysticism and Meditation," in *Mysticism and Philosophical Analysis,* ed., Steven T. Katz (New York; Oxford University Press, 1978),170-99; Jones (2018) and Marshall (2005), according to Gellman, they researched other important aspects of the extrovertive mystical experience and repudiated Stace's point of view. As referred to by Gellman, op. cit., 8. However, Forman accepted Stace's opinion positively and said that Stace was a deconstructionist who interpreted sources without the influence of his religious background. See "Paramartha and Modern Constructivists on Mysticism:

experience is the *nirvana* enlightenment. As aforementioned, in enlightenment, the *nirvana* enlightenment is a higher stage than enlightenment, which stage is obtaining wisdom, although the above quote by Suzuki did not distinguish between enlightenment and the *nirvana* enlightenment, but considered a natural progress of enlightenment into a complete stage of the same enlightenment. In my research, I would like to examine enlightenment in two stages: the *nirvana* enlightenment being higher stage than enlightenment; this is a point that I agree with Stace—that the introvertive mystical experience, which is the same as the *nirvana* enlightenment, is higher stage than the extrovertive mystical experience, which could be considered similar to enlightenment, acquiring wisdom state. I shall probe into these different stages of enlightenment in more detail when I analyze the stories corresponding to these stages of enlightenment.

Stace first examined the extrovertive mystical experience by selecting several countries' mystical experience sources to compare them. The meaning of Stace's extrovertive mystical experience is the mystic feels the One or the Oneness by his or her sense in exterior, and he or she feels It as divine Reality, that he or she feels enormous happiness and becomes ineffable.[162] This extrovertive mystical experience is said to be given once, so it cannot be reexperienced.[163] The general meaning of the

---

Epistemological Monomorphism Versus Duomorphism," *Philosophy East and West* vol. 39, no. 4 (October 1989): 411.

[162] Gellman, "Mysticism," 8.
[163] Stace, *Teachings of the Mystics*.

extrovertive mystical experience is that he or she feels a mystical experience by sensory cognizance, which means he or she feels a god's existence or seems to have the union with nature in exterior.[164]

Stace's introvertive mystical experience means the mystic achieves pure consciousness that he or she reaches unitary consciousness that does not hold any phenomenal form.[165] Forman calls Stace's "unitary consciousness" as "pure consciousness event" (PCE), and it denotes the mystic emptying one's consciousness; in other words, the contents of the consciousness (i.e., thought, sense, image, etc.) are empty so that only pure consciousness remains.[166] Stace claimed that when the mystic achieved "unitary consciousness," he or she felt sacredness that enabled him or her to be happy and ineffable about the experience.[167] The introvertive mystical experience is said to be able to reexperience,[168] which means when a mystic's spiritual level reaches to the point of entering the introvertive mystical experience or the *nirvana* enlightenment at will, the mystic can reexperience it at any time one wishes. The general meaning of the introvertive mystical experience is that the mystic's consciousness cuts off from the sensory cognizance that the mystic feels emptiness or the Universal Self or God.[169]

---

[164] Gellman, op. cit., 4.

[165] Ibid., 8.

[166] Loc. cit.

[167] Ibid.

[168] Stace, *Teachings of the Mystics*.

[169] Gellman, "Mysticism," 5.

Usually mystics of Eastern religions experience emptiness or the Universal Self, and mystics of Western religions God, but among mystics of Eastern religions, Buddhists, mostly experience emptiness; however, among Hindus, it depends on their sect— one may experience the Universal Self, and the other a god. Among mystics of Western religion, they generally experience Jesus or God, but the Catholic mystic Eckhart and his followers are said to experience the Godhead,[170] in which state, the Trinity is yet to be present but dormant; thus, their mystical experience seems rather similar to emptiness in Buddhism. Henceforth, in the introvertive mystical experience, it is difficult to claim whether all mystical experiences are the same or different. As Rudolf Otto mentioned, mankind's spiritual experiences were generally similar, so it seemed their mystical experiences also were similar; nevertheless, he contended that similar mystical experiences only corresponded to very few exceptional mystics (i.e., Plotinus of Greece, Shankara of India, Eckhart of Germany, and mystics of Mahayana Buddhism), that we need more comparative research on cross-cultural perspective of mystical experiences.[171] Based on his point of view, mystical experience could be different among the mystics, and it depends on their levels of religious cultivation. In the case of Eckhart, as I will examine in more detail in the following sections, he can be perceived as one who transcended his religious boundary, and he can be considered a mystic of the world. In the following sections, I shall compare Eckhart's extrovertive and introvertive

---

[170] Stace, *Teachings of the Mystics,* Eckhart's sermon 22, 27, pp. 156, 157 respectively; commentary, pp. 157, 160, 162.

[171] Rudolf Otto, op. cit.

mystical experiences with *The Upanishads* and the Korean sources in the *Samgook Yusa*.

2.2.1 Comparative Research on the Extrovertive Mystical Experience of Eckhart and Jitong

Gellman mentions that Stace's extrovertive mystical experience means the mystic feels the One or the Oneness by his or her senses in the exterior and feels It as divine Reality that he or she feels enormous happiness and becomes ineffable.[172] The corresponding source that illustrates Stace's definition of the extrovertive mystical experience is the following example of Eckhart's extrovertive mystical experience.[173]

> All that a man has here externally in multiplicity is intrinsically One. Here all blades of grass, wood and stone, all things are one. This is the deepest depth and thereby am I completely captivated.[174]

In the example, says Eckhart, all things that exist in nature are intrinsically One. Eckhart adopts the term *One*, which is a pantheistic term used by Plotinus. This is unusual. For a

---

[172] Gellman, "Mysticism," 8.

[173] Meister Eckhart (1260–1328), born in Germany, entered the Dominican Order at a young age and became the Saxony and Bohemia areas' head of the order. As he experienced deep philosophy and mysticism, he accepted the pantheistic mystical theory, which caused him to be criticized by the Church; thus, he was designated a heretic posthumously. *The Teachings of the Mystics*, 139.

[174] Otto, op. cit., 61.

Catholic mystic, the term *God* would be more natural. So if it were changed to correspond with Catholicism, it would be like "intrinsically from God."[175] However, Eckhart chose to express the term *One*, which demonstrates that he was truly a world mystic who transcended all boundaries of his religion, culture, language, period, etc. His usage of the pantheistic term *One* was one of the reasons for him to be designated as a heretic posthumously. However, he chose to be truthful to his experience. Here, Eckhart expresses a variety of things that exist externally to appear to be One, and he feels the Oneness from the depth of his heart; also because of how various things appear to him as united in One, he is completely fascinated by it. He feels the One externally by sense, so it is the extrovertive mystical experience.

In the following text, Otto mentions that Eckhart expresses his true insight, which does not distinguish contrast among different entities.[176]

> Say, Lord, when is a man in mere "understanding" (in discursive intellectual understanding). I say to you: "When a man sees one thing separated from another." And when is a man above mere understanding? That I can tell

---

[175] Stace also mentioned that some mystics used the term *One* instead of *God*, but generally, Western mystics use *God* more than *One*. *The Teachings of the Mystics*, 16.

[176] Otto, op. cit., 45.

you: "When he sees all in all, then a man stands beyond mere understanding."[177]

In the above example, says Eckhart, when a man understands a variety of all things as a separate thing, he merely understands things. But when he perceives those separate things as a whole or as the Oneness, he is beyond understanding. In other words, through his true insight, he can understand what is beyond nature; however, he still senses the Oneness in the exterior and feels the Oneness as Reality. Thus, he is explaining the extrovertive mystical experience.

There is another source that expresses a similar notion as Eckhart. Marcus Aurelius Antonius, a second-century Stoic, contended how the multifarious nature of things originated from the One.[178] According to him, the essence of an entity is contained in various objects, but the principal essence is the One; in the same way, a soul is possessed in many different types of people, but the essence of the soul is the One.[179] When I compare Eckhart's and Aurelius's remarks, Eckhart is experiencing the essence of the One by his feelings; in other words, he is experiencing the Oneness by his senses. However, in the case of Aurelius, it is difficult to know whether he is experiencing the Oneness by his senses or know It by his wisdom. Nevertheless, both Eckhart and Aurelius are indicating the same entity called the One or the Oneness, which signifies

---

[177] Ibid., 45-46.

[178] *Marcus Aurelius Antonius and Marcus Tullius Cicero*, trans. Sung-sook Kim (Seoul: Dongseo Moonhwasa, 2013).

[179] Ibid.

Eckhart's and Aurelius's realization of the One or the Oneness seems to transcend country, religion, language, and period.[180]

The next example is Jitong's enlightenment experience, which is similar to Eckhart's extrovertive mystical experience. Stace mentioned that although there were many introvertive mystical experiences in Asian sources, there was hardly any extrovertive mystical experience in Asian sources.[181] Jitong's enlightenment experience falls under the definition of the extrovertive mystical experience.

> When he [Jitong] became a monk at seven years old, a crow came to him and said, "Go to Youngchui Mountain and become a disciple of Nangji." When he heard that, he went to the mountain and was resting under a tree in a deep mountain valley. Suddenly, he saw a strange looking man approaching him and said, "I am

---

[180] It may be a little far-fetched to say two sources, which were written originally in two different languages, German and Latin, were interpreted as the same based on the translated versions; however, with the hypothesis of the translations being correct, we can perceive that they mean the same universal entity, the One or the Oneness, which is transcendent of country, religion, language, and period. And this is also a valid point to one of Otto's viewpoints of Eckhart's mystical experience being similar to Plotinus of Greece. Plotinus was a Neo-Platonist whose common ground with Stoics could be Platonic philosophy on universal nature. Also refer to. A. N. Marlow, "Hinduism and Buddhism in Greek Philosophy," *Philosophy East and West* vol. 4, no. 1 (April 1954): 35–45; Sung-sook Kim, *Marcus Aurelius Antonius*.

[181] Walter T. Stace, *Mysticism and Philosophy* (London: The Macmillan Press, Ltd., 1960).

Bohyun Bodhisattva and want to give you the Buddhist precepts." After he gave it to Jitong, he disappeared. Then, <u>all of a sudden, Jitong felt his mind expanded and united with nature, and his wisdom was highly awakened to the level of reaching *Nirvana*</u>.[182]

According to the story, we can hypothesize Jitong was desperately running around Youngchui Mountain looking for Nangji, based on the allusion of "[he] was resting under a tree in a deep mountain valley." It seemed that the young monk was all over the mountain looking for Nangji and got tired, so he was resting under a tree. In this situation, Jitong was resolute in finding Nangji, so his mind was all united with that purpose. His concentrated mind might have affected sympathy from a deity. The story said, "Suddenly, he saw a strange looking man approaching him." In this expression, his experience could be mystical as suggested by the words as, *suddenly*, *saw*, and *strange-looking person*. These words hinted his experience was not ordinary, possibly a different world experience. These words denoted Jitong was suddenly having a mystical experience. Moreover, the strange-looking person was a Buddhist saint, Bohyun Bodhisattva; thus, after Jitong received the Buddhist monk's precepts from him, his mind expanded and united with nature, and his wisdom was awakened highly. In this situation, it is possible to perceive his mind expanded and united with nature, or the One or the Universal Self. It seems that Jitong's

---

[182] A part of the summary from the Jitong story; Ilyeon, *Samgook Yusa*, 548.

mind expanding and uniting with nature is similar to Eckhart seeing the One or the Oneness. The difference between Jitong uniting with nature, or the One, or the Universal Self, and Eckhart seeing the One or the Oneness was that Eckhart did not express directly that he was united with the One but connoted seeing multifarious things as the One. However, he mentioned that what he saw as multifarious things as the One, he felt it from deep down in his heart; so his expression seems to be a different experience, but in actuality, Eckhart is suggesting a similar experience, in which he is experiencing the union with the One; in the case with Jitong, with nature, or the Universal Self. Jitong united with nature or the Universal Self, or the One, by expanding his mind as felt by his senses, thus, it corresponds to the extrovertive mystical experience, in which he feels sacred reality or nature externally by his senses. Therefore, Jitong is expressing the extrovertive mystical experience, just like Eckhart's extrovertive mystical experience in the aforementioned examples. Their similar extrovertive mystical experiences seem to reinforce Otto's contention that Eckhart's mystical experiences were similar to the Mahayana Buddhist mystics' experiences.

2.2.2 Comparative Research on the Introvertive Mystical Experiences of Eckhart, Ruysbroeck, Jinjeong, and Princess Bari

In comparing the introvertive mystical experience among different sources, I shall analyze Eckhart's, Ruysbroeck's, and Jinjeong's introvertive mystical experiences or the *nirvana* enlightenment first, then I will compare Jinjeong's and Princess

Bari's introvertive mystical experiences; thus, I can compare both cross-culture and cross-genre sources to find similarity or dissimilarity between them.

Stace's introvertive mystical experience means the mystic obtains pure consciousness, which denotes phenomenologically emptying the mystic's consciousness contents; thus, the mystic achieves "unitary consciousness."[183] The general meaning of the introvertive mystical experience is by completely cutting off from sensory cognizance, the mystic experiences either emptiness or the Universal Self or God's existence.[184] This means that after all the contents in the consciousness (i.e., form, thought, volition, image, etc.) are emptied, pure consciousness arises; therefore, this pure consciousness state is called "emptiness," "the Universal Self," "the One," "the Infinite," "God," etc.; however, Stace avoided using the terms for such a state, *pure consciousness*, as *God* or *the One*, but he rather called it "undifferentiated unity"; in other words, when the mystic achieves "unitary consciousness" or pure consciousness, that state is, as he called it, "undifferentiated unity."[185] Stace perceived that there some hypocrisy existed when the mystic emptied all contents of consciousness, and so obtained pure consciousness, yet the mystic was feeling peacefulness or ineffableness; moreover, Western religion mystics expressed having the union with God, while Eastern religion mystics alluded to having the

---

[183] Gellman, "Mysticism," 8.

[184] Ibid., 5.

[185] Stace, *Teachings of the Mystics*, 20–21.

union with the Universal Self or the One or the emptiness.[186] Eckhart expressed differently from other Western mystics. He contended that when he achieved pure consciousness, he had the union with the Godhead, which is a state alluded to by the Catholics as the Trinity not yet materialized but in the state of dormancy; hence, it was possible to view the Godhead as the emptiness. Therefore, Eckhart's introvertive mystical experience could be deemed as a world mystic who transcended religious boundaries.

However, Steven T. Katz, who is a leading Constructivist, negates the experience of "pure consciousness."[187] The reason for his negation is that the meaning of words themselves are more important than expressed or interpreted words; this is because, he says, words' meaning can be found in the context of a certain situation.[188] For example, Katz argues that *nothingness* in Buddhism "does not mean a god but it refers to 'emptiness,' which transcends all existential states"; however, Eckhart, who is the Catholic mystic, asserting *nothingness* as the same as Buddhist *nothingness* is inappropriate understanding.[189] Moreover, Katz contended that "'nothingness,' as *nichts* in Eckhart's language is the same as the Buddhist *Mu*, for the Christian mystic such as Eckhart seeks the re-birth of his soul now purified through

---

[186] Ibid., 22.

[187] Katz, "Language, Epistemology, and Mysticism," 46.

[188] Ibid., 46–47; even in the recently edited book, he asserts the same view. Steven T. Katz, "General Editor's Introduction," in *Comparative Mysticism: An Anthology of Original Sources*, ed. Steven T. Katz (Oxford: Oxford University Press, 2013).

[189] Katz, "Language, Epistemology, and Mysticism," 53.

its immersion into the *Gottheit,* whereas the Buddhist seeks *sunyata* as the transcendence or liberation from all selfhood"; and also the meaning of *self* "needs close scrutiny in its eastern and western and Buddhist Christian context, if these comparisons are to make sense."[190] Katz's contention of necessity in examining exact words' meanings in context is a very important point to address.

Nevertheless, after Katz's negation of the existence of pure consciousness, Robert K. C. Forman argued for the existence of pure consciousness, and Forman criticized the way the Constructivist used language to analyze the mystical experience and to make decisions based on it was inappropriate, especially the introvertive mystical experience, which was being experienced in the state of consciousness being completely shut down; therefore, in such a situation, analyzing it in terms of language expression was not pertinent.[191]

In my point of view, Katz's assertion of Eckhart's expression of *nothingness*—which he is trying to "seek the re-birth of his soul new purified through its immersion into the *Gottheit*"; thus, it is different from Buddhist *emptiness*, which is seeking "the transcendence or liberation from all selfhood"[192]—seem convincing based on Eckhart's sermons. However, what Eckhart pursues in the Godhead is not different from what Buddhist mystics are seeking in the emptiness to liberate from themselves.

---

[190] Ibid.

[191] Forman, "Introduction: Mysticism."

[192] Katz, "Language, Epistemology, and Mysticism," 53.

It seems that Eckhart's Godhead is similar to the Buddhist *mu* (nothingness). The Godhead Eckhart is referring to is the point where the Christian Holy Trinity has not yet appeared but dormant, and it is completely emptied or in a desert state that there is no action. In the following example, Eckhart voices how perfect it would be to be thrown into that desert.

> In this way the soul enters the unity of the Holy Trinity, but it may become even more blessed by going further, to the barren Godhead, of which the Trinity is a revelation. <u>In this barren Godhead, activity has ceased</u> and therefore <u>the soul will be most perfect when it is thrown into the desert of the Godhead, where both activity and forms are no more, so that it is sunk and lost in this desert where its identity is destroyed</u>...[193]

In the above example, Eckhart is expressing the state of lost identity, which alludes to complete dissolution of the self, and this is similar to entering *Nirvana* in Buddhism. Stace also mentioned that Eckhart was expressing the introvertive mystical experience, which is the same as the *nirvana* enlightenment.[194] It seems the Godhead Eckhart is referring to means complete dissolution of the self, *tatha-ta* (suchness) rather than the *nirvana* enlightenment while alive; thus, it is very similar to entering *Nirvana* for Buddhists. Consequently, Eckhart seeking the Godhead was not much different from the Buddhists seeking

---

[193] Eckhart, sermon 22; Stace, *Teachings of the Mystics*, 156.
[194] Ibid., 17–22, 83, 156.

mu (nothingness) in order to enter *Nirvana* permanently. Eckhart probably did not read Buddhist text in the thirteenth to the fourteenth centuries in Europe, yet he highly likely experienced pure consciousness, the introvertive mystical experience or the *nirvana* enlightenment, which was the same as what Buddhist monks experienced. Therefore, in his sermons, some pantheistic theories (i.e., monistic view) were included. This was possible because his mystical experience had transcended country, religion, culture, language, period, etc. His introvertive mystical experience well coincided with the Mahayana Buddhist monks' *nirvana* enlightenment that Otto's contention, in which Eckhart's mystical experience was similar to mystics of Mahayana Buddhism, is defensible.[195] Moreover, Steindl-Rast alludes to Eckhart's mystical experience in the Godhead as the same original source, where the Buddhist mystics experience "nothingness."[196]

There is another Christian mystic who mentioned the similar notion of the Godhead, that is, Jan van Ruysbroeck, who alluded to having a similar mystical experience as Eckhart's; thus, he also referred to the Godhead in his mystical experience writings.[197] However, his interpretation of the mystical

---

[195] Rudolf Otto, op. cit.

[196] David O'neal, ed. *Mister Eckhart, from Whom God Hid Nothing* (Boulder, CO: New Seeds Books, 2005).

[197] Jan van Ruysbroeck (1293–1381) was born around Brussels and later became one of the great Flemish mystics. Until he was fifty, he served as a cathedral chaplain in Brussels. After he retired from the position, he relocated to a countryside near Brussels and devoted his life to mysticism. Stace, *Teachings of the Mystics,* 158–9.

experience was more in line with the Church's guideline, so he was never designated as a heretic.[198] The following example conveys his notion of the Godhead and the same identity with God quite well.

> And after this there follows <u>the union without distinction</u>. For you must apprehend the Love of God not only as an outpouring with all good, and <u>as drawing back again into the Unity; but it is also, above all distinction</u>, an <u>essential fruition in the bare Essence of the Godhead</u>. And in consequence of this enlightened men have found within themselves an essential contemplation which is <u>above reason and without reason, and a fruitive tendency which pierces through every condition and all being, and through which they immerse themselves in a wayless, abyss of fathomless beatitude, where the Trinity of the Divine Persons possess their Nature in the essential Unity</u>. . .
>
> For by this fruition, <u>all uplifted spirits are melted and noughted in the Essence of God, which is the super-essence of all essence</u>. <u>There they fall from themselves into a solitude and an ignorance which are fathomless; there all light is turned to darkness;</u> there the three Persons give place to the Essential Unity,

---

[198] Stace, *Teachings of the Mystics*, 160.

and <u>abide without distinction in fruition of essential blessedness</u> . . .<u>Yet all living spirits are one fruition and one blessedness with God without distinction.</u> For there all uplifted spirits are, in their superessence, one fruition and one beatitude <u>with God without distinction; and there this beatitude is so onefold that no distinction can enter into it.</u> And this way prayed for by Christ when He besought His Father in heaven that all His beloved might be made perfect in one, even as He is one with the Father through the Holy Ghost. And this I think the most loving prayer which Christ ever made for our blessedness.[199]

As in Ruysbroeck's mystical writing example alludes to the highest mystical experience, which is the introvertive mystical experience or the *nirvana* enlightenment, there are some similar elements with Eckhart's mystical experience (i.e., the notion of the Godhead and the same identity with God). Ruysbroeck alludes the Godhead as "the essential Unity where Trinity of the Divine Persons possess Their Nature," "the Essence of God," "the superessence of all essence," "fathomless," "darkness," etc. Hence, his allusion is similar to Eckhart's Godhead, from which the aforementioned example says, "The Trinity is a revelation . . . activity has ceased"; Eckhart distinguished "the difference between God and the Godhead is the difference

---

[199] Jan van Ruysbroeck, *The Adornment of the Spiritual Marriage*, trans. C. A. Wynschenck, DOM (London: J. M. Dent and Sons, Ltd., 1916), 244–46, as quoted by Stace, *Teachings of the Mystics*, 173–4.

between action and nonaction."²⁰⁰ Thus, he and Ruysbroeck were referring to the Godhead, wherein the Holy Trinity is in a dormant state. Then Ruysbroeck also implied monism, which signifies the same identity as God. For example, "And after this there follows the union without distinction." In this part, he refers to the same identity with God because he says, "the union without distinction," which means the same identity. But in the next line, he also implies distinction. For example, "But it is also, above all distinction, an essential fruition in the bare Essence of the Godhead"; therefore, in this part, he may be alluding to one moment, he has the union with God without distinction, and in another moment with distinction. In other words, his union with God is intermittent. This experience is also similar to Eckhart's, in which he mentioned in his sermon that holding the union with God had taken much of his strength of concentration that the union lasted intermittently.²⁰¹

Afterward, Ruysbroeck also alludes to the introvertive mystical experience or the *nirvana* enlightenment, similar to what Eckhart implied in the above example, such as the following: because they are in "the bare Essence of the Godhead,". . . "enlightened men have found within themselves an essential contemplation which is above reason and without reason, and a fruitive tendency which pierces through every condition and all being, and through which they immerse themselves in a wayless abyss of fathomless beatitude, where the Trinity of the Divine Persons possess Their Nature in

---

[200] Stace, *Teachings of the Mystics,* sermon 27, p. 157.

[201] Ibid., sermon 3, p.150.

the essential Unity. . ." In this part, Ruysbroeck seems to be referring to the mystics in the state of being beyond reason because the mystics' consciousnesses completely fell into the state of *nirvana*. Moreover, he alludes to the dissolving of the self in the Godhead: "For by this fruition, all uplifted spirits are melted and noughted in the Essence of God, which is the superessence of all essence. There they fall from themselves into a solitude and an ignorance which are fathomless." In this instance, Ruysbroeck is referring to the mystics' consciousnesses melting and becoming nothing by falling into the fathomless Godhead. This part is also very similar to Eckhart's implication of falling to the Godhead. For example, "In this barren Godhead, activity has ceased and therefore the soul will be most perfect when it is thrown into the desert of the Godhead, where both activity and forms are no more, so that it is sunk and lost in this desert where its identity is destroyed . . ." The difference in their Godheads is their allusion: to Ruysbroeck, the Godhead is "the Essence of God," which is "the superessence of all essence"; whereas to Eckhart, the Godhead is "desert," where all activities have ceased. However, they are in agreement that enlightened beings falling into the Godhead and losing their identities are an ideal mystical state, which is the introvertive mystical experience and also the *nirvana* enlightenment.

In the following, I shall examine Asian sources that express the introvertive mystical experience or the *nirvana* enlightenment and compare the sources with Eckhart's and Ruysbroeck's introvertive mystical experiences. First, I will analyze the introvertive mystical experience mentioned in *The Upanishads*.

"Katha Upanishad"[202] is constructed in the form of dialogues between Yama, who is the king of the nether world, and his disciple Nachiketas discussing the topic of how to achieve the highest state, how to have the union with gods or the Universal Self (*Brahman*), how to obtain immortality, etc.

> When the five organs of perception become still, together with the mind, and the intellect ceases to be active; that is called the highest state.[203]

In the above example, Yama tells Nachiketas how to obtain the highest state, which also can be viewed as achieving the introvertive mystical experience or the *nirvana* enlightenment. In order to acquire the highest state, all sensory functions as well as the mind and the intellect have to be completely closed from distraction. Yama's explanation also coincides with the general definition of the introvertive mystical experience, which is "by completely cutting off from sensory cognizances, the mystic experiences either emptiness or god's existence."[204]

Paramananda, who translated and commentated the text, mentioned that the teacher is explaining how to achieve "the transcendental vision": in other words, one's outgoing senses, that is, "seeing, hearing, smelling, touching, tasting; the restless mind and the intellect: all must be indrawn and quieted. The state of equilibrium thus attained is called the highest state,

---

[202] "Katha Upanishad" is known to be one of the best Vedas, which explains its philosophy in Western language translation. Paramananda, *Upanishads*, 21.

[203] Ibid., part 6, section 10, p. 59.

[204] Gellman, "Mysticism," 5.

because all the forces of one's being become united and focused; and this inevitably leads to supersensuous vision."[205] Therefore, the meaning of "the mystic being in the highest state" is that the mystic is in a completely inactive state by shutting all sensory cognizances, the mind and the intellect; by doing so, the mystic can view gods or has the union with the Universal Self or emptiness. This highest state "Katha Upanishad" expresses is not much different from what Ruysbroeck mentions in the above example about all uplifted spirits falling into the Godhead. For example, says he that "all uplifted spirits are melted and noughted in the Essence of God, which is the superessence of all essence. There they fall from themselves into a solitude and an ignorance which are fathomless; there all light is turned to darkness."[206] In this instance, "all uplifted spirits are melted and noughted in the Essence of God" means their sensory cognizances are closed, so their existence became like nothing and melted in the Godhead. Then, says he that "they fall from themselves into a solitude . . . is turned to darkness." He is alluding to the state of their sensory cognizances being indrawn completely so that their existences are like nothing. They are like in solitude and ignorance because their senses, minds, and intellects are completely shut down; thus, they are in the states of fathomless and darkness. In this part of the example, he does not denote uplifted spirits having the union with God after all their sensory cognizances, minds, and intellects indrawn completely, which caused them to be melted and abode in darkness; he alludes them to have fallen into the

---

[205] Paramananda, "Katha Upanishad," 59.

[206] Jan van Ruysbroeck, op. cit., 173.

Godhead, which seems rather similar to be in nothingness. The mystical state Ruysbroeck mentions in this example is about the introvertive mystical experience, which is like the highest state mentioned in "Katha Upanishad." Obtaining the highest state is not only about having transcendental vision upon gods or having the union with gods or the Universal Self, but it also means abiding in the state of nothingness. Moreover, Ruysbroeck's expression of mystical experience in the Godhead coincides with the general definition of the introvertive mystical experience, which is "by completely cutting off from sensory cognizances, the mystic experiences either emptiness or the Universal Self, or God's existence."[207] Therefore, Ruysbroeck's expression of falling into the Godhead and "Katha Upanishad" mentioning how to obtain the highest state are alluding to the similar introvertive mystical experience or the *nirvana* enlightenment.

The next is about Yoga, which is like entering the state of introvertive mystical experience.

> This firm holding back of the senses is what is known as Yoga. Then one should become watchful, for Yoga comes and goes.[208]

In the example, says Yama, by controlling the sensory cognizance, one can enter the highest state; but it is difficult to hold on to the control of the sensory cognizance. Thus, staying in the highest state continuously is difficult. To this statement, Paramananda commentated the following:

---

[207] Gellman, "Mysticism," 5.
[208] Paramananda, "Katha Upanishad," part 6, section 11, p. 59.

> Yoga literally means to join or to unite the lower self with the Higher Self, the object with the subject, the worshiper with God. . . . When this is accomplished through constant practice of concentration and meditation, the union takes place of its own accord. But it may be lost again, unless one is watchful.[209]

Based on these examples, we can perceive the meaning of Yoga is the same as the introvertive mystical experience or the *nirvana* enlightenment. Furthermore, Eckhart's expression about the introvertive mystical experience is also similar to the meaning of Yoga. The following example is Eckhart's sermon on the introvertive mystical experience.

> To rid the mind of all sensations, images, thoughts, etc., requires great strength. Since the soul cannot thus put out its strength continuously, its union with God can only be intermittent.[210]

In the above example of "Katha Upanishad," says Yama, "firm holding back of the senses is what is known as Yoga," and unless one is watchful, this "Yoga comes and goes." This is very similar to Eckhart's remark, in which he says that "to rid the mind of all sensations, images, thoughts, etc. requires great strength" and holding on to that state is very difficult, so the union with God stops time to time. How can we explain

---

[209] Ibid.

[210] Eckhart's sermon 3; Stace, *Teachings of the Mystics*, 150.

these remarkable similarities between two different countries, religions, languages, and periods' texts: the one by Yama, who probably was a Hindu philosopher, and the other by Eckhart, a Catholic priest and a mystic, with around 2,500–3,000 years of lapse? One possible way of understanding this phenomenon would be that their mystical experiences were similar; hence, they were expressing similar contents. Although we need more comparative research, so far, what Otto asserted—Eckhart's mystical experience was similar to Plotinus of Greece,[211] Shankara of India, who was the head of one of Hindu sect, and Mahayana Buddhism mystics—is convincing. In the next section, I shall analyze a Korean Mahayana Buddhism monk's introvertive mystical experience to see if there is a similarity with the above sources. The text is the Jinjeong story, recorded in the *Samgook Yusa*.

After Jinjeong became a Buddhist monk under the teaching of Uisang, which was about three years since he left home, he heard the news of his mother's death; then "he sat in the lotus posture, fell into meditation, and only woke up after seven days."[212] To this, other people in the temple hypothesized three different situations. One person supposed he tried to assuage his pain of losing his mother by falling into a long meditation; then another person mentioned "he visited home to observe his deceased mother while he was in meditation," yet the other said that "by acting in this way, he prayed for his deceased

---

[211] See Marlow, "Hinduism and Buddhism"; Sung-sook Kim, *Marcus Aurelius Antonius*.

[212] Ilyeon, "The Jinjeong Story," 573.

mother's soul's peacefulness in the other world."[213] I contend that Jinjeong probably did all three, which was hypothesized by others. To Jinjeong's state in deep meditation, Won-joong Kim, the translator of the *Samgook Yusa*, mentions that he was in "the state of unity."[214] To put it another way, his state of unity is the same as what "Katha Upanishad" mentions: "When the five organs of perception become still, together with the mind, and the intellect ceases to be active; that is called the highest state."[215] Jinjeong was in the highest state by being in the state of his perception, mind, and intellect completely shut off; thus, he was able to maintain equilibrium and assuage his pain arising from losing his mother. Moreover, he might have been able to see his deceased mother. According to the commentator of "Katha Upanishad," Paramananda, "all must be indrawn and quieted" all sensory perceptions, such as seeing, hearing, touching, etc., then one can become united and focused; when this happens, one can have "supersensuous vision."[216] Perhaps Jinjeong achieved this state of unity by being indrawn with his perceptions, mind, and intellect; thus, he achieved the unity and was able to see his deceased mother.

Furthermore, "Katha Upanishad" offers a clue as to how Jinjeong was able to visit his home being in the state of deep meditation. "Katha Upanishad" says that when one is united

---

[213] Ibid.

[214] Ibid., footnote 2.

[215] Paramananda, "Katha Upanishad," part 6, section 10, p. 59.

[216] Ibid.

with the Self in the heart during the meditation, there is not any place one cannot go.

> Though sitting, It travels far; though lying, It goes everywhere. Who else save me is fit to know that God, who is [both] joyful and joyless?[217]

To this, Paramananda commentated the following:

> The Self is all pervading, hence It is that which sits still and that which travels, that which is active and that which is inactive. It is both stationary and moving, and It is the basis of all forms of existence . . .[218]

Jinjeong was probably in the state of unity like this by uniting with his Self in his heart; by doing so, he was able to visit his home and saw the state of his deceased mother's soul and knew what to do to help her to ascend to heaven. Jinjeong falling into seven days of meditation is not much different from other mystics (i.e., Eckhart and Ruysbroeck expressing about the introvertive mystical experiences or the *nirvana* enlightenment), based on the teachings of the above "Katha Upanishad." By comparing the above example texts' introvertive mystical experiences, we can perceive what the Perennialist insist, which is that the introvertive mystical experiences transcend the period, country, culture, language, etc., is a valid point, although more

---

[217] Ibid., part 2, section 21, p. 37.
[218] Ibid.

cross-culture comparative research is needed. At least, what Otto contended—Eckhart's mystical experience was similar to Plotinus of Greece, Shankara of India, and mystics of Mahayana Buddhism—deem to be reasonable.

A. N. Marlow mentioned that there was affinity between Hinduism and Buddhism with Greek philosophy.[219] He perceived there were many similar elements in the Hindu Pantheon with early Greek's, and sacrifice mentioned in the *Rg Veda* with the rituals of Homer; moreover, he also argued that Orphism, which influenced Pythagoras and Plato, was more akin to *The Upanishads* or Hindu mysticism than any other ancient philosophy.[220]

> The aim of Orphism seems to be the liberation of the soul from the chains of the body, and this is to be achieved by asceticism, but man must pass through many lives before he achieves final freedom. This is very far, indeed, from genuine Greek religion of any period, but almost exactly the predominant view of the *Upanishads* . . . It has been remarked that the aim of Orphism, the realization by man of his identity with God, would have appeared blasphemous insolence to a sixth-century Athenian.[221]

---

[219] Marlow, op. cit.

[220] Ibid., 39–40.

[221] Ibid., 40; footnote 33; Marlow also referred to W. K. C. Guthrie, *Orpheus and Greek Religion* (London: Methuen, 1935), 236–7.

Marlow further asserted that the belief in transmigration, which influenced Pythagoras, probably came from an Eastern source, especially *The Upanishads*; furthermore, said he, based on some similarities between "the Brahmin teaching, Orphism, and Pythagoreanism, one can hardly resist the speculation that in the *Upanishads* and in the doctrines and practices based on them we may have a clue to the Greek mysteries."[222] Afterward, Marlow asked how there could be such similar philosophical notions among Eastern and Western cultures?; he supposed it might have been possible by Persian presence in ancient Greece and later by Alexander's expedition into the East, which enabled cultural exchanges between them; therefore, it was possible the teachings of *The Upanishads* might have influenced other ancient Greek philosophers.[223]

However, in terms of the introvertive mystical experience discussed in the above examples, the Perennialist insist that mystics' experiences are beyond cultures, languages, periods, countries, religions, etc., which seem to be referring to mankind's possession of pure consciousness that would enable them to have a similar mystical experience, that is, the introvertive mystical experience or the *nirvana* enlightenment. Properly speaking, in order to experience pure consciousness, the mystics need to cultivate themselves beyond enlightenment, which is the stage of obtaining wisdom. They need to pursue the introvertive mystical experience or the *nirvana* enlightenment in order to experience pure consciousness. And this state is

---

[222] Marlow, "Hinduism and Buddhism," 41.

[223] Ibid., 45.

mostly achieved by ascetics of Eastern and Western religions. This was one of the reasons Stace considered the introvertive mystical experience was more fully matured, a higher stage of mystical experience.[224] This was also mentioned by Wonhyo, as aforementioned in chapter 1: to ascend to the heavenly realm, one must cultivate one's whole life as a Buddhist ascetic and follow more precepts than secular Buddhists. The mystic experiences pure consciousness through the introvertive mystical experience or the *nirvana* enlightenment at one's will, then one would likely join *Nirvana* or the heavenly realm anytime one is willing. Hence, we can suppose all mankind is capable of experiencing pure consciousness through entering the introvertive mystical experience or the nirvana enlightenment regardless of how different we are in terms of culture, period, language, religion, etc.; however, pure consciousness is not easily reachable by an ordinary secular person's pursuit because it requires highly advanced and vigorous spiritual training, as aforementioned in the example of "Katha Upanishad" about one achieving the highest state, which is being in pure consciousness. This is why my comparative research sources are mostly ascetics' mystical experiences of different religions. What Marlow argued was that there was a possibility of cultural exchanges between the East and the West since the ancient period; thus, the Eastern philosophy text, *The Upanishads*, might have influenced their thought and religious practice since long ago. This explains why Neo-Platonist, Hindu, and Buddhist mystics share some similarities, but what about Christians, like Eckhart, whose mystical experience was similar to mystics of Neo-Platonism,

---

[224] Stace, *Teachings of the Mystics*.

Hinduism, and Mahayana Buddhism? This probably had to do with Eckhart's mystical experience reaching the highest point, which was the experience of the pure consciousness, like other mystics who had reached their highest state; thus, they expressed the same notion of their mystical experiences.

Up to this point, I have examined comparative sources on the mystical experiences of Eckhart and Ruysbroeck, who were the Catholic mystics, with teachings of *The Upanishads* and the Korean Buddhist monks, Jitong's and Jinjeong's mystical experiences and found similar elements between them. In the next part, I shall probe into an orally transmitted shamanic song, "Princess Bari," to compare it with the other introvertive mystical experiences (i.e., Jinjeong's) to find out whether their experiences also share some common elements. I deem "Princess Bari" also alludes to Princess Bari obtaining the *nirvana* enlightenment or the introvertive mystical experience before she becomes the Goddess of Necromancer.

"Princess Bari" is an enlightenment story, in which she travels to the other world to look for the water of life and the herbs of life for her dying parents. During her travel to the other world, she meets the shaman god Musang, who guards the Seocheon Flower Field, where the water of life and herbs of life exist; then she marries him to gain what she needs and returns to this world and revives her parents with the water of life and the herbs of life. Afterward, she resigns from the secular world to become the Goddess of Necromancer. The story's climax is the mystical union of the shaman god Musang and Princess Bari, which I deem to be her acquiring the *nirvana* enlightenment or the introvertive mystical experience.

However, the different element of Princess Bari gaining the *nirvana* enlightenment from Jinjeong is that she has the sacred union with the god Musang, instead of having indrawn her senses, mind, and intellect within herself and thus has the unity within her like Jinjeong's *nirvana* enlightenment. Princess Bari's sacred union with the god is rather similar to a Christian mystic having the sacred union with Jesus. Furthermore, it is similar to Nohill, the Buddhist monk, having the sacred union with Avalokitesvara in the Nohill and Daldal story, which I will explain in the following chapter. Nevertheless, the answer to different attributes in mystical experience is well explained by Evelyn Underhill. According to her, unlike ordinary secular followers of different religions, mystics share similar religious experiences, but what these mystics encounter during their mystical experiences could be different from their actual religions' images that arise from their theologies.[225] She mentioned that the important point was how these mystics were aware of their gods, and what kind of relationship they had with their gods—whether they were in love or possessed by them—communion with their gods were necessary elements of mysticism.[226] The following are different characteristics of how mystics feel about their gods: "Plotinus rapt to the 'bare pure One'; St. Augustine's impassioned communion with Perfect

---

[225] Evelyn Underhill, "The Essential of Mysticism," in *Understanding Mysticism*, ed. Richard Woods (Garden City, NY: Image Books, 1980), 28.

[226] Loc. cit.

Beauty; Eckhart declaring his achievement of the 'wilderness of God'; . . . Ruysbroeck describing his achievement of 'that wayless abyss of fathomless beatitude where the Trinity of divine persons possess their nature in the essential Unity' . . ."[227] Therefore, the way mystics portray the image of gods may be different, but they are all aware of their relationship with the gods. The way Princess Bari has a relationship with the god Musang is permanent communion with the god. In the story, Princess Bari is to marry him for one hundred years and bears seven sons for him, which signifies she becomes a permanent family member of the god; hence, she can be deemed the mystic who has permanent communion with the god.

Subsequently, the story tells that she goes to the other world by walking, which could be alluding to two different possibilities: the one may be referring to her physical walking to get to the other world, and the other may be denoting her spirit taking a flight to the other world.[228] As the aforementioned example of "Katha Upanishad": "Though sitting, It travels far; though lying, It goes everywhere";[229] thus, she may be going to the other world sitting, in the meditative state, just like Jinjeong, who fell into deep meditative state for seven days, yet

---

[227] Ibid. 29.

[228] Stephen Owen, trans. and ed. *Anthology of Chinese Culture: Beginnings to 1911* (New York: W. W. Norton & Company, 1996), 176–81. Owen mentions that a shaman's spirit journey to the other world is similar to an adept Daoist's spirit journey. A good example of his remark is Qu Yuan's "Far Roaming," which is contained in the "Lyrics of Chu." Ibid.

[229] Paramananda, "Katha Upanishad," part 2, section 21, p. 37.

he probably was able to go home to see his deceased mother or tried to lead his deceased mother to heaven, but he could not for some obstacles.

The main difference in the Princess Bari story having the introvertive mystical experience or the *nirvana* enlightenment with other sources is that Princess Bari has the sacred marriage in the other world. This probably has to do with her sacred function, in which she effectuates the role of transporting the deceased souls to the other world. Hence, she has to go to the other world and get married to the god of the other world to legitimize her sacred function. Moreover, the other world or the nether world is a symbolic place to experience the introvertive mystical experience or the *nirvana* enlightenment. Even with Jinjeong's *nirvana* enlightenment, being in seven days of meditation, he could have visited the other world, where his deceased mother's soul probably resided, and got to know the situation she was in and tried to lead her to heaven. Jinjeong's *nirvana* enlightenment is recorded tersely, whereas Princess Bari's *nirvana* enlightenment is explained in detail since it is a shamanic song and still being practiced in the shamanic rituals even nowadays. Therefore, they appear to be completely different; but in reality, they could have the same *nirvana* enlightenment—the only difference being the nature of gods they are united in. For example, Princess Bari is in the union with the shaman god Musang, whereas Jinjeong with his Self and the Universal Self or the emptiness. Furthermore, as in Suzuki's quote that aforementioned in the beginning of this chapter, which mentions that the enlightened beings progressed into the *nirvana* enlightenment by being free from all bindings in the world and "landing on the other shore of the stream of *samsara*, where all things are viewed in their state of suchness, in the way of purity."[230] Princess Bari and Jinjeong deem to have visited "the other shore of the stream of *samsara*," which is the other world, and return to this world. This is like Er visiting the other world after his death in war and returning to life again, telling about his experience of the other world in "Myth of Er," which is a story I will explain in more detail in the next chapter. Hence, my contention is that both Jinjeong's and Princess Bari's *nirvana* enlightenments or the introvertive mystical experiences are similar in nature but appear to be different because of the way they are articulated in different genres.

In summary of chapter 2, the meaning of enlightenment can be understood in two ways: the general meaning, in which he/she gains wisdom, so he/she understands the way nature and mankind operate in the world; the other is the Buddhist term, such as gaining the *nirvana* enlightenment; thus, one can enter *Nirvana* at one's will. Even in entering *Nirvana*, there are two ways to understand the term: one is *tatha-ta* (suchness), which signifies the deceased soul completely joins the state of *Nirvana* that it is never fated to reincarnate in this world; the other is what the schools of the philosophy of mysticism contend—one can enter the *nirvana* enlightenment or the introvertive mystical experience while alive for a few minutes, hours, or days.

---

[230] Suzuki, op. cit., 130.

In this chapter, I examined Eckhart's and Jitong's extrovertive mystical experiences first and found similar elements between their experiences. Afterward, I introduced what is currently being debated among different schools of Western philosophy of mysticism—what it is like to experience the introvertive mystical experience or the *nirvana* enlightenment while alive. There are two extreme schools of thought, the Perennialist and Constructivist: the Perennialist is the one who contends for the common core theory, which asserts that mystics' experiences are basically the same regardless of their different backgrounds (i.e., countries, religions, periods, languages, cultures, etc.), but their interpretations are different; the Constructivist argues for the diverse theory, which persists mystics' experiences are all different. Walter T. Stace was one of the head pioneers of the Perennialist, who introduced the way to research mysticism in philosophy; and he analyzed the mysticism in the extrovertive mystical experience, and the introvertive mystical experience, which was the same as the nirvana enlightenment.[231] Stace argued that the introvertive mystical experience or the *nirvana* enlightenment was a more fully matured enlightenment experience than the extrovertive mystical experience, with which point of view I agree. Then for the sources to analyze the introvertive mystical experience, I referred to Eckhart's sermons, Ruysbroeck's mystical writing, "Katha Upanishad," and the Jinjeong story, and I compared their mystical experiences and found out that they were expressing about the same introvertive mystical experience or the *nirvana* enlightenment. Consequently, these sources well reflect what

---

[231] Stace, *Teachings of the Mystics*, 17–22, 83.

Otto contended: Eckhart's mystical experiences were similar to Plotinus of Greece, Shankara of India, and mystics of Mahayana Buddhism; thus, his assertion is cogent although more cross-culture comparative research is needed.

I also compared the shamanic song "Princess Bari" with the Jinjeong story for the *nirvana* enlightenment experience and found out some similarities between them albeit they appear to be different on the surface due to the nature of different genres' articulation. In the next chapter, I shall examine the methods of gaining enlightenment suggested in the Nohill and Daldal story and the Jitong story in the *Samgook Yusa* and "Princess Bari."

CHAPTER 3

THE ENLIGHTENMENT METHODOLOGIES REPRESENTED IN THE *SAMGOOK YUSA* AND "PRINCESS BARI"

The way to gain enlightenment represented in the *Samgook Yusa* stories is mainly based on Buddhist ascetics following the Hinayana (the Lesser Vehicle) Buddhism cultivation method (the Hinayana method) or the Mahayana (the Greater Vehicle) Buddhism cultivation method (the Mahayana method); then the ascetics obtain a god's or goddess's response, which will lead them to obtain enlightenment. In the Hinayana method, ascetics strictly maintain their precepts, practice vigorous meditation, afterward awaken their *kundalini* and activate their seven *chakras*, which will lead them to the union with a god or a goddess, like the Shiva and Shakti union in their *sahasrara chakra* (the crown of the head);[232] thus, they gain enlightenment. The other Hinayana method represented in the source is that ascetics could not have awakened their *kundalini*, but they could have the union with their Self (*Atman*) and the Universal Self (*Brahman*) or a god or a goddess in their *anahata chakra* (the heart).[233] The texts referring to the highest state or the *nirvana* enlightenment or the introvertive mystical experience I mentioned in chapter 2 are

---

[232] See footnote 73.
[233] Gopi Krishna, *Kundalini*.

109

mainly about having the union with their Self (*Atman*) and the Universal Self (*Brahman*), One, nature, or God. Eastern religions' ascetics usually express having the union with the Universal Self, nature, emptiness, a god or a goddess; and Western religions' ascetics mention they have the union with God or the Godhead.

The ascetics who cultivate in the Mahayana method usually practice vigorous meditation and devote themselves in welfare services for others as well; they also strive to awaken their *kundalini* and have the union with a god or a goddess in their *sahasrara chakra*, like the union of Shiva and Shakti. What they strive to achieve in enlightenment is the same as the Hinayana method cultivating ascetics; however, with the Mahayana method of cultivating ascetics in the *Samgook Yusa* stories, some of them are married, so the way they follow their precepts may not be as strict as the Hinayana method of cultivating ascetics. Nevertheless, they lead the life of serving public welfare; thus, they accumulate virtue, from which would enable them to gain a god's or a goddess's response easily. Hence, they can gain enlightenment more easily than the Hinayana method of cultivating ascetics. A good example story of this situation that I will examine in this chapter is the Nohill and Daldal story. Afterward, I will analyze the Jitong story, which does not mention either the Hinayana or Mahayana cultivation method, but it alludes to him gaining enlightenment by a response from Bohyun Bodhisattva, which I mentioned in chapter 2, as universally common, the extrovertive mystical experience. Jitong's enlightenment experience arises from his sacredness, which is more related with mankind's nature than any specific religious cultivation method.

The shamanic song "Princess Bari" can be perceived as the story of Princess Bari acquiring *nirvana* enlightenment by cultivating the Mahayana method, if viewed from the Buddhist perspective. However, from the viewpoint of traditional Korean thought, she can be deemed to obtain enlightenment by the way of *poongrhu* (*poongrhudo*) because the song contains not only elements of shamanism and Buddhism but also Confucianism, immortality, Hinduism, and the ancient Mesopotamian purification ceremony as well as heroism; and it seemed that *poongrhudo* enabled such different religious elements to be syncretized into the shamanic song "Princess Bari."

According to Moon-tae Kim, the Nohill and Daldal story signifies how different cultivation methods (i.e., the Mahayana and Hinayana methods) enabled their enlightenment: Nohill gains enlightenment first by obtaining Avalokitesvara's response, and Daldal with the help of Nohill.[234] Kim asserts that since Avalokitesvara responded to Nohill, who cultivated the Mahayana method, the story seems to suggest Avalokitesvara prefers an ascetic who practices the Mahayana method; however, he points out that it rather depends on who is able to affect the Bodhisattva's sympathy by showing their painstaking cultivation rather than which cultivation method the ascetics adopt, based on the Nohill and Daldal story and other stories he examined about the issue of obtaining enlightenment by a

---

[234] Moon-tae Kim, "Deukdo Yangsang," 293.

god's response.²³⁵ Then he quotes, "When there is affection, there must be a response, which means feelings are shared; and the utmost virtue moves a deity."²³⁶ Kim interprets the quote as "The affection is done by mankind, and the response to it by Buddha; in other words, water cannot ascend to the sky nor the moon can descend to the ground, yet it is like the moon shines all over the lake."²³⁷ Furthermore, says he that this "alludes to only after an ascetic spent painstaking cultivation, Buddha is affected to respond to it, which demonstrates the ascetic is sharing feeling with the deity or can move the deity to respond; and this relationship is not only referring to Buddhists and Buddha but it also to all other religions' followers and their deities."²³⁸ The Nohill and Daldal story signifies the same relationship. In order to obtain enlightenment, a deity's response is needed; whether the ascetics follow the Hinayana or Mahayana method, they must affect a deity to respond to their wishes to acquire their enlightenment. Nohill gains enlightenment by helping a young woman, who is the avatar of Avalokitesvara; thus, Nohill acquires Avalokitesvara's response. For this, Kim contends that the story well represented "*Gameung Dogyo,*"²³⁹ which I quoted above. Kim's argument—in which ascetics' cultivation method is not essential, but how they affect the god's or goddess's response by showing their

---

²³⁵ Ibid.

²³⁶ "*Gameung Dogyo,*" as quoted by Moon-tae Kim, op. cit., 300–1.

²³⁷ Loc. cit.

²³⁸ Ibid. Gang-ok Lee also asserts that either Buddha's or Bodhisattva's response is needed in order to obtain enlightenment, op. cit., 224.

²³⁹ Moon-tae Kim, "Deukdo Yangsang," 300-1.

painstaking cultivation effort is crucial—seems more valid for other enlightenment stories than the Nohill and Daldal story because in the Nohill and Daldal story, their different cultivation methods are directly related with how they affect the Bodhisattva's response, which leads them to their different degree of enlightenment. Therefore, the story specifically suggests Avalokitesvara preferred the Mahayana cultivation method. This is only a natural outcome because the Bodhisattva belief arose with Mahayana Buddhism; hence, Nohill, who helps the avatar of Avalokitesvara, obtains enlightenment by the response of Avalokitesvara is well represented in the story. Gopi Krishna—who was a twentieth-century Indian spiritual teacher and had awakened his *kundalini* by meditation method, thus gained the nirvana enlightenment—also mentioned that the ascetic's good heart was absolutely necessary in order to affect a divinity's response to help the ascetic gain enlightenment.[240] In the Nohill and Daldal story, the main distinction between them is their hearts. Nohill displays a warmhearted Buddhist ascetic, while Daldal a coldhearted one. Thus Ilyeon, the compiler and the commentator of the *Samgook Yusa*, also conveyed that the ascetics' hearts were directly related to acquiring the deity's response in this story.

---

[240] Gopi Krishna, op. cit., 102; in here, Krishna refers to the *Prana*, which is life energy, instead of a divinity.

3.1 The Enlightenment Methodology Represented in the *Samgook Yusa*

The following is a brief summary of the Nohill and Daldal story:

> In a village called Seoncheonchon lived two men, Nohill-Budeuk and Daldal-Barkbark, who were extraordinary and strived to gain enlightenment. When they became twenty years old, they shaved their heads and became Buddhist monks. They were married, so they had to support their families, but they realized life was transitory, so they left their families and went to a deeper mountain valley to obtain enlightenment to become Buddha. Before they left their families, in one night, they had the same dream, in which "*baekhoguang*[241] came from the West, and within the light, a golden arm came down to rub the two men's forehead."
>
> At last they moved to Baekwol Mountain. Nohill settled in a hermitage near water, under a stones-hill on the east ridge, to cultivate his enlightenment to become Mireuk Buddha. Daldal settled in *sajaarm* (teacher's hermitage) on the north ridge to cultivate his enlightenment to

---

[241] *Baekhoguang* is *baekho* light, which is a white shining light that exists between the eyebrows of the Buddha. Ilyeon, "The Nohill and Daldal Story," *Samgook Yusa*, footnote 5, 359.

become Amita Buddha. When they cultivated for a little less than three years (Silla King, Sungdeok, eighth year, 709 CE), in the evening, a beautiful woman, looking about twenty years old, came to Daldal's hermitage and asked to stay overnight since she could not go on in the mountain at night. However, Daldal was afraid that she might contaminate his hermitage, so he told her to leave his hermitage without caring for her safety at night. Then she came to Nohill's hermitage to ask if she could stay overnight. Nohill was worried about a woman staying in his hermitage, but he was more concerned about her safety at night; thus, he wanted to find out what her real intention by asking her several questions. At this, the woman realized that he had a warm heart who cared for mankind's agony, so she told him the truth that she came there to help him obtain enlightenment. Nohill then permitted her to stay in his hermitage overnight. When she was in the room, Nohill turned his back from her and was chanting under a dim light; all of a sudden, she asked him to lay some hays on the ground since she was about to give birth. After she gave birth, she asked him to help her with the bath. Nohill sympathized with her situation that he brought in warm water to give her a bath. All of a sudden, the bathwater turned gold color, so Nohill was shocked. Then she told him to take a bath in the gold water. When he followed, suddenly, his mind was awakened, and his skin color turned to gold. Then she asked him to sit on the lotus seat next to him. When he followed, she said, "I am Avalokitesvara. I came to help you gain enlightenment," then she disappeared.

At this point, Daldal was expecting Nohill probably was seduced by her; thus, he broke the monk's precepts. On the contrary to his expectation, Nohill was sitting on top of the lotus seat and became Mireuk Buddha. Daldal was shocked and asked him what happened. Nohill explained everything about her. At this, Daldal lamented his foolishness and asked Nohill to help him also to obtain enlightenment. Then Nohill told him that there was still water left in the washing container, so he told him to take a bath. When Daldal took a bath, he also became Amita Buddha. When these two Buddhas were sitting in front of each other, people in the village heard the news and came to worship them. Then they gave the people Buddhist lectures and disappeared by riding clouds.

When Silla King Gyungdeok reigned (755 CE), he wanted to worship them by building a temple called Baekwolsan Namsa. He placed Mireuk Buddha in the Geumdang and Amita Buddha in the Gangdang. However, when he made Amita Buddha, there was not enough gold paint left to finish Amita Buddha's gilding that Amita Buddha had smeared.[242]

In the story, the words that alluded to two different Buddhist ascetics' characteristics were the locations of their hermitages, although Moon-tae Kim perceives their location might be related with their meditation methods.[243] Nohill stayed in a hermitage on the east side where the sun rises, Daldal on the north side where a chill wind blows. Moreover, Nohill's hermitage was located near water under a stones-hill, which alluded his characteristic was as strong as stones but with flowing water like compassion; Daldal's place was called *sajaarm* (teacher's

---

[242] Ilyeon, "The Nohill and Daldal Story," 358-63 summary.

[243] Moon-tae Kim mentions that in the records of the *Hyangjeon* (The records of the local people), Daldal is located in a hermitage on the south side, and Nohill on the north side; however, Ilyeon gainsaid that three times, the records were incorrect. Ilyeon argued that Nohill stayed in hermitage on the south side and Daldal on the north side. Kim suggests that the reason Ilyeon argued about their locations in that way might have to do with their cultivation methods, which are directly related with their suggested locations. Kim says that "I cannot be absolutely sure, but the way Ilyeon perceived Daldal's hermitage on the north side represented Shinsoo's northern sect of meditation method, which espoused gaining enlightenment through slow progress; whereas Nohill's hermitage on the south side alluded to obtaining enlightenment suddenly, which was related to Haeneung's southern sect of meditation. Moreover, Daldal, who appeared lofty, stayed in the north and awakened slowly, which method symbolized northern sect of meditation; and Nohill, who seemed to have transcended attitude, stayed in the south and awakened suddenly, which method signified the southern sect of meditation." Op. cit., 302.

hermitage), which symbolized an austere monk. Thus, locations of their hermitages signified different characteristics of the ascetics. As Ilyeon commentated at the end of the story, "The memo, the beautiful lady gave to Daldal was pitiful, lovable, and an earnest request that even had the air of an angel from heaven."[244] However, considering the characteristic of Daldal, suggested by his hermitage location, no matter how pitiful and lovable the woman was, she could not arouse his compassion. He only thought about obtaining enlightenment, so he rigorously cultivated his meditation without caring for others. On the other hand, where Nohill stayed, stones and water were placed harmoniously; thus, it suggested he had strong volition like stones and softness like water, which enabled him to empathize with other people. Thus, when the young woman asked to stay in his room overnight, he did not reject her right away like Daldal but asked her several questions to find out her real intentions. He might have doubted why such a young woman was in a deep mountainside at night. So he wanted to find out whether her coming to his hermitage was to ruin his monk's precepts or not by asking questions. Thus, the woman realized his intention and told him directly that she came there to help him gain enlightenment knowing he had compassion for other people.

In the story, how two ascetics had different attitudes toward the woman was to symbolize the different ideals between the Hinayana and Mahayana cultivation methods. Daldal, who never aroused compassion toward the woman in a difficult situation,

---

[244] Ilyeon, "The Nohill and Daldal Story," 364.

but only worried that she might corrupt his hermitage, thus told her to leave the area; such an attitude was to symbolize the Hinayana cultivation method. However, Nohill aroused compassion toward the woman in hardship and thus told her to stay there, although he was worried that he could be ruined from obtaining enlightenment if he broke the monk's precepts. Thus, he took a considerable risk, like falling from a cliff if he stepped on the wrong side of the ground, which would be like ruining his soul for eternity. Therefore, when she was in his room, he turned around from her and was chanting continuously, not to lose his concentration on the purpose of acquiring enlightenment. By showing such compassion toward the young woman, who was the avatar of Avalokitesvara, regardless of his risk of ruining the chance of obtaining his enlightenment, he was taken highly by Avalokitesvara. Thus Nohill's attitude toward the young woman symbolized the ideal of the Mahayana cultivation method, which emphasized compassion for others is equally important as his acquiring enlightenment.

In the story, whether the ascetics could arouse compassion toward the young woman was directly related to whether they could have a union with the deity. Because she was the avatar of Avalokitesvara, arousing compassion for her could offer them a chance to unite with Avalokitesvara, who could help them obtain enlightenment. The emotion Nohill aroused was pity, which empathized with the feeling of the young woman, who enabled them to unite together. And the allusion to their spirits being united together was articulated as taking a bath together: the bathwater symbolizes spirits. This is just Ilyeon's figurative expression to allude they were united spiritually. Moreover, the bathwater turned gold color, which signified the water held Avalokitesvara's rays, that is, wisdom. The gold is the most valuable mineral. If we compare gold in mankind, it signifies wisdom, which is the most valuable attribute. Therefore, Nohill taking a bath in gold water with the woman who was the avatar of Avalokitesvara means he united spiritually with Avalokitesvara and gained her rays, or lights, which suggests brightness or wisdom; thus, he was deemed to obtain enlightenment. Furthermore, another interpretation is possible. The symbol of Nohill taking a bath together with Avalokitesvara in gold water could mean he spiritually united with the goddess in his *sahasrara chakra* (the crown of the head). As Nohill was shocked by the bathwater turning to gold color, he could have been astounded by looking at the lights in his *sahasrara chakra*. The gold also symbolizes lights. Thus, Nohill might have spiritually united with her in his *sahasrara chakra*, just like the union of Shiva and Shakti. The story mentioned Nohill's head became very clairvoyant and his skin turned to gold when they took the bath together; this could mean his body received some kind of light. In other words, he saw the lights in his *sahasrara chakra* and lights from other parts of the body. Most of all, his enlightenment was the *nirvana* enlightenment, as suggested by the lotus seat given by Avalokitesvara. The lotus seat symbolizes *prajna paramita*, in which the highest wisdom, *prajna*, one gains first; then by performing virtue, which is required to enter *Nirvana*, one gains *paramita*.[245] Hence, Nohill practiced the Mahayana cultivation method, which enabled him to arouse compassion

---

[245] Zimmer, *Myths and Symbols*, 98-100.

for the woman, and it symbolized his virtue, so he could be seen as gaining both wisdom (*prajna*) and virtue (*paramita*), that he gained the *nirvana* enlightenment. Moreover, the lotus seat is the throne of Buddha, so Avalokitesvara giving him the lotus seat alludes that he has gained the *nirvana* enlightenment like Buddha.

However, Daldal was said to take a bath in the remaining gold water by himself and became Amita Buddha, but his enlightenment was suggested to be not as perfect as Nohill's enlightenment because he lacked compassion, which signified virtue. The meaning of Daldal taking the bath alone symbolized that he did not have the union with Avalokitesvara. He could have united with his Self in his heart. But his union with the Self might not have been as perfect as Nohill's union with Avalokitesvara since it was recorded that when King Gyungdeok built the Buddhist temple to pay a tribute to their enlightenment, Amita Buddha, who symbolized Daldal, was not finished perfectly with gilding that had some unfinished spots. This suggested Daldal's enlightenment was not as complete as Nohill's enlightenment.

To this, Pyung-hwan Cho mentions that "Daldal was able to gain enlightenment and became Amita Buddha with the help of Nohill"; also, says he that Gwangdeok, who sang "Wonwang saengga," practiced the Hinayana cultivation method and ended up going to Seobang Jeongto, the earthly paradise in Western Pure Land, where Amita Buddha was known to reside. But by practicing the Hinayana method, "they were only interested in their own salvation and could not gain Buddhahood who had intention to lead mankind to salvation."[246] Furthermore, he criticized the ascetics who espoused Amita Buddha's paradise, Seobang Jeongto, as superior to Mireuk Buddha's paradise, Dosolcheon, the heavenly paradise, because the ascetics who wished to become Amita Buddha practiced the Hinayana cultivation method.[247]

I deem Ilyeon alluded Nohill's enlightenment as superior to Daldal's enlightenment. Nohill practiced the Mahayana cultivation method and obtained the *nirvana* enlightenment, which symbolized gaining both wisdom and virtue, to be able to enter *Nirvana*, and he became Mireuk Buddha, who was known to reside in the heavenly realm, Dosolcheon. However, Daldal practiced the Hinayana cultivation method and became Amita Buddha, who was known to stay in the earthly paradise in Western Pure Land, with the help of Nohill, but he was lacking in virtue; thus, he could not obtain as perfect enlightenment as Nohill did. Based on Ilyeon's allusion to preferring Nohill's enlightenment, Ilyeon probably perceived Mireuk's paradise, Dosolcheon, the heavenly realm, as superior to Amita's paradise, Seobang Jeongto, the earthly realm. Gang-ok Lee also contends that the purpose of Ilyeon representing Nohill possessing compassion, which enabled him to help the young woman, was what he deemed to be Mahayana Buddhism monk's proper behavior as he represents a Bodhisattva.[248] It appears that the enlightenment story of Nohill and Daldal figuratively expressed

---

[246] Pyung-hwan Cho, "Mita Sasang," 359, 364.

[247] Ibid., 357–360.

[248] Gang-ok Lee, "Choolga Deukdodam," 233.

what Ilyeon considered the most ideal way of cultivating was to follow the Mahayana cultivation method and criticized those who followed the Hinayana cultivation method.

However, Moon-tae Kim contends that Ilyeon did not necessarily prefer the Mahayana cultivation method, as what appeared in the Naksan Yidaesung story. As for Wonhyo, who practiced the Mahayana method, and Uisang, the Hinaya method, Ilyeon did not suggest which method was superior, but he rather introduced a variety of different cultivation methods.[249] I agree with him on some part of his point of view, but not totally agree with him; there are enlightenment stories that Ilyeon did not signify his preference upon which method Buddhist ascetics followed, such as the Naksan Yidaesung story; however, there are also stories which he specifically suggested his preference for the Mahayana cultivation method. Ilyeon covertly expressed the ideal way for a Mahayana Buddhist monk to behave as an ideal Bodhisattva. I deem what Ilyeon tried to convey in his viewpoint on the most critical Mahayana Buddhism monk's exemplary behavior representing a Bodhisattva in the stories was expressed in the book's last chapter with the filial piety theme in the Jinjeong story and the Daesung story.

Jinjeong became a Buddhist monk who was skilled at falling into deep meditation under Uisang's teaching. After three years passed since he left home, he heard the news of his mother being deceased; he could not bear the sadness of his mother's passing, that he entered deep meditation and did not wake up until seven

---

[249] Moon-tae Kim, "Deukdo Yangsang," 306.

days passed.²⁵⁰ I argued in chapter 2 that the state Jinjeong was in for seven days of deep meditation was the introvertive mystical experience or the *nirvana* enlightenment. Moreover, Jinjeong's state of deep meditation enabled him to assuage his pain of losing his mother and to see his deceased mother's soul; then he probably tried to guide her soul to enter the heavenly realm, but he could not for some obstacles, which might have been her lack in wisdom or virtue. Thus, he woke up from the meditation and told his teacher, Uisang, something. Consequently, Uisang invited three thousand disciples to Buddhist sutra lectures in Chudong for ninety days; when Uisang finished the ninety days of lectures, Jinjeong's deceased mother appeared in Jinjeong's dream to tell him that she was born in heaven.²⁵¹ The way Jinjeong made it possible to transport his deceased mother to heaven was his ability to enter deep meditation, which is the *nirvana* enlightenment; by doing so, he was able to see what prevented her from entering heaven. Based on the context of the story, it was possible that Jinjeong told Uisang about what was his mother's obstacle in entering heaven; thus, it seemed that Uisang resolved her obstacle by giving the ninety days of lectures and was able to make her born in heaven.

Furthermore, as the actual title of the Jinjeong story being "Hyoseon Ssangmi" (Jinjeong's filial piety and good deeds are equally beautiful), he probably helped other decedent souls to be transported to nice places by utilizing his ability to enter the *nirvana* enlightenment at his will, just like he helped his mother

---

[250] Ilyeon, "The Jinjeong Story," 573.

[251] Ibid., 573–4.

enter heaven by getting rid of her obstacle. Thus, his acquiring the *nirvana* enlightenment effected a major role in transporting his deceased mother's soul to heaven and probably other people's deceased souls too. Based on the story, Ilyeon perhaps wanted to illustrate Jinjeong as his ideal role model of Bodhisattva, who obtained the *nirvana* enlightenment and was able to help his mother and other people, and he wished to convey the proper way for an enlightened Buddhist monk to behave in society. The Daesung story conveys a similar message of a Buddhist monk representing a Bodhisattva's ideal.

> Daesung lived with his mother but was very poor that he worked for the household of Bokan, who gave Daesung a small portion of land to farm. One day, Jeomgae, who was well-known Buddhist monk for his virtuous way, came to Bokan's house to ask for donation for "*yooklunhui*"[252] prayer gathering in the Buddhist temple, Heunglunsa.
>
> Bokan donated fifty rolls of hemp cloths. Then Daesung heard what Jeomgae told Bokan, "If you donate one, you will get it back ten thousand times." After Daesung came back home, he told his mother that he did not donate

---

[252] *Yooklunhui* is a prayer gathering for a higher stage of the transmigration of souls. There are six cycles (hell, a hungry ghost, animals, birds, human beings, and heaven) of reincarnation; in this prayer event, human beings repent their accumulated sins by doing good deeds and pray not to fall below the human beings' stage.

much in his past life, so he was born poor in the present life. Therefore, he suggested to his mother, how about donating all of the farmland he received from Bokan to the Buddhist temple to have a better future in the afterlife. His mother agreed to his suggestion. So he donated everything. Then, not too long after, Daesung died and reincarnated as the prime minister's son.

When he was born, he held a tag with his name 'Daesung' written in his hand, so other people got to know he was the past life Daesung reincarnated. Thus they found Daesung's past life mother and brought her to the prime minister's house and lived together. When he grew up, he also became the prime minister of Silla and built a famous Buddhist temple, the Boolgooksa, for his present-life parents, and a Buddhist stone grotto, the Seokgoolarm, for his past-life parents.[253]

The story illustrated how Daesung donated everything he had to a prayer event, *yooklunhu*i, held in the Heunglunsa Buddhist temple by a virtuous monk, Jeomgae, and he reincarnated to a much-improved status, later became the country's prime minister, and built famous Buddhist architecture for both his past-life and present-life parents; thus, he was able

---

[253] Part of summary from the Daesung story; Ilyeon, *Samgook Yusa*, 575-6.

to perform loyalty to his country and filial piety to his parents. However, in the story, the figure who enabled Daesung to perform both loyalty and filial piety was the virtuous monk named Jeomgae. The meaning of his name, Jeomgae, alludes to "open the way gradually." So to speak, he was the figure who could improve somebody's way of life. Daesung probably was awakened all of a sudden when he heard Jeomgae tell Bokan, "If you donate one, you will receive ten thousand times more." Hence, he could see the reality of his present-life situation and decided to make some changes. Especially, the figure who was performing *yooklunhui* was Jeomgae, who probably influenced Daesung's reincarnation. Jeomgae was known for his virtuous way at that period in Silla; and Daesung perhaps had faith in what Jeomgae said. Thus, he was able to donate everything he had for a better life in his afterlife. Jeomgae must be a Buddhist monk who had obtained the *nirvana* enlightenment. So he was able to see how to improve Daesung's afterlife when he passed away. Jeomgae must have been a similar figure, like Pyohoon, who appears in the Pyohoon story. As Pyohoon ascended to heaven to ask the Heavenly Emperor on behalf of King Gyungdeok's wish to have a male heir to his throne, it was possible Jeomgae also ascended to the heavenly palace to promote Daesung's improved reincarnation.

I deem from both Jinjeong's and Daesung's stories that Ilyeon wanted to express figuratively the proper ways for Buddhist monks to behave as representing an ideal Bodhisattva. In other words, Ilyeon wished to tell other monks to obtain *nirvana* enlightenment so that they could gain the ability to help mankind to perform filial piety and also create occasions for mankind to be reincarnated in a promoted-life situation. He deemed this is the true ideal Bodhisattvas' way of Mahayana Buddhism. In order to emphasize his message to others, he included filial piety and promoted-reincarnation stories as the concluding chapter of the *Samgook Yusa*. Therefore, in the *Samgook Yusa*, as Moon-tae Kim suggests, there are enlightenment stories that introduce several different methods of obtaining it, but there are also stories that emphasize Ilyeon's preferred way of enlightenment method and their proper conducts after they gained enlightenment.

The next story wherein I will analyze the enlightenment methodology is the Jitong story. As aforementioned in chapter 2, Jitong's enlightenment experience is the extrovertive mystical experience, which is similar to Eckhart's extrovertive mystical experience. The way Jitong obtains enlightenment by the response of Bohyun Bodhisattva has nothing to do with either the Mahayana or Hinayana cultivation method. It rather illustrates his purity of mind, which had arisen from his sacredness, united into one mind, thus affecting Bohyun Bodhisattva's response; hence, he experienced his mind being united with nature or the Universal Self. So to speak, Jitong's purity of mind and earnestness united into one mind, which caused Bohyun Bodhisattva's response to make Jitong gain enlightenment.

Jitong was also one of the ten disciples of Uisang. When he was a child, he was a training monk, then he became a monk when he reached seven years old; at that time, a crow came to him and said, "Go to Youngchui Mountain and become a disciple of Nangji," so he went to the mountain and was resting under a tree. Then suddenly, Bohyun Bodhisattva appeared and gave him the Buddhist monk's precepts; as soon as he received it, he felt "his mind expanded, and his wisdom was awakened greatly."[254] The translator of the text, Won-joong Kim, says that the wisdom Jitong gained was so profound that he could even enter *Nirvana*.[255] Because Jitong's pure and earnest mind was united into one mind, it easily affected Bohyun Bodhisattva's compassion to arise and empathize with him. Therefore, Jitong's wisdom was greatly awakened by the Bodhisattva's response.

Jitong became a Buddhist monk at seven years old and was able to hear what a crow said: "Go to Youngchui Mountain and become a disciple of Nangji," which alluded to his mind being pure that he could easily be in the state of uniting with nature or the Universal Self. Furthermore, it is apparent that in Youngchui Mountain, how eagerly Jitong was looking for the old monk Nangji. Therefore, Bohyun Bodhisattva was easily empathized with Jitong's situation. Bohyun Bodhisattva is known as who "sits on the right side of Shakyamuni that the Bodhisattva's compassion leads mankind to salvation."[256] Consequently, Jitong obtained enlightenment due to his pure and earnest mind united into one mind, which enabled Bohyun Bodhisattva's compassion to arise and helped him to acquire great wisdom.

---

[254] Ilyeon, "The Jitong Story," 548.

[255] Ibid., footnote 2.

[256] Ilyeon, "Heunglunsa Byuck-e Guirin Bohyun Bosal," *Samgook Yusa*, 325.

> When there is affection, there must be a response.
>
> When this happens, everything will be understood:
>
> That is, the utmost virtue affects a deity.[257]

Based on the above example, we can perceive that Jitong's painstaking efforts, purity, and sacredness were also essential elements affecting Bohyun Bodhisattva's response. When Jitong met Nangji, he said, "I am Nangji. Just now a crow came to the main building and told me that 'a sacred child will arrive soon to become your disciple, so you must go out to the front to receive him.' So I came here for you."[258] In this conversation, the crow told Nangji that Jitong was a sacred child, which could be understood as Jitong was known in the world of nature or the Universal Self as a sacred child. Therefore, Jitong's purity and sacredness were equipped to be easily united with nature or the Universal Self and also caused to arise Bohyun Bodhisattva's compassion for him. The purity, sacredness, and earnestness are not related with any one specific religious cultivation method, but they are common natures of religiously cultivated mankind. Therefore, they are common elements of mankind following different religions in the world. However, Jitong encountering Bohyun Bodhisattva is a Buddhist element. This is because Jitong is a Buddhist monk. If Jitong were a Catholic priest, he would have met a Catholic saint. Consequently, the difference in which deity he or she is encountering has to do with different

---

[257] "Gameung Dogyo," as quoted by Moon-tae Kim, op. cit., 300.

[258] Ilyeon, "The Jitong Story," 548.

religious practices. But in the case of Jitong's enlightenment itself, it could be similar regardless of the different religious practitioners because his enlightenment had arisen due to his purity and sacredness united into one mind. This is a common element among different religions' followers. Hence, the Jitong story is different from the Nohill and Daldal story, which clearly dichotomizes between the Mahayana Buddhism and Hinayana Buddhism cultivation methods. Jitong's enlightenment method is a common element among different religious practitioners.

In the next part, I will examine the shamanic song "Princess Bari," how her enlightenment method is similar to or different from the above sources I have analyzed. Princess Bari did not leave to the other world for her spiritual cultivation but left to seek the water of life for her dying parents. Then in the other world, she met the unanticipated shaman god Musang and had the sacred marriage with him, after which she gained the water of life and returned to this world to revive her dying parents. When I study the main plot from the Buddhist point of view, Princess Bari seemed to gain her enlightenment by cultivating the Mahayana method; however, considering "Princess Bari" is the shamanic song, it is supposed to contain only shamanic element, yet it embraces several other religious elements, especially the enlightenment experience itself does not reflect shamanism; it rather illustrates Hinduism. Therefore, I shall examine her enlightenment methodology in the aspect of the ancient Korean religion, *poongrhudo*, which tolerated all different religious elements.

3.2 The Enlightenment Methodology Represented in "Princess Bari"

"Princess Bari" is a shamanic song, but it contains several religious elements besides shamanism. It embraces elements of shamanism, Buddhism, Confucianism, immortality, Hinduism, and the ancient Mesopotamian purification ceremony, as well as heroism that it truly represents the ancient Korean religion, *poongrhudo*, which accepted all different religious elements.

Princess Bari is born as the last and the seventh daughter of a king who is desperately waiting for a male heir to his throne; but due to her parents getting married in an inauspicious year, they just have a daughter every time. Hence, when Princess Bari is born as the seventh daughter, her father abandons her in a boat in the sea out of rage for having another daughter. However, Shakyamuni saves her and finds her foster parents to raise her. Moreover, he helps her to enter the other world to find the water of life. Examining the main plot of the story, "Princess Bari" is closely constructed with Buddhist elements. Therefore, probing the methodology of how Princess Bari gains enlightenment would be an interesting comparative source with the *Samgook Yusa* enlightenment stories, which mainly contain Buddhist monks' enlightenment stories.

In the *Samgook Yusa*, there is not an enlightenment story about a Buddhist nun, although there are several stories about goddesses (i.e., Seondo Sungmo, Avalokitesvara, Cheonsu Daebi, etc.), but these stories do not mention how they gained their enlightenment before they became goddesses. Therefore, examining how Princess Bari gains enlightenment before she becomes the Goddess of Necromancer could be meaningful. I deem the way Princess Bari gains enlightenment is not different from the way Nohill gains enlightenment. Nohill gains enlightenment by having the union with the deity, Avalokitesvara, which is the same as how Princess Bari obtains enlightenment by having the sacred marriage with the shaman god Musang. There is another possible similarity between these stories: just like Nohill, Princess Bari may have awakened her *kundalini* and activated her seven *chakras* that she seemed to have the union with the god Musang in her *sahasrara chakra* (the crown of the head). This element of union with a deity is the same attribute in how the ancient Korean shamans or shamanesses, by dancing, had the union with a god or a goddess during the ancient Korea's national founding day celebration, which many Korean scholars consider an archetype of *poongrhudo*.[259] The difference in methodology of inducing the deity to have the union in "Princess Bari" is that she does not dance in a ceremony but performs house chores (i.e., carries water for three years, makes fire for three years, and chops wood for three years) to pay the price of the water of life and the herbs of life to revive her dying parents. However, her nine years of performing house chores can be considered as her purification stage to get ready for the union with the god Musang. Thus, the methodology of inducing the union with a deity is different between the shamaness in the ancient ritual and Princess Bari, but the way they acquire enlightenment by having the union with a deity is the same.

---

[259] Dong-shik Yu, *Poongrhudo*, 42.

Dong-shik Yu's point of view upon the function of *poongrhudo* is a little different. He contends that "*poongrhudo* is not a name of certain ancient religion: its thought and culture rather enabled to accept foreign religions and to develop them into a place of cultural gathering"; furthermore, says he that it has been "the principle of Korean spirit; *poongrhudo* was not just the spirit existed in ancient Korea, but it has been Korean spirit which had formed the foundation of Korean cultural history."[260] Moreover, says he that the Korean religious culture can be viewed as built upon indigenous shamanism, which was founded with *poongrhudo*'s mentality and accepted all other foreign religions (i.e., Buddhism, Daoism, Confucianism, and Christianity); thus, it developed into a further sublimated cultural gathering place.[261] However, he asserts that based on a certain period's need, one religion played a more dominant role than the others: for example, says he, "in the ancient period, shamanism played dominant role, in the Silla and Goryeo periods Buddhism, in the Joseon period Confucianism, and in the present Christianity began to dominate Korean culture."[262]

I perceive "Princess Bari" is built upon *poongrhudo* because I also agree with Yu's contention I referred to in above. The shamanic song "Princess Bari" is structured upon shamanism, yet it syncretized different religious elements (i.e., Buddhism, immortality, Confucianism, Hinduism, and the ancient Mesopotamian purification ceremony), which were transmitted

---

[260] Ibid., 59–60.

[261] Ibid., 72.

[262] Loc. cit.

to Korea in different periods; thus, it can be considered the song was transformed into the present form by accepting the ideology of *poongrhudo*. The Princess Bari story is based on the Joseon period, but when I analyze the story's structural elements, it alludes to ancient Silla's historical and cultural attributes. Thus, it is possible to view the way Cheol-su Cho contends that the earliest archetype of the story could have formed in the ancient Silla Kingdom period.[263] In addition, during the Silla period, *poongrhudo* was at the peak of its development due to *hwarangdo*, which utilized *poongrhudo* as their foundation ideology. Considering the archetype of "Princess Bari" might have formed in the ancient Silla Kingdom and incorporated different religious elements, even Hinduism and the ancient Mesopotamian purification ceremony, which might have been transmitted by religious figures who came to Silla along with merchants of their countries,[264] the shamanic song can be perceived to contain *poongrhudo*'s ideology of syncretizing different religious elements.

According to Sung-arm Hong, "there are two ways to examine how *poongrhudo*'s ideology is absorbed in literature": one is by examining the ideology of *poongrhudo*, including immortality in literature, and another is by analyzing "the spirit of *poongrhudo* which derived from *poongrhudo* expressed naturally in literature."[265] I will examine Sung-arm Hong's first point of view in analyzing Princess Bari's enlightenment methodology.

---

[263] Cheol-su Cho, *Godae Mesopotamia*.

[264] Loc. cit.

[265] Sung-arm Hong, "Poongrhudo-ui Yinyum," 237.

In "Princess Bari" of the Gyung-jae Bae's version, the story begins with the element of shamanism. It is the Joseon Dynasty period; thus, Confucianism was the state religion, and shamanism was extremely oppressed. However, before the king and the queen got married, they sent courtiers to the shamaness's house to predict a felicitous wedding date. If they waited one year, it would be their most prosperous year, making it possible to have three princes; but they could not wait a year, so they married in the least auspicious year, which prophesied to have seven daughters. After they got married, the queen was pregnant, so they sent courtiers to the shamaness's house to foretell whether the queen would have a son or a daughter. They always get the same response from the shamaness: the queen would have a daughter because they married in an untimely year. The same story repeats seven times until the seventh daughter, Princess Bari, is born.

It is prophesied from the story's onset that they would have seven daughters because they married in an inauspicious year; however, they ignored the shamaness's prophecy completely and were hoping for different outcomes. Nevertheless, they always got disappointed by the expected results. Following any other religion besides Confucianism during the Joseon period was considered heresy and illegal, yet the king and the queen even sent courtiers to the shamaness's house whenever they were wondering about the gender of the queen's baby. Hence, from the story's beginning, it is suggested that the custom of religious hypocrisy existed during that period. The shamanistic element is apparent to the point of the queen's pregnancy with Princess

Bari. The next part of the story alludes to a heroic mythical element.

When the queen is pregnant with Princess Bari, she has a dream that seems to predict she will have a son, yet the baby turns out to be a girl. The king, desperately waiting for a son to make his heir, cannot control his rage that he throws the baby away in the rear garden. When that happens, a magpie flies over to her and protects her with its wings.

> When he throws the baby girl away in the rear garden of the back mount and turns away,
> the mount is quiet, and the pond is peaceful.
> All of a sudden wind blows away.
> A magpie unknown whence it comes flies down,
> with one wing supports the baby in the ground,
> with the other wing covers the baby.[266]

This story element is similar to the ancient Korean myth of the Goguryeo Kingdom founder, Saint King Dongmyung: it said that since he was born from an egg, his father thought it was the omen of bad luck, so he threw him away in the road, yet no animal stepped on him; thereafter, he threw him away in the field, then birds flew over to protect him.[267] Saint King Dongmyung was well-known for establishing the Goguryeo Kingdom. The Princess Bari story embracing such a heroic

---

[266] Kim and Hong, "Seoul, Gyung-jae Bae's," 130

[267] Bu-shik Kim, "Goguryeo Bonki," *Samgook Saki*, commentary by Jong-sung Kim, vol. 13 (Seoul: Janglark, 2004), 192.

mythical element alludes that her life would be heroic.[268] Dae-seok Seo also perceives that this type of motif in which "the queen's dream of a prosperous son before the birth and animals protecting the abandoned baby are not shamanic originated elements; they were rather borrowed from classical heroic novels;" so to speak, he contends that to make Princess Bari's life story sublime, the heroic element was added to the account.[269] Moreover, the allusion of birds protecting the baby could be interpreted as her being protected by a god because birds symbolize a god's messenger. Up to this point of the story, a heroic mythical element is expressed. From the next part of the story is the Buddhistic element.

The king watches the birds protecting the abandoned baby in the rear garden, yet he cannot bear the misery of seeing her born as a girl instead of a boy that he places her into a precious chest, places it in a boat, and throws it into the sea permanently. At this point, again a bevy of magpies gather around her and protect her. Shakyamuni happens to be around the sea with his disciples and watches a bevy of magpies gathered around the boat, where auspicious air is also visible. Thus, he sends his disciples to find out what is happening out there. His disciples come back and report to him a girl is in a chest in the boat. Now Shakyamuni also expresses disappointment after hearing "It is a girl in the chest."

There is a precious chest.

---

[268] Dae-seok Seo, "Bari Gongjoo Yeongoo," 241.
[269] Ibid., 236.

> If the child were a boy,
> I could make him my disciple.
> Since it is a girl, no need.²⁷⁰

Shakyamuni is disappointed because where Princess Bari is located, there is the air of auspiciousness, so it is evident that she is a special figure, but she is not a boy; thus, she cannot become his disciple. Because Princess Bari was born as a girl, she is abandoned by her father and cannot become a disciple of Shakyamuni either; nevertheless, the story alludes that a god knows her, so she is destined to live an extraordinary life, becoming the Goddess of Necromancer.

After Shakyamuni saves her from the boat, he also finds her foster parents, Biri Gongdeok grandpa and grandma, to raise her.

> Then how about raising her?
> Grandpa and Grandma say,
> in the spring, summer, and autumn, we stay outdoors.
> In the winter, we stay in a cave.
> If you raise her,
> you will get food to eat, clothes to wear.
> You will also get a cottage to stay, naturally.²⁷¹

Shakyamuni, who is a god of Buddhism, saves the life of Princess Bari, who becomes the Goddess of Necromancer; this as well may have a special allusion. It could be referring

---

²⁷⁰ Kim and Hong, "Seoul, Gyung-jae Bae's," 133.
²⁷¹ Ibid.

to Korean shamanism, which survived Confucian oppression in the Joseon period by uniting with Buddhism and receiving aid from Buddha. From Biri Gongdeok grandpa and grandma raising Princess Bari changes to the compound elements of shamanism and Confucianism. The story tells that Princess Bari is a prodigy who can read and understand texts even without learning when she reaches eight to nine years old. I wonder why the story includes the motif of her being a prodigy and literate in a shamanic song. Not only does the story express that she is a prodigy in the letter, but it also signifies that she obeys the symbol of her parents, which may connote that the Confucian practice of filial piety must be followed. At this age, she asks her foster parents where her natural parents are. They say, at first, her natural parents are heaven and earth; when the princess does not believe that, they say the giant bamboo tree is her father, and the quince tree in the backyard is her mother. Princess Bari still does not believe their answers but considers them as the symbol of her parents and pays respectful visits three times a day. This motif in the story represents the Confucian element, which emphasizes filial piety to parents as a duty.

However, on the other hand, paying respect to the tree may allude to her receiving some kind of shamanism training. The tree being the symbol of her parents, she paid it respect and visited it three times a day, which could signify a remnant custom of ancient shamanism worshiping a tree as a god. Heonseon Kim suggests a different meaning in this. The way Princess Bari's foster parents answer who her natural parents are, at first, heaven and earth, then they themselves, at last, the giant bamboo tree and the quince tree,²⁷² may suggest special meaning; so to speak, Kim argues that they are trying to explain to her the logic of nature by showing "all life is produced from the nature of heaven and earth, then it goes through growth and death, and finally it returns to nature."²⁷³ Furthermore, he asserts that "the essential motif in travel to the other world is the ability to control production and extinction."²⁷⁴ Therefore, he perceives this story element could be an allusion to Princess Bari receiving a training in the philosophical understanding of life and death ahead of her travel between this world and the other world.²⁷⁵ It is certain that the princess is learning something is suggested by saying that she is able to read and understand texts that she never learned. This alludes that she is preparing for her heroic life; on the other hand, she is receiving some training to become the Goddess of Necromancer.

Moreover, a conspicuous element in this motif is Confucianism; that is, Princess Bari pays respect and visits the tree three times a day, which is deemed a symbol of her parents. However, the shamanic element is tacitly suggested; in other words, her paying respect and visiting the tree three times a day could imply the ancient shamanic custom of tree worship, so she might have received some shamanic ritual training while she was growing up. Hence, it is possible to perceive

---

²⁷² The order in which Princess Bari's foster parents tell her who her natural parents are could be different from one variation to the another.
²⁷³ Heon-seon Kim, "Bari Gongju-ui Yeosung Shinhwa," 30.
²⁷⁴ Loc. cit.
²⁷⁵ Ibid.

that during Princess Bari's childhood, she lived a dualistic way of life in shamanism and Confucianism, symbolizing the reality of shamanism in the Joseon period. During the period, shamanism was considered heresy and strictly prohibited by the law.[276] Therefore, what shamans and shamanesses could have done without compromising the Confucian element in their shamanic song. Consequently, they probably had to incorporate the Confucian element in "Princess Bari."

The next story motif indicates the immortality element. When the king and the queen become gravely ill, they have the same dreams, in which six blue-clothed boys fly over to their palace and tell them they are the messengers of the Jade Emperor in Heaven. They prophesy that the king and the queen will die at the same hour on the same day because they abandoned the child, the Jade Emperor in Heaven knows.

> Both the king and the queen have the same dream
> at the same hour, on the same day.
> Six blue-clothed boys fly in the court of the palace
> and pay respect to them.
> Are you people or ghosts?
> Not even a bird can fly in here.
> Why did you come in?
> We are not people nor ghosts.

---

[276] Gooksa Pyunchan Wewonhui, comp., "Eumsa, Seungsang, Geotchirae-deungui Biruhan Poongsok-ul Cheoljeohe Geumji Shikida," *Joseon Wangjo Sillok*, Sejong 76, 19th year, February 14, 1437, the fourth article.

We came as messengers of the Jade Emperor in Heaven
to take your name tablets.
Keep them in the Island of Poong-doct.
. . .
Due to committing the sin of abandoning the child,
the Jade Emperor in Heaven knows,
if you become ill, at the same hour, on the same day,
you will die, at the same hour, on the same day.[277]

Then they tell the way to resuscitate their lives. They must find the abandoned child and let her search for the water of life, where the god Musang guards, brings the water, and has them drink it; then they can revive. In this motif, terms (i.e., the Jade Emperor in Heaven, the Emperor's messengers of the blue-clothed boys, the water of life, which revive their lives, etc.) are closely associated with becoming immortals. Therefore, this part of the story can be considered the immortality element.

The next story motif again reflects the Confucian element. When Princess Bari becomes fifteen years old, her parents become gravely ill. Hence, they send people to find the princess and bring her back to the palace. Her parents ask all their daughters to find the water of life for them, but they all refuse the request out of fear, except Princess Bari. She is willing to

---

[277] Kim and Hong, "Seoul, Gyung-jae Bae's," 136.

go to the other world for her parents, out of gratitude for her mother, who had kept her in her abdomen for ten months. This element signifies the Confucian value. She is not raised by her natural parents, so she is not obligated to risk her life by going to the other world; yet based on the Joseon period's Confucian ideology, no matter what, fulfilling filial piety is an absolute duty of children. This Confucian value was added to the story probably to reflect the period's ideology in "Princess Bari." Up to this point of the story, it represents its acceptance in the elements of heroism, Buddhism, immortality, and Confucianism based upon the foundation of shamanism. The next part of the story again reflects a shamanic element.

When Princess Bari goes to the other world, the Seocheon Flower Field, the road is very rough and far; thus, she wields the metal baton to contract space to shorten the distance she needs to travel.

> She wears metal hat, holds metal baton
> . . .
> Wields the baton once, goes to thousand *li*.
> Wields it twice, goes to two thousand *li*.
> Wields it thrice, goes to three thousand *li*.[278]

Then a different version articulates she is more fully equipped with metal implements.

---

[278] Ibid.,139–140. The actual measurement of 1 *li* is about 0.4 km, but this is symbolically indicating she is traveling to a faraway place.

> As you wish, grant silk clothes, metal general, metal backpack,
> metal shoes, metal baton, metal hat . . .
> Wields the metal baton once, goes to thousand *li*.
> Wields it twice, goes to two thousand *li*.
> Wields it thrice, goes to three thousand *li*.[279]

This story motif makes it possible to infer that when Princess Bari lived with her foster parents in a deep mountain, she might have learned some shamanism training. And her foster parents were found by Shakyamuni, who wanted to make her his disciple if she were a boy. He could not raise her as his disciple, so he found her foster parents who lived in a deep mountain. They could have been a shaman and shamaness since they lived away from people in a deep mountain. Hence, it is possible Princess Bari might have gotten some shamanism training there. However, Dae-seok Seo asserts that even Princess Bari did not receive any training, she could still wield the metal baton for contracting space since she was supposed to hold the supernatural power, just like Saint King Dongmyung was supernaturally skillful in archery even without learning it.[280] Heon-seon Kim contends that Princess Bari, who is able to go to the other world, is suggested by her ability to utilize metal implements (i.e., metal baton, metal shoes, and metal backpack etc.), of which he perceives them as magical tools.[281] Furthermore, says he that metal implements were originally used

---

[279] Kim and Hong, "Seoul, Deok-soon Moon's," 167.

[280] Dae-seok Seo, "Bari Gongjoo Yeongoo," 246.

[281] Heon-seon Kim, "Bari Gongju-ui Yeosung Shinhwa," 31.

by the northeast Asia shamans; however, using the method of contracting space, Princess Bari can be deemed as articulating the essence of giant goddesses in ancient Korea, and they were the goddesses of shamans and shamanesses.[282] Based on Seo's and Kim's opinions, Princess Bari seems to be fully prepared to go to the other world, being able to utilize magical tools; and when she returns from the other world with the water of life, she is destined to become the Goddess of Necromancer or the goddess of shamans and shamanesses, as already suggested from the onset of her journey to the other world.

In the next part of the story is the Buddhist element again. After Princess Bari travels some distance, she reaches the place where Shakyamuni preaches with Jijang Bodhisattva and Amita Buddha. Here, Princess Bari voices her firm determination to go to the other world to find the water of life for her dying parents, even if she dies there. Shakyamuni is impressed by her resolution that he gives her a magical implement, the *rahwa*. With the *rahwa*, the princess could change the sea into land to cross and change rough mountains to plains; thus, she could easily walk a long distance. Moreover, on the way to the other world, Princess Bari shakes the *rahwa* to release decedent souls imprisoned in hell. Hence the *rahwa* carried out the major role in her travel to the other world.

> You came three thousand *li* in plains roads,
> but how are you planning to go through
> rough roads of three thousand *li*?

---

[282] Ibid.

> Even if I die on the way, I still will go.
> I will give you the *rahwa*, take this with you.
> There will be a big sea, then shake this.
> The big sea will become land.
> There is a metal castle with thorns reaching the sky.
> She remembers what Buddha told her and shakes the *rahwa*. . . .
> Opens eighty-four thousand doors of hell,
> sends the ones who are to become ten underworld judges.
> Send the ones who are to go to hell there . . .
> Some follow Princess Bari,
> go to Western Pure Land, the World of Nirvana.[283]

In the above example, Princess Bari receiving the *rahwa* from Shakyamuni and using it to release the deceased souls imprisoned in hell to different levels of the other world (i.e., the underworld, Western Pure Land, and *Nirvana*) is the Buddhist element. One of the main rituals in Buddhism is translocating decedent souls from hell to higher stages of the other world.

The next story motif is about Princess Bari meeting the shaman god Musang. This part illustrates a different attribute from aforementioned shamanism, heroism, Buddhism, Confucianism, and immortality elements. As Princess Bari passes the doors of hell, she shakes the *rahwa* and releases more decedent souls captured in hell. Then she reaches the center of the other

---

[283] Kim and Hong, "Seoul, Gyung-jae Bae's," 141.

world; there stands god Musang. This center of the other world is the Seocheon Flower Field, where the water of life exists. The god Musang is the god of the other world, based on the description of his giant stature.

> His height is about to reach the sky.
> His face is about a round food tray.
> His eyes are about lamps.
> His nose seems to be a bottle being hung by a line.
> His hand is about the back of a cow.
> His foot is about one meter.[284]
> So shocking and scary, she steps back and bows three times.[285]

The description of the god is not only of a giant, it is hyperbolic of the *Seoyuck* (western region) people.[286] Thus, from this part of the story, cultural and religious elements of the

---

[284] The story says his foot size is in Korean measurement—three *ja* and three *chi*—which calculates to be about one meter.

[285] Kim and Hong, "Seoul, Gyung-jae Bae's," 142.

[286] Cheol-su Cho perceives that the description of the god seems to be the *Seoyuck* people. In here, the *Seoyuck* means from any Western region of ancient Korea to the Near East. Cho argues that the god Musang appears to symbolize Talhae, who was a prince from the Yongsung Kingdom and was known to be extremely tall. Op. cit. In the *Samgook Yusa*, there is a record about Talhae, who came to Silla by a ship that was full of seven types of precious goods. Among them, it is said they might have been glass items. Ilyeon referred to the *Samgook Saki's* record that mentioned the Yongsung Kingdom was somewhere in Japan, but Dong-hwan Lee perceives it in the Southern Oceania region, where they have a dragon as their totem. Thus, Korean scholars have different points of view on where the Yongsung Kingdom was. Ilyeon, *Samgook Yusa*, 76, footnote 1, 5.

Seoyuck is prominent. Princess Bari travels far west to reach the other world and meets the god who guards the water of life and the herbs of life in the Seocheon Flower Field. The god Musang, who is the god of the other world, asks if Princess Bari brought money for the water of life and the herbs of life. When she answers no, he asks her to draw water for three years, make fire for three years, and cut trees for three years.

> If you come here for the sake of filial piety, did you bring money for the water?
> Did you bring money for the herbs? I have forgotten it completely.
> Draw water for three years, make fire for three years, cut trees for three years.[287]

The above example tells she needed to pay the water of life and the herbs of life by carrying out house chores for nine years; after she had spent nine years doing what he asked her to do, he asked her to get married and bear seven sons. Thus, the nine years of house chores seemed to be preparatory stages to get married to the god.

> After three times of three years, a total of nine years lived there.
> God Musang says,
> when I see you in the front, you are a woman.
> When I see you from the back, you look like our king's body.
> How about we get married

---
[287] Kim and Hong, "Seoul, Gyung-jae Bae's," 142.

and bear seven sons before you return?

If that is required for my filial piety to my parents, o.k.[288]

Whether the nine years of house chores were her purification stages to get the union with the god, or good deeds to accumulate for her virtue, which needed to qualify for the union with the god, it was what Princess Bari must pay for. However, I wonder why the god asked her for seven sons. When I recall the Princess Bari story is mainly concerned with how she becomes the Goddess of Necromancer, having the union with the god and bearing seven sons must be closely related with the process of her becoming the goddess. I deem the symbolic meaning of the seven sons as what human beings have, seven *chakras*.[289] Hence, this may be alluding to Princess Bari having the sacred marriage to the god Musang, which signifies having her enlightenment experience; as aforementioned, Nohill having the union with Avalokitesvara and gaining the *nirvana* enlightenment. And Princess Bari bearing seven sons could be referring to activating her seven *chakras* and efficacies obtained from them. Furthermore, the seven sons, which I deem her seven *chakras*, may be referring to her having the union with the god Musang at her *sahasrara chakra* (the crown of the head) like the union between Shiva and Shakti[290] because the god specifically asks for the seven sons, which may be alluding to her seven *chakras*' activation, which will eventually make her

---

[288] Ibid.

[289] Gopi Krishna, *Kundalini*, 170.

[290] See footnote 73.

achieve transcendental consciousness. In addition, Princess Bari having the sacred union in the other world with her *chakras* being fully activated can be considered she has acquired the *nirvana* enlightenment.

I deem the sacred marriage motif in "Princess Bari" as related with the Indian Hinduism element, in which Brahmins seeking enlightenment by meditation practices, awakening their *kundalini* and activating their *chakras*' function.[291] The story seems to allude that Princess Bari goes through nine years of a purification process, then has the sacred marriage to the god Musang, which is also possible to perceive she has awakened her *kundalini* in order to have the sacred union in her *sahasrara chakra*, just like the union of Shiva and Shakti. Then the god asks her to bear seven sons, which seems to be alluding to her seven *chakras* being activated; thus, she gains efficacies of them. Gopi Krishna also mentioned that after he had awakened the *kundalini*, for fifteen years he went through physical changes, then he was able to achieve his transcendental consciousness.[292] In order to acquire transcendental consciousness, not only the *kundalini* has to be awakened but also *chakras* have to be activated to induce physical changes. Hence, the god asking for seven sons seems to signify her seven *chakras*' activation, which will eventually make her obtain transcendental consciousness. Especially the reason I deem the princess to have awakened the *kundalini* is because she is the seventh daughter, and the number seven symbolizes

---

[291] Gopi Krishna, op. cit.

[292] Ibid., 236.

wisdom.[293] According to Gopi Krishna, when one awakens the *kundalini*, one's transcendental consciousness can discover a source that shows light inside the body, and the source of the light is what grants joy and wisdom.[294]

There is another reason I deem this sacred marriage motif is related to Hinduism; it is because in the Deok-soon Moon's version of "Princess Bari," she later becomes a Bodhisattva protecting an Indian king at the end of the story. Dae-seok Seo mentions that the function of the Bodhisattva of an Indian king is also the goddess of shamanesses.[295] However, if there is no story motif related to Hinduism in "Princess Bari," her becoming the Bodhisattva guarding the Indian king at the end of the story does not make sense. Because Princess Bari has the sacred marriage with the god Musang, which is similar to the union between Shiva and Shakti, she could become the Bodhisattva protecting an Indian king at the end of the story. In "Princess Bari," the Buddhism element is overtly represented, but the Hinduism element is covertly suggested; thus, it can be perceived that both Buddhism and Hinduism elements are embraced in the shamanic song. This is not unusual, as Gopi Krishna and Heinrich Zimmer suggested, in India, that up until the middle age, Buddhism and Hinduism had the same purpose in religious practices: for example, they both sought after *Nirvana*, their methods of yoga practice leading to enlightenment was the same, starting with *dharana*, then progressing to *dhyana*

---

[293] See footnote 6.

[294] Gopi Krishna, op. cit., 208.

[295] Dae-seok Seo, op. cit., 207, footnote 7.

and *samadhi*.²⁹⁶ The main difference in Buddhism is that they established the tradition of monks and nuns who could solely practice religious cultivation, and some theological differences; that is, Buddhists espouse non-ego²⁹⁷ while Hindus believe in true ego (*Atman*, the reality of the Self). However, in terms of the basic aspect of Indian philosophy, in which one achieves freedom from illusion, Maya-Shakti, and by practicing meditation, one becomes a divinity, are what both Hindus and Buddhists have sought after.²⁹⁸

Consequently, the Princess Bari story can be perceived to include both Buddhism and Hinduism elements. Especially in the Deok-soon Moon's version, wherein Princess Bari becomes the Bodhisattva protecting an Indian king at the end of the story; it is possible because Princess Bari has the union with the god, who has similar attributes to Shiva. Shiva originally differed from other Hindu gods—Indra (thunder), Agni (fire), Vayu (wind)—who were staying in the middle of Mount Meru in the heavenly realm, according to the *Vedas*: Shiva was the god of the forest; he carried a bow and arrows, and the deceased souls were thought to be following him.²⁹⁹ The way Shiva was accepted in the Hindu tradition was that he defeated an evil king who took Mount Meru and expelled all Hindu gods; Shiva, by using his bow and arrows, made it possible for the Hindu gods to return to Mount Meru and reestablished the world order; thus,

---

296 Gopi Krishna, *Kundalini*; Zimmer, *Myths and Symbols*.
297 Suzuki, "Basics of Buddhist Philosophy," 127-8.
298 Zimmer, op. cit., 195.
299 Ibid., 185–6.

he got to be joined as one of the Hindu gods.[300] Another name for Shiva is Lord of the Deceased, which seems to be similar to the god Musang, who is the god of the other world, where the deceased souls stay. Moreover, where the god Musang stays is the Seocheon Flower Field; these characteristics are similar to Shiva, who is the god of the forest and the lord of the deceased. Furthermore, Princess Bari gains the ability to transport the deceased souls after she has the sacred marriage to the god Musang, which seems to hold similar attributes as Shakti, who materializes her husband's, Shiva's, power.[301]

The next part of the story illustrates how she changed to a divine being after she had the sacred marriage to the god. Princess Bari said that she dreamed her parents had passed away, so she had to go back home fast. Then the god Musang says,

> The water you were drawing is the water of life.
> Take on your gold general.
> The tree you were chopping is for revival of bones and flesh.
> Take it with you.[302]

> In that case the water you drew is the water of life.
> The weed you were chopping is for opening eyes.
> In the back hill of the rear garden has three kinds of plants:
> for breath revival, for bone revival, for flesh revival,

---

[300] Ibid., 186.

[301] Ibid., 193.

[302] Kim and Hong, "Seoul, Gyung-jae Bae's," 143.

three kinds of flowers, starlike, put them in your eyes.
The herbs for opening the eyes, embrace it in your body.
The water of life, put it in your mouth.
When you came, you were a metal general.
When you return, you are a gold general.³⁰³

In these examples, the former, Gyung-jae Bae's version expresses more laconic than the latter, Deok-soon Moon's, but the meaning is similar. In the Moon's version, the meaning of "for breath revival, for bone revival, for flesh revival . . . put them in your eyes. / The herbs for opening the eyes, embrace it in your body. / The water of life, put it in your mouth," is Princess Bari's body has transformed that she became as the water of life and the herbs of life. And the allusion of "When you came, you were a metal general. / When you return, you are a gold general." is that she definitely changed and has gained divinity. The allusion of gold equals divinity is also expressed in the Nohill and Daldal story. In the story, the bathwater changed to gold water, which implied Avalokitesvara's light or wisdom imbued into Nohill; thus, it signified Nohill gained enlightenment. In the same way, the god Musang refers to Princess Bari as the gold general, which could be denoting her enlightened state and transformation to a divinity. In Western tradition, gold signifies wholeness or completeness, in which complete opposite elements (i.e., masculinity and femininity, the sun and the moon, the heaven and the earth, etc.) unite together

---

³⁰³ Kim and Hong, "Seoul, Deok-soon Moon's," 171.

to achieve wholeness or completeness.[304] In other words, the god of the heavens (the sun) and the mother goddess, who symbolizes the earth (the moon), uniting would be like the sacred marriage, which makes them whole or complete.[305]

Hwan-hee Kim also perceives the marriage motif in "Princess Bari" as the sacred marriage, which enables Princess Bari gaining wholeness by uniting her masculine and feminine elements in the process of individuation, as Jung contended.[306] Jung's individuation process is focused on the human psychological aspect of wholeness, whereas the other religious view (i.e., Mahayana Buddhism) of completeness or the enlightenment process is more focused on the spiritual aspect although they are aiming for the same goal.

In Western literature, the story that indicates marriage as gaining enlightenment, comparable to "Princess Bari," is the *Cinderella*. In the *Cinderella*, the story ends with the marriage between Cinderella and the prince, which could be alluding to her ego having the union with her alter-ego, represented as the prince, which has been existing in her unconsciousness; and this is Jung's theory of gaining wholeness in the human psyche. If I interpret it from the Hindu perspective, Cinderella's marriage with the prince is comparable to the Shiva and Shakti union: Shiva symbolizing the prince and Shakti Cinderella. Anne Baring perceives the *Cinderella* as the story of discovering

---

[304] Hwan-hee Kim, "Shamanist Myth," 20.

[305] Dong-shik Yu, *Poongrhudo*, 60.

[306] Hwan-hee Kim, "Shamanist Myth," 23; Individuation is Jung's theory. See Jung, *Redbook*.

wisdom by having the sacred union between "the highest feminine and masculine qualities in the soul," which are symbolic of being queen and king, Cinderella and the Prince, respectively.[307] By doing so, says she, Cinderella discovers her illumination or divinity that exists within herself.[308]

The *Cinderella* story, which has been told all over the world, was collected and culled into 345 variations and published by the Folk-Lore Society in 1893.[309] The book includes Andrew Lang's foreword, who was the president of the Folk-Lore Society at that time. In the foreword, he said that he disagreed with M. Cosquin's point of view, in which the *Cinderella* story began in India because there were few similar elements, that is, young heroines who were mistreated and later recognized by their shoes; it existed in several cities in India.[310] But Lang claims that the main plot of the *Cinderella* was about a jealous stepmother and stepsisters who mistreated Cinderella, who was the daughter of the deceased wife, and Cinderella got married in higher social status with the help of magic, but Cinderella hid, so later she was found by shoes or a ring, then her stepmother and stepsisters got punished, and Cinderella had a happy wedding ceremony at the end. Lang argued that this plot could be syncretized with many

---

[307] Anne Baring and Jules Cashford, *The Myth of the Goddess: The Evolution of an Image* (London: Arkana, Penguin Books, 1993), 656.

[308] Ibid.

[309] Marian Roalfe Cox, *Three Hundred and Forty-Five Variants of Cinderella, Catskin, and Capo'Rushes, Abstracted and Tabulated, with a Discussion of Medieval Analogies, and Notes* (1893; reprint, London: Forgotten Books, 2014).

[310] Ibid.

other elements to produce variations; however, in Indian sources, there were not enough plots to give them credit.[311]

The author of the book, Marian Roalfe Cox, also criticized Henry Charles Coote, who asserted in his book, the *Folk-Lore Records,* that the *Cinderella* type of stories first began in India, from Vedic myth, and later included in the *Rg Veda,* as symbolic meanings of astronomy (i.e., the sun and the moon).[312] However, Anne Baring agrees with the viewpoint of Harold Bayley, who argued that the *Cinderella* was a story about the changes of consciousness, and the origin of such a story could be found in Gnostic or Sumerian and Egyptian myths.[313] The reason Baring perceives the *Cinderella* as the story about spiritual transformation is that the main plot has mystical elements, in which Cinderella is mistreated by her stepmother, but with the help of her godmother or the fairy-mother, she transforms into a different figure; and there is a prince who starts an adventure to find his bride, and at the end, there is a royal wedding.[314] Baring contends that in the *Cinderella,* similar elements can be found in the moon myth, which existed in the bronze age, as the ritual of plentifulness: a goddess and her partner had the sacred marriage (i.e., Inanna and Dumuzi of Sumer, Ishtar and Tammuz of Babylonia, Aphrodite and Adonis of ancient Greece, Sophia and King Solomon in Gnostic myth, etc.); then

---

[311] Ibid.

[312] Loc. cit.

[313] Baring and Cashford, op. cit., 655; Harold Bayley, *The Lost Language of Symbolism* (1912; reprint, London: Forgotten Books, 2015).

[314] Baring and Cashford, *Myth of the Goddess,* 656.

she argues that based on those myths, feelings, and experiences that have existed in mankind, in general, were imbued to make the story of the *Cinderella*.³¹⁵ She says that Cinderella wearing shabby clothes and doing all house chores are like Inanna's story about descending to the nether world, in which, although Inanna was the queen of heaven and earth, she descended to the underworld and passed through seven doors and lost all good-quality clothes, and later got killed and got hung on nails on the wall; still, Enki, who was the god of subterranean water and the god of wisdom, helped Inanna to revive; hence, she returned to the world with light; moreover, Baring asserts that the Inanna and Cinderella stories have some common elements, such as, Cinderella was in a desperate situation, but with the help of her godmother or the fairy-mother, she transformed into another figure and met the prince and got married to him; thus, her social status was promoted, just like Inanna was able to ascend to the world with lights with the help of Enki.³¹⁶ Baring argues that Cinderella is an allegory of light, which all mankind possess in their consciousness, but due to her squalid clothes in exterior, that light is being hidden.³¹⁷ Harold Bayley also mentioned this light by referring to a book, the *Brahma Knowledge*, and said that in the human's heart, there is a 1.5cm sized light, and the name of Cinderella symbolizes this light.³¹⁸ "Katha Upanishad" refers to this light as non-smoking light, which has existed from the past to the present and will exist in the future, and it calls

---

³¹⁵ Ibid., 658.
³¹⁶ Ibid., 657.
³¹⁷ Ibid., 658.
³¹⁸ Bayley, op. cit., 138-9, footnote 1, and 190.

Purusha (the Self) and Divinity.³¹⁹ This light is what mystics call "the germs or seeds of Divinity" that depending on how one strives to conquer the Self, the light "may be fanned into a flame, the flame into a fire, the fire into a star, and the star into the sun."³²⁰ Hence, the meaning of Cinderella could be perceived as "the ignited light on seeds of Divinity," but it depends on the variations, the light could be understood as a star or the sun: to be more specific, *ella* in *Cinderella* originated from *Ele* in Greek, which signifies "one who shines" or "giver of light"; thus, the name of the son of Apollo is *Eleuther*, and *Helios* is the another name of the sun, and *Selene* means the moon, etc.; all carry the same root syllable.³²¹ Baring also contends that the name of Cinderella signifies "light and fire" in the blackness of the night sky.³²² Furthermore, says she, this light symbolizes wisdom; by uniting with love, it achieves the union between masculinity and femininity of the soul; this union is the sacred marriage between a goddess or a queen and a king, Cinderella and the Prince, respectively.³²³ Also the union symbolizes one's mind or soul's completeness or wholeness; thus, such a highly achieved soul's condition is deemed as gaining enlightenment.

According to Bayley, Cinderella, as one who achieved enlightenment, was symbolized by the dress she wore to the ball being held in the palace: it depends on the variants of the

---

[319] Paramananda, "Katha Upanishad," chapter 12–13, p. 50.

[320] Bayley, op. cit., 41.

[321] Ibid., 192.

[322] Baring and Cashford, op. cit., 656.

[323] Ibid.

Cinderella, it is told her dress shined like the sun, so people could not look at her directly; moreover, her chariot going to the ball was said to be shined like a "golden chariot" or a "splendid chariot."[324] He perceived these allegories of Cinderella's dress and the chariot as her stage of awakening and the achievement of the highest wisdom in the soul.[325] In addition, says Baring, in the *Cinderella*, there are allusions to her awakening by her dress worn to the ball, that is, "blue like the sky," "woven of the stars of heaven," "made of all the flowers in the world"; and an expression, such as the pumpkin she brought transformed into a golden chariot—all these refer to her last stage in the alchemical transformation that will lead her to the royal marriage or sacred marriage to the prince.[326] In other words, by getting married, she gains the wholeness of her mind or soul, which also symbolizes her enlightenment. Getting gold in the last stage signifies acquiring enlightenment. This is the same allusion aforementioned in the Nohill and Daldal story: King Gyungdeok made Nohill as Mireuk Buddha and Daldal as Amita Buddha and alloyed Buddhas with gold to signify they had gained enlightenment. Furthermore, in "Princess Bari," the god Musang tells her she has changed from metal to gold alluding to her gaining enlightenment or divinity. Gold also symbolizes the sun thus conveys brightness. When one gains gold, one is deemed to achieve brightness, which refers to wisdom. Therefore, gaining gold means obtaining enlightenment.

---

[324] Bayley, op. cit., 224.

[325] Ibid., 196.

[326] Baring and Cashford, op. cit., 656.

Baring also mentions there is another reason the *Cinderella* has been pervading in Western countries. As aforementioned, the original meaning of *Cinderella* was that the light exists in mankind, but it is covered by many forms of life accumulated in darkness that people are not aware of the light's existence in themselves; therefore, the *Cinderella* was written in the form of an old fairy tale to inform people about the existence of the light within themselves, so they can discover their divine origin.[327] I deem this process of discovering divine origin as obtaining enlightenment. However, enlightenment in the *Cinderella* is different from "Princess Bari," which alludes to the *nirvana* enlightenment. The *Cinderella* is about acquiring wisdom and accomplishing the wholeness of the soul or mind, although in this respect, it alludes similar attributes to "Princess Bari." The *Cinderella* can be perceived as the early stage of enlightenment albeit the wisdom Cinderella obtains could symbolize the same stage of wisdom Jitong had gotten in the Jitong story. Won-joong Kim, who translated the story, tells Jitong obtained great wisdom, which could even enable him to enter *Nirvana*; thus, he suggests Jitong's wisdom is such a high stage of accomplishment. Also in the Nohill and Daldal story, when Nohill gained enlightenment, Avalokitesvara told him to sit on the lotus seat, which suggested his enlightenment was like becoming Buddha; thus, it alluded to a higher stage of enlightenment, such as the *nirvana* enlightenment. However, in the *Cinderella*, the story connotes gaining wisdom, and she becomes a whole person and ends the story. There is not an allusion to *Nirvana*. Therefore, it can be understood as the story of acquiring enlightenment, but

---

[327] Ibid., 657–8.

not as the *nirvana* enlightenment. When one can enter *nirvana* enlightenment at one's will, that stage is considered the highest level of enlightenment.

Aforementioned examples of Eckhart's, Ruysbroeck's, and Jinjeong's *nirvana* enlightenments or the introvertive mystical experiences indicate the highest level of enlightenment. In this point of view, the Princess Bari story also can be deemed as acquiring the *nirvana* enlightenment because she can go back and forth to the other world and this world at her will to translocate decedent souls. Princess Bari born as the seventh child symbolizes she is born with wisdom. The number seven represents wisdom.[328] The story supports this view by mentioning that "she is known by a god," and she is able to read texts without learning at eight to nine years old. Hence, it is possible to view Princess Bari as having wisdom from the onset of her life. Young-lan Jang wonders, "Princess Bari was already a goddess, then she reincarnated as a human being and went through many ordeals then prevailed those hardships and became a goddess again. However, the shamanic song does not reveal why the goddess was reincarnated as a human being."[329] I deem Princess Bari reincarnated to gain *nirvana* enlightenment. She was born with wisdom: so to speak, the earlier stage of enlightenment. Then, she travels to the other world, meets the god Musang, and gains divinity and legitimacy to transport decedent souls by having the sacred marriage to him, which is

---

[328] See footnote 6.

[329] Young-lan Jang, "Hangook Shinhwasok-ui Yeosung-ui Juchae Uishik-gua Mosung Shinhwa-ui Jeonbokjeok Kijae," *Hangook Yeosung Cheolhark* (Hangook Yeosung Cheolharkhui) 8 (2007): 161.

the *nirvana* enlightenment. Afterward, she returns to this world, becomes the goddess who can translocate the deceased souls from this world to the other world.

Baring mentions that the theme of gaining wisdom, which is, enlightenment, has commonly existed since ancient times, in Sumerian myth, Egyptian alchemy, Greek myth and mysticism, Jewish wisdom-related literature, etc.; then in the middle ages, they were generally known as mysticism and have been considered one of the most precious thoughts among mystics of Christianity, Judaism, and Islam. However, during the dark ages of the medieval period, mysticism was considered heresy, so many mystics faced their lives being in danger that they made a wisdom-related story like the *Cinderella* to maintain the knowledge covertly.[330] The Princess Bari story seems to share a similar situation. During the Joseon Dynasty period, shamanism was considered heresy and was thus oppressed extremely by Confucian scholars. Hence, it seemed the shamanic song "Princess Bari" had to syncretize all other religious elements to appear like *poongrhudo*, in order to maintain its religious tradition. If "Princess Bari" only contained shamanic element, it would not have been able to survive in the Seoul and Gyunggido regions: from the beginning of the Joseon period, all other religions, except Confucianism, were considered heresy that they expelled all shamans and shamanesses from the capital region.[331] Therefore, "Princess Bari" probably had

---

[330] Baring and Cashford, op. cit., 658.

[331] Gooksa Pyunchan Wewonhui, comp., "Moogyuck-ui Poongsok-gua Eumsa-reul Geumhada," *Joseon Wangjo Sillok*, Sungjong, vol. 88, 9th year, (January 20, 1478), sixth article.

to accept other religious elements in the Seoul and Gyunggido variations to survive in the central regions. According to Hyun-seol Cho, morals of shamans expressed in the Hamheung region's variations of "Princess Bari" are different from the Seoul and Gyunggido as well as different regions' variations: the Seoul, Gyunggido, and different regions' variations illustrate externally Confucianism and internally Buddhism, but the Hamheung region's variations indicate anti-Confucianism and anti-Buddhism; hence, he perceives that the Hamheung region's variations seem to be the oldest version, which contains the original shamans' morals.[332] As Cho indicates, the original story might not have included other religious elements, but due to contemporary political and social environmental influences, it probably had to accept all other religious elements, to make it appear to be the characteristic of *poongrhudo*.

Therefore, "Princess Bari" and the *Cinderella*, which are the enlightenment stories, not necessarily representing orthodox religions of the period, share a similar situation and were propagated to the mainstream people. I perceive the marriage theme in "Princess Bari" and the *Cinderella* are very similar allusions to the sacred marriage, which signify them obtaining enlightenment. Princess Bari is able to reach the other world, the Seocheon Flower Field, where the god Musang keeps the water of life and the herbs of life, with the help from Shakyamuni; whereas Cinderella gets help from her godmother or the fairy-mother, transforms herself, and meets the prince.

---

[332] Hyun-seol Cho, "Baridaeki-wa Mu-ui Yoonli," *Gookmoonhark Yeongoo* (Gookmoonharkhui) 37 (2018).

The different elements in these stories are that Princess Bari meets the god Musang in the other world, whereas Cinderella, the prince in this world. In this regard, I deem Princess Bari acquires the *nirvana* enlightenment, but Cinderella wisdom, which is enlightenment. As aforementioned, in order to obtain *nirvana* enlightenment, one should be able to enter *Nirvana* or the other world at one's will. The example stories of Jinjeong, Eckhart, and Ruysbroeck illustrate their entering the *nirvana* enlightenment, or the introvertive mystical experience, with their wills while alive. As I described in chapter 2, Princess Bari's travel to the other world could be a similar allusion to her spiritual flight as Jinjeong's nirvana enlightenment. Hence, I deem Princess Bari's travel to the other world is about her having the *nirvana* enlightenment.

In terms of how Princess Bari gains the *nirvana* enlightenment is like Indian Hindu Brahmins seeking the *kundalini* awakening and *chakras* activating, then having the union similar to Shiva and Shakti in their *sahasrara chakra*; likewise, Princess Bari has the union with the god Musang in her *sahasrara chakra*, just like Shiva and Shakti. As I mentioned, the god Musang has some similar attributes to Shiva; thus, it is possible to hypothesize Princess Bari with Shakti. Cinderella also plays the role of a goddess after she achieves transformation with the help of her fairy-mother; she gets to marry the prince, which symbolizes her enlightenment. The way Princess Bari and Cinderella progress to get enlightenment is similar, too. Princess Bari does house chores for nine years (i.e., draws water for three years, makes fire for three years, and chops wood for three years). Then tells the story that she bears seven sons after the marriage to the god; this seems to be alluding to her seven *chakras*' activation process. Thus, the princess spends almost two decades of painstaking efforts to gain her divinity. However, there is a question: why does she bring the water of life from the *Seoyuck*? And why does she have to go to the other world, the Seocheon Flower Field, to bring the water of life? I deem the water of life the princess brings from the other world is the symbol of her acquiring the *nirvana* enlightenment. She is able to gain enlightenment after she travels to the other world, the Seocheon Flower Field. Therefore, her travel to afar regions, the *Seoyuck*, or the other world, or the Seocheon Flower Field, is directly connected with her obtaining the *nirvana* enlightenment. According to Zimmer, when one is seeking some kind of religious cultivation, one can hear one's inner voice guiding one's soul when one travels to a faraway place from one's home.[333] Zimmer mentioned that one must be away from one's accustomed environment and be in a completely different condition, then one can hear one's inner voice and accept its guidance; moreover, said he, the secret that is inherent in one's interior can be known by foreigners.[334] Hence, Princess Bari also travels to a faraway place, the *Seoyuck,* and discovers the god Musang, who may have existed in her even before, and has the sacred marriage, like the union between Shiva and Shakti; consequently, she gains the *nirvana* enlightenment and becomes a divinity and acquires legitimacy in transporting decedent souls to the other world.

---

[333] Zimmer, *Myths and Symbols*, 221.
[334] Ibid.

Cinderella also had to do all house chores because her stepmother ordered her, and she did all other sundry work when other people asked her to do so. Even in the *Cinderella's* different variations, Baring also mentions that her devotion to what others ask her to do is consistently stressed.[335] Cinderella goes through many ordeals before she marries the prince or before she gets enlightenment. The different element in the *Cinderella* is that the story ends by getting married to the prince or by getting enlightenment. However, in "Princess Bari," she gains the *nirvana* enlightenment in the other world, then she returns to this world and revives her deceased parents; thus, the story includes the element of making benefits of her enlightenment in this world. This may be due to the fact that "Princess Bari" is still being performed in the shamanic rituals even to the present.

In comparing different endings of "Princess Bari" and the *Cinderella*, we can perceive two types of enlightenment stories: one is like "Princess Bari," which represents offering some benefits to society after she gains enlightenment, and the other, is like the *Cinderella*, ends the story when she obtains enlightenment. Even the Nohill and Daldal story, like the *Cinderella*, ends the story when they gain enlightenment. However, the characters in the Samso-Guaneum story, Wolmyung story, Pyohoon story, Jinjeong story, and Daesung story, like "Princess Bari," they effectuate some benefits to society they live in after acquiring enlightenment. Therefore, enlightenment stories can be analyzed in two ways: one story up to obtaining the enlightenment process; and the other, after

---

[335] Baring and Cashford, *Myth of the Goddess*, 656.

acquiring enlightenment, what kind of benefits the enlightened ones carry out in society.

From the next part of "Princess Bari," the story again represents the Buddhistic element, that is, the "cause-and-effect" and "the deceased souls' translocation." On the way back to this world, Princess Bari watches how the deceased souls are separated by the boats going to *Nirvana* and hell.

> Souls in that boat, in the past-life,
> performed filial piety to parents and
> loyalty to the country,
> good to siblings and family.
> Wow it is so sad to see them depart.
> In the first ritual, receive seonhengja.
> In the second ritual, receive janbujeong.
> In the third ritual, receive sajae samsung.
> Receive suaeseolmoon, daeseolmoon,
> yeonjudang, ssanggetsaeram.
> Receive silver coin, gold coin.
> Go to Western Pure Land, to *Nirvana*.
> The boat is going by chanting.[336]

> Souls in that boat, in the past-life,
> they were traitors to their country,
> bad to their siblings, . . .
> Souls in that boat are crying on the way to
> all kinds of infinite numbers of hells.[337]

---

[336] Kim and Hong, "Seoul, Gyung-jae Bae's," 143-4.
[337] Ibid., 144.

The former example expresses going to *Nirvana* and the latter to hell. Heon-seon Kim perceives that "They are deeply imbued with Buddhist thought of how the deceased souls lived while alive affect their afterlife."[338] However, in shamanism, when it comes to dealing with death, it is not so clearly divided into whether decedent souls lived in goodness or badness while alive, it rather depends on whether decedent souls received the shamanic rituals or not.[339] Moreover, Seon-young Yu also deems this motif as the Buddhist viewpoint of the afterlife.[340] She mentions that the shamanist point of view in the afterlife has nothing to do with how they lived in the past, whether they had merits or not, and whether they had religions or not, "having the afterlife is like the law of nature which is recognized as the natural process of return; that is, like nature when things die, they return to nature, so mankind were perceived to follow the same law of nature."[341] Subsequently, she contends that the reason for such a shamanist outlook in the afterlife, perhaps, has to do with the origin of shamanism, which was a primitive religion, and it has not been established in systemic religion.[342] Furthermore, in terms of the shamanist view of the nether world, they do not specifically express where the nether world is but calls it by different names (i.e., Myungbu, Hwangcheon, Seocheon Seoyuckkook); however, in the above example, the story motif illustrates the deceased souls who lived virtuously go

---

[338] Heon-seon Kim, "Jeoseung-ul Yeoheng haneun," 166.

[339] Ibid., 165–6.

[340] Seon-young Yu, "Hangookyin-ui Joogeumguan," 153.

[341] Ibid., 157.

[342] Ibid.

to *Nirvana* but lived in a vice to hell; thus, their destinations are different by their merits, which can be considered the Buddhistic element.[343]

However, I do not think that the afterlife of the deceased souls being divided by *Nirvana* and hell based on how they lived while alive is only the Buddhist viewpoint of the afterlife. Seon-young Yu perceives that shamanism is primitive religion and has never been established in doctrine; thus, it has not set up its perspective in the afterlife, which could be related to how the deceased souls lived while alive. However, the shamanistic view of the afterlife is somewhat similar to that of ancient Mesopotamia (i.e., Sumer, Assyria, and Babylonia); they thought how well they received their postmortem rituals made a difference in their afterlife rather than how they lived while alive.[344] Their similar points of view in their afterlife perhaps had to do with their emphasis on ritual performances rather than practicing doctrine. The afterlife, being divided into heaven and hell, existed not only in Buddhism but also in ancient Greek philosophy. The example story "Myth of Er" is included at the end of the *Republic* by Plato.[345] The Myth of Er story is about what Er experienced after he died in battle but returned to life and told about his experience in the other world. The story tells that one who lives justly while alive will go to heaven and

---

[343] Ibid., 154, 157.

[344] J. Edward Wright, *The Early History of Heaven* (Oxford: Oxford University Press, 2000).

[345] The Myth of Er story was referred to as one of the Myths of Plato. See John Alexander Stewart, MA trans., *The Myth of Plato* (1905; reprint, London: Forgotten Books, 2013).

choose one's next life as one wishes and get to be reincarnated in this world. But, on the other hand, the one who lives unjustly while alive will go to the underworld and get to be punished. The myth also includes how an astronomical body is operated in this world. However, the main theme is one must live justly; otherwise, one will get punished. Thus, the myth illustrates that the cause-and-effect relationship in the afterlife is very similar to the Buddhist afterlife. The following is the introduction of the myth, which expresses the cause-and-effect relationship about the afterlife.

> He [Er] was slain in battle, and ten days afterwards, when the bodies of the dead were taken up already in a state of corruption, his body was found unaffected by decay, and carried away home to be buried. And on the twelfth day, as he was lying on the funeral pyre, he returned to life and told them what he had seen in the other world. He said that when his soul left the body he went on a journey with a great company, and that they came to a mysterious place at which there were two openings in the earth; they were near together, and over against them were two other openings in the heaven above. In the intermediate space there were judges seated, who commanded the just, after they had given judgment on them and had bound their sentences in front of them, to ascend by the heavenly way on the right hand;

and in like manner the unjust were bidden by them to descend by the lower way on the left hand; these also bore the symbols of their deeds, but fastened on their backs. He drew near, and they told him that he was to be the messenger who would carry the report of the other world to men, and they bade him hear and see all that was to be heard and seen in that place. Then he beheld and saw on one side the souls departing at either opening of heaven and earth when sentence had been given on them; and at the two other openings other souls, some ascending out of the earth dusty and worn with travel, some descending out of heaven clean and bright. And arriving ever and anon they seemed to have come from a long journey, and they went forth with gladness into the meadow, where they encamped as at a festival; and those who knew one another embraced and conversed, the souls which came from earth curiously inquiring about the things above, and the souls which came from heaven about the things beneath. And they told one another of what had happened by the way, those from below weeping and sorrowing at the remembrance of the things which they had endured and seen in their journey beneath the earth (now the journey lasted a thousand years), while those from above were describing heavenly delights and visions of inconceivable beauty. The story, Glaucon, would take too long to tell; but the sum was this:—He said that for every wrong which they had done to anyone they suffered tenfold; or once in a hundred years—such being reckoned to be the length of man's life, and the penalty being thus paid ten times in a thousand years.[346]

Based on the above myth, we can understand how one lives in this world will decide whether one goes to heaven or hell. Moreover, Socrates tells in the myth, if one commits one unjust action, one will get it back ten times of what one had committed. This definitely explains the logic of cause-and -effect on how one lived while alive affects one's afterlife. Shamanism mainly focuses on the rituals of appeasing the deceased souls, so it does not emphasize whether they lived justly or unjustly as long as the deceased souls receive sumptuous rituals, then the souls are thought to be transported to the other world safely. But the shamanic song "Princess Bari" contains the theme of the deceased souls either going to *Nirvana* or hell based on how they lived in this world; it illustrates it was syncretized with the Buddhist view of the afterlife.

From the next story, again the shamanic song indicates the story being mixed with the shamanic and Buddhistic elements.

> What kind of boat is the one without a guide?
> That boat is ridden by the souls in the past

---

[346] Plato, "The Republic," 454-5.

without offspring thus going to the sea.[347]

Over there, the boat is on a rock without light, without the moon.
What kind of boat is on a rock without a guide?
The deceased souls in the boat are the ones who died without offspring and during childbirth, thus they did not receive any rituals, such as, seonwangjae,
49 days memorial, sajasamsung, jinogi, and saenam.
They are lost where to go, thus it is on a rock without a guide.
Wow, that is very sad.
Amo mangjae, Princess Bari, in order to translocate them,
she got on the boat,
by chanting Amita Buddha, Jijang Bodhisattva,
to *Nirvana*, to the world of ten directions,
to the Lotus World, translocate them.[348]

The latter example, Deok-soon Moon's version, illustrates that Princess Bari translocates the deceased souls who did not receive any shamanic ritual because they died without offspring or died during childbirth. It indicates she translocates them to nice places (i.e., *Nirvana* or the Lotus World). However, the former version, Gyung-jae Bae's (recorded 1937), does not have the motif of Princess Bari translocating the deceased souls to

---

[347] Kim and Hong, "Seoul, Gyung-jae Bae's," 144.
[348] Kim and Hong, "Seoul, Deok-soon Moon's," 172-3.

the other world on the way back to this world. The Deok-soon Moon's version is a later one (recorded 1966), and it includes Princess Bari revealing compassion toward the deceased souls who died without offspring or who died during childbirth. This must be related with her sacred function, which may have to do with childbirth, added later.

The motif of translocating the deceased souls to *Nirvana* or the Lotus World could be seen as being influenced by the Buddhist view of the afterlife. According to Heon-seon Kim, Princess Bari is known to translocate the deceased souls to the Lotus World, which is one of *Nirvana*; thus, it is only possible when the Buddhist view of the afterlife, *Nirvana* and hell, have been syncretized with the shamanist view of the afterlife.[349] Shamanism originally did not have the notion of heaven and hell. They called the other world with various names, as Seon-young Yu indicates in the aforementioned article, which mostly related with nature: in the postmortem, they thought of returning to nature as a natural process; however, in the Deok-soon Moon's version, it mentions that Princess Bari translocates the deceased souls who died without offspring or who died during childbirth to *Nirvana* or the Lotus world. In order to include this motif in the song, shamanism must be embraced with Buddhism to designate her role in translocating the deceased souls to *Nirvana* or to the Lotus World.

The story motif of translocating the deceased souls in the Deok-soon Moon's version also alludes to Princess Bari's fertility

---

[349] Heon-seon Kim, "Jeoseung-eul Yeoheng Haneun," 166.

function. In the song, she sees several different kinds of boats that carry the deceased souls to the other world on the way back home. However, she has compassion for the deceased souls who died without offspring or who died during childbirth; this may signify that they are related to her sacred function. Heon-seon Kim contends that Princess Bari gained the ability to take the deceased souls to the other world by traveling there to find the water of life to revive her parents in this world; by doing so, she can also bring the deceased souls from the other world to this world.[350] Princess Bari brings her husband, the god Musang, and their seven sons, as well as the water of life and the herbs of life, which are known to be the essence of resuscitating dead people in this world. Kim perceives this motif of translocating the deceased souls as symbolizing her function to bring them from the other world and revive them in this world.[351] I agree with Kim's point of view. The meaning of her bringing her husband, the god Musang, to this world, who used to be the gatekeeper of the other world, the Seocheon Flower Field, where the water of life and the herbs of life exist, could be that she had gained divine authority to bring the deceased souls from the other world and can revive them in this world with the water of life and the herbs of life. A story that mentions bringing something from the other world to this world appears in the Sumerian myth "Inanna and Enki: The Transfer of the Arts of Civilization from Eridu to Erect."[352]

---

[350] Ibid., 165.

[351] Ibid., 160.

[352] Samuel Noah Kramer, *Sumerian Mythology: A Study of Spiritual and Literary Achievement in the Third Millennium B.C.*, rev. ed.

According to Samuel Noah Kramer, Inanna, the queen of heaven, goes down to see the subterranean water god, Enki, known for his wisdom, to learn how to make her city, Erech, prosper.[353] When Enki sees Inanna, he is so impressed by the way she looks that he instructs Isimud, his messenger, how to prepare a hospitable table:

> Come, my messenger, Isimud, give ear to my instructions,
> . . .
> Have Inanna enter the Abzu of Eridu,
> Give her to eat barley cake with butter,
> Pour for her cold water that freshens the heart,
> Give her to drink date-wine in the "face of the lion,"
> . . .
> At the pure table, the table of heaven,
> Speak to Inanna words of greeting.[354]

Thus, Isimud follows his instruction. Then, during the occasion, Enki and Inanna enjoy drinks and become happy; hence, he exclaims,

> "O name of my power, O name of my power,
> To the pure Inanna, my daughter, I shall present . . .,

(Philadelphia: University of Pennsylvania Press, 1972), 65–68.

[353] Ibid., 65.

[354] Loc. cit.

Lordship, . . . -ship, godship, the tiara exalted and enduring,
the throne of kingship."

Pure Inanna took them.

"O name of my power, O name of my power,
To the pure Inanna, my daughter, I shall present . . .
The exalted scepter, staffs, the exalted shrine, shepherdship, kingship."

Pure Inanna took them.[355]

Kramer illustrated that by repeating like this several times, Enki gave to Inanna "over one hundred divine decrees which are the basis of the culture pattern of Sumerian civilization."[356] Inanna took these divine decrees to prosper her city by loading them to the "Boat of Heaven" and headed toward her city, Erech; in the meantime, Enki sobered up and regretted what he had given to Inanna and tried to prevent her boat reaching the city; however, with the help of a god, Ninshubur, she arrived at Erech and allotted divine decrees to the people and made the city prosper.[357]

---

[355] Ibid., 66.
[356] Ibid.
[357] Ibid., 66–68.

Cheol-su Cho perceives these divine decrees Inanna brought from Enki were similar in nature to what Hwan-ung brought, three Cheonbuyin (the symbol of divine authority), from which to administer people in over three hundred sixty matters, when he descended from heaven to the earth in "Dangoon Myth," which was recorded in the *Samgook Yusa* about the oldest Korean kingdom, Gojoseon.[358]

> Once upon a time, one of Hwanyin (the Heavenly God) sons, Hwan-ung, had an ambition to rule people on the earth. The Heavenly God understood his wish and looked down on Taebaek Mountain area, where it seemed to be appropriate to benefit people; thus he gave Hwan-ung three Cheonbuyin and let him descend to this world to administer people.
>
> Hwan-ung descended to the Tree of Shindan, which was on top of Taebaek Mountain with three thousand people and called this area Shinsi (the city of god). The people called him the Heavenly King, Hwan-ung. He brought with him Poongbaek (the wind control master), Woosa (the rain control master), and Woonsa (the clouds control master) and administered people over three hundred sixty matters, i.e.,

---

[358] Cheol-su Cho, *Godae Mesopotamia*.

grain, life, disease, punishment, goodness, badness, etc., and edified the people.[359]

There is a similarity between what Inanna brought from the other world, over one hundred divine decrees to prosper a city, and what Hwan-ung brought to this world from the heaven, three symbols of divine authority to administer over three hundred sixty matters of people's lives (i.e., grain, life, disease, punishment, goodness, badness, etc.) and to edify the people. In the ancient Sumerian myth, it is called "divine decrees," and in the ancient Korean myth, "divine authority" (Cheonbuyin) to administer matters. Hence, both myths seem to be referring to similar divine decrees. The dissimilarities between them are the nature of gods: Enki is the god of subterranean water, and Hwanyin is the god of heaven. This probably is related to the origin of the people who believe in the gods. The people who believe in the god of subterranean water were probably people who originated in the desert, wherein the subterranean water is essential to their survival. The people who believe in the god of heaven were probably from the north or colder region. So the nature of their gods is different by the location of the people's origin. Furthermore, the number of divine decrees is different. Inanna brought over one hundred divine decrees to prosper the city Erech, whereas Hwan-ung's divine authority over three hundred sixty matters seems to be alluding to prospering a kingdom. Thus, the number of divine decrees or authority a god is holding seems to be connoting its divine responsibility, either over a city or a kingdom.

---

[359] Part of Dangoon Myth, "Gojoseon"; Ilyeon, *Samgook Yusa*, 36–37.

However, what Princess Bari brings from the other world is her husband (the god Musang, who was the god of the other world), their seven sons, the water of life, and the herbs of life, which are directly related with reviving the deceased souls. Hence, the allusion of what Princess Bari brings to this world has to do with divine decree or authority to bring back the deceased souls to life in this world. A good example for her divine decree would be her role in resuscitating her dead parents with the water of life and the herbs of life she obtained in the other world.

> Gather up fresh energy to repel dead energy.
> Open the seven layers of [their] clothes.
> The herbs to revive the breath, put them in for the breath.
> The herbs to revive the bones, put them in the bones.
> The herbs to revive the flesh, put them in the flesh.
> The herbs to revive the eyes, put them in the eyes.
> The water of life, put it in their mouths.
> They revive at the same hour, on the same day.[360]

The above example illustrates Princess Bari reviving her deceased parents with the herbs of life and the water of life. However, before she begins to apply the herbs of life and the water of life, she repels her parents' dead energy with her fresh energy. This is a certain indication of her having gained enlightenment. As the god Musang mentioned before she

---

[360] Kim and Hong, "Seoul, Gyung-jae Bae's," 145.

departed the other world, "You came as a metal general, but you return as a gold general," which is an allusion that she transformed spiritually and obtained enlightenment. This is in alchemy "metal transformed to gold"; thus, it is referring to her change in spiritual condition, which is also related with her fresh energy. Therefore, she used her pure energy to fight off her parents' dead energy before she applied the herbs of life and the water of life. If Princess Bari did not gain enlightenment and just became the goddess by marrying the god Musang and bearing the seven sons, such expressions as "Gather up fresh energy to repel dead energy" would not make sense. This articulation is possible because she spent many years in spiritual cultivation and acquired enlightenment; thus, the god said that she changed from metal to gold. However, the way she gained divine decree or authority to bring the deceased souls back to life was probably by marrying the god Musang, who was the gatekeeper of the other world, the Seocheon Flower Field. As aforementioned, the god Musang is like Shiva, and Princess Bari, Shakti, that as Shakti uses Shiva's power as his consort, Princess Bari can also use the god Musang's divine authority as his wife. Therefore, in the above example, Princess Bari brings around her deceased parents to life with her fresh energy, which arises from her long years of spiritual cultivation as well as the herbs of life and the water of life she brought from the other world, the Seocheon Flower Field, by which also alludes to the divine authority she obtained to resuscitate mankind in this world.

The story that contains a similar motif of reviving the deceased souls with the herbs of life and the water of life is the ancient Mesopotamian, Sumerian myth, "Inanna Descent to the Nether World."[361] I mentioned briefly in the chapter about Anne Baring's point of view that Cinderella's wretched life condition is like Inanna's descent to the underworld, in the part I compared "Princess Bari" with the *Cinderella.* I discussed a brief outline of the story without mentioning the herbs of life and the water of life. Here is another plot from Kramer's text as follows: Although Inanna was the queen of heaven, she descended to the nether world for unknown reasons; there she tempted to take the throne of the queen of the nether world and failed; thus, she got killed and ended up hanging on a nail in the wall; however, she instructed her messenger Ninshubur what to do if she did not return; hence, Ninshubur asked all gods to help revive her, but all refused except Enki, who sent two creatures to bring her back to life; when those creatures descended to the nether world and sprinkled the water of life and the herbs of life on the corpse of Inanna, she revived and ascended to this world.[362]

In the Inanna story, the motif of her reviving after two creatures sprinkled the water of life and the herbs of life is very similar to Princess Bari resuscitating her deceased parents with the water of life and the herbs of life. Based on these similarities, Cheol-su Cho suggests that there might have been some connection between the ancient Mesopotamian myth and the ancient Korean myth.[363] However, the different element in these stories is the location of the other world. In the Inanna story, the

---

[361] Samuel Noah Kramer, *Sumerian Mythology,* 84–96.

[362] Ibid., 86-87, part of summary.

[363] Cheol-su Cho, *Godae Mesopotamia.*

other world is underground, whereas in Princess Bari's *Seoyuck*, which signifies indefinite plains in the western region, it is also the Seocheon Flower Field, where the water of life and the herbs of life exist. This location of the other world has to do with the Korean points of view on the other world, which they perceive to be far west plains rather than underground.

Moreover, Cho perceives the main characters in the Princess Bari story reflect the actual historical figures: for example, the shaman god Musang, to whom Princess Bari married to, might symbolize the historical figure Talhae, who enthroned kingship as a son-in-law of King Namhae in the ancient Silla Kingdom period.[364] According to historical records, Talhae was a prince from the Yongsung Kingdom[365] and came across by a ship, and he was known to be very tall and muscular, like herculean type; thus, it is possible to perceive he might have been a *Seoyuck* person as Cho claims.[366] Furthermore, the *Samgook Yusa* records that when Talhae's ship arrived in the ancient Silla period, many magpies gathered around his ship, so it caught the attention of an old woman, who discovered a chest with a boy inside, who was a young Talhae.[367] This motif is very similar to Princess Bari being abandoned in a boat with a chest, and magpies gathered around her boat; thus, it caught the attention of Shakyamuni, and she was rescued by him. Hence, "Princess Bari" not only contains the heroic element of Saint King Dongmyung but also embraces

---

[364] Loc. cit.

[365] See footnote 286 of chapter 3.

[366] Ilyeon, *Samgook Yusa*, 76–79.

[367] Ibid., 76.

a similar element of King Talhae's ship, with a chest inside being discovered by a third figure. Subsequently, Cho further connotes Princess Bari to symbolize Queen Seondeok, who enthroned kingship as a princess in the Silla Kingdom: he alludes that Princess Bari going to the other world to obtain the water of life and the herbs of life for her parents seem to convey she is effectuating the role of a prince who is preparing to become the king; therefore, he contends that the archetype story of "Princess Bari" might have formed based upon those two historical figures.[368] Cho's supposition of "Princess Bari" archetype story to be formed in the ancient Silla is fascinating. It is possible to perceive since two historical figures' identities being shared with the attributes of the main characters in "Princess Bari." Dae-seok Seo also mentions that, in general, orally transmitted literature are perceived only as holding hints upon matters related to the transmission and variation; thus, research about historical matters deem to be impossible; however, says he that these "transmission and variation also accomplish within history, and they reflect matters related to the period; therefore, in orally transmitted literature coexist matters relate to the ancient as well as the present, and depends on how we analyze the literature, we can find historical meanings."[369] Based on Seo's opinion, Cho's argument in considering the earliest possible archetype story of "Princess Bari" to be formed in the ancient Silla Kingdom seems convincing.

---

[368] Cheol-su Cho, *Godae Mesopotamia*.

[369] Dae-seok Seo, "Bari Gongjoo Yeongoo," 254.

In addition, Cho argues that the motifs in the Inanna story (she being revived after two creatures sent by Enki sprinkled the water of life and the herbs of life) and in the Princess Bari story (she bringing back her parents to life after she applied the water of life and the herbs of life) are similar to a priest performing a purification ceremony to repel evilness by spraying the water of life on an impure body in ancient Mesopotamia.[370] Therefore, he contends that based on the purification ceremony and Princess Bari's parents celebrating afterward being revived seem to convey the story's main theme signifies the tradition of *Byucksa Jingyung* (expelling the evils and celebrating the effects) that had existed in the ancient Silla Kingdom.[371] It appears that Cho hypothesizes the archetype story of "Princess Bari" might have formed in the ancient Silla period, and reviving the deceased souls with the water of life and the herbs of life as a purification ceremony; thus, the main theme of "Princess Bari" is about expelling the evils and celebrating the effects. If we consider only "the water of life and the herbs of life" element in the story, Cho's argument seems legitimate. However, as I examined in above, the Princess Bari story contains several religious elements, and the story's main theme is how Princess Bari gains divine authority by traveling to the other world, as Cho also mentions, and how she obtains the ability to translocate the deceased souls to the other world, as well as bring them to this world, and revive them. The only possible way to understand such syncretized religious elements in a story would be the influence of *poongrhudo*, which has existed ever since ancient Korea.

---

[370] Cheol-su Cho, op. cit.

[371] Ibid.

Sung-arm Hong mentions that "*poongrhudo* is a religion that formed within the framework of Korean society by knowing what is the proper way to behave as a human being. It is not dogmatic and accepts the best alternatives and possible to change when it is needed; therefore, it is a very flexible religion."[372] Because *poongrhudo* is very flexible, it can accept any foreign religious element as long as it is beneficial and creates harmony within society. Hence *poongrhudo* can be understood as Hong asserts: "It is the religion which espousing harmony, moderation, and for a wholeness, thus it can only be expressed as 'wondrous harmony'."[373] Like Hong's contention of *poongrhudo* as holding the elements of different religions in wondrous harmony, the Princess Bari story embraces different religious elements of shamanism, Buddhism, Confucianism, immortality, Hinduism, and the ancient Mesopotamian purification ceremony, as well as heroism marvelously: by doing so, it illustrates how she obtains divinity; thus, she is still being worshiped in the shamanic rituals of translocating the deceased souls even up to the present. Based on such syncretized religious elements in the Princess Bari story, we can deem the methodology that Princess Bari adopted to gain her enlightenment is *poongrhudo*. As Cheol-su Cho contends, it is possible the archetype story of "Princess Bari" might have formed in the ancient Silla period; then it could be perceived—as it paralleled with the history of *poongrhudo*—that it has been the one of the longest surviving shamanic songs in Korea. The possibility of such a long survival of "Princess Bari"

---

[372] Sung-arm Hong, "Poongrhudo-ui Yinyum," 226-7.
[373] Ibid., 235.

may have to do with its nature of embracing different religious elements, which reflects the ideal of *poongrhudo*.

In summary of chapter 3, I examined the enlightenment methodologies represented in the Nohill and Daldal story and the Jitong story in the *Samgook Yusa* and an orally transmitted shamanic song, "Princess Bari." The Nohill and Daldal story illustrates Nohill followed the Mahayana Buddhism cultivation method and Daldal Hinayana Buddhism cultivation method. Nohill gains the *nirvana* enlightenment by obtaining the response from Avalokitesvara, whereas Daldal seems to gain enlightenment with the help of Nohill, but his enlightenment is alluded to be not as perfect as Nohill's, perhaps due to not receiving the response directly from Avalokitesvara. Based on the Nohill and Daldal story, Ilyeon covertly conveys the ideal of a Mahayana Buddhist monk representing a Bodhisattva, which he deems the proper way to behave in Mahayana Buddhism. The Jitong story voices Jitong gaining enlightenment after he receives the Buddhist monk's precepts from Bohyun Bodhisattva. The story does not mention which cultivation method he follows, but his enlightenment experience is more in common with what is worldly known as "the extrovertive mystical experience," in which he experiences the god, nature, or the Universal Self with his sense perception. And his mystical experience seems to have arisen from his sacred mind being united with nature or the Universal Self; hence, his enlightenment experience does not fall under any specific religious cultivation method, but it rather reflects a commonly existing element among different religious followers.

The Princess Bari story indicates she gains the *nirvana* enlightenment by having the sacred marriage to the shaman god Musang in the other world. This is a shamanic song; thus, it could be deemed to contain only shamanic elements; however, after I probe into the construction of the stories containing different religious elements (i.e., shamanism, Buddhism, Confucianism, immortality, Hinduism, and the ancient Mesopotamian purification ceremony), as well as heroism, it rather illustrates the syncretized nature that the song can be perceived as influenced by *poongrhudo*, which has existed since ancient Korea. However, the way Princess Bari gains enlightenment itself is by traveling to the other world to find the water of life and the herbs of life for her dying parents, and by having the sacred marriage to the shaman god Musang, who is the guardian of the Seocheon Flower Field, where the water of life and the herbs of life exist, she gains the *nirvana* enlightenment. This is a similar allusion to how Nohill gains the *nirvana* enlightenment, in which he has the union with Avalokitesvara. In both the Nohill and Daldal and the Princess Bari stories, there are also possibilities of Nohill and Princess Bari gaining the *nirvana* enlightenment by the *kundalini* awakenings and their *chakras* being activated that they might have the union with the goddess and the god in their *sahasrara chakras*, just like the union of Shiva and Shakti. Moreover, Princess Bari's union with the god Musang resembles the Western source, the *Cinderella*, in which Cinderella marries the prince at the end. The difference between them is that the *Cinderella* symbolizes gaining wisdom, which is enlightenment; however, in "Princess Bari," it alludes the princess is already born with wisdom, but by traveling to the other world, she gains the *nirvana* enlightenment, or the introvertive mystical experience, which is known to be a fully matured stage of enlightenment.[374] The Princess Bari story contains several religious elements, but when analyzing her enlightenment experience alone, it indicates a similar aspect by having the sacred union with the deity, as the Buddhist monk Nohill gains his enlightenment and Cinderella obtains her enlightenment. Therefore, their enlightenment experiences transcend religion, culture, period, language, etc., although more cross-culture and cross-genre comparative research are needed.

---

[374] Stace, *Teachings of the Mystics*.

CHAPTER 4

THE NECESSITY IN GAINING ENLIGHTENMENT SUGGESTED IN THE *SAMGOOK YUSA* AND "PRINCESS BARI" STORIES

What is the necessity in gaining enlightenment suggested in the stories of the *Samgook Yusa* and "Princess Bari"? If one obtains enlightenment, then one can offer one's efficacy to society. In other words, the enlightened person's wisdom and sacred energy can be used to benefit people. Moreover, the enlightened one's efficacy can be utilized in different ways. For example, the Pyohoon story in the *Samgook Yusa* indicates Pyohoon can ascend to heaven and communicate with the Heavenly Emperor and convey King Gyungdeok's request to have a male heir to his throne. Thus, he effectuates the role of intermediary between the Heavenly Emperor and the king. In the Samso-Guaneum story, the head monk of the Buddhist temple, the Joongsengsa, already acquired the union with his Self (*Atman*) and the Universal Self (*Brahman*) that he can accomplish things as he planned. In the Wolmyung story, Wolmyung also achieved the union with his Self and the Universal Self that when he plays the flute, he plays with his consciousness being in meditation, which causes the sound of it to be so mesmerizing that the people who are listening to it feel as though a passing moon even stops to listen to his flute playing. In the Jinjeong story, he can translocate the deceased souls by falling into deep meditation and being in the union with his Self and the Universal Self. In the Daesung story, a respectful monk, Jeomgae, translocates Daesung from a very humble status to the Silla Kingdom's prime minister's son after Daesung died. Hence, he enabled Daesung to become famous for building a well-known Buddhist temple, the Boolgooksa, for his present-life parents and the Buddhist stone grotto, the Seokgoolarm, for his past-life parents. This is possible because Daesung meets a greatly enlightened Buddhist monk, Jeomgae.

Moreover, "Princess Bari" also mentions how she can translocate the deceased souls after she has traveled to the other world and by marrying the god Musang. As aforementioned in chapter 3, the sacred marriage in the other world is the allusion to her *nirvana* enlightenment. Thus, after she gains the *nirvana* enlightenment, she can translocate the deceased souls to the other world and bring the deceased souls to this world and revive them. Therefore, the efficacies of enlightenment are expressed in several ways in the stories. Consequently, in chapter 4, I will probe into the necessity of gaining enlightenment suggested in the stories I mentioned above and other texts in three parts: (1) One can communicate with a divinity. (2) One can obtain spiritual power by having the union with the Self and the Universal Self or a god. (3) One can translocate the deceased souls to a higher realm, thus offering them salvation.

4.1 Communicating with a Divinity Is Possible

The following example explains how Pyohoon carried out an intermediary role between the Heavenly Emperor and King Gyungdeok:

> King Gyungdeok in the Silla Kingdom did not have an heir to his throne, so he asked Pyohoon to request his wish to have a male heir to the Heavenly Emperor. Thus, Pyohoon ascended to heaven and conveyed the king's wish to the Heavenly Emperor; then, the Heavenly Emperor said that a daughter was possible but not a son.
>
> Thereafter King Gyungdeok wished to change the daughter to the son. Hence, Pyohoon ascended to heaven again and expressed the king's wish. At this, the Heavenly Emperor said that if he changed to a son, the kingdom would fall into chaos. When Pyohoon was about to descend, the Heavenly Emperor said that "The matters of heaven and mankind should not be known, but you are visiting heaven like your neighbor and reveal the secret of the heavenly way, so from now on, you are forbidden to ascend here."
>
> At last, King Gyungdeok was able to have a male heir by his second queen; then, the king passed away when his son was eight years old.

Thus, his son enthroned the kingship as King Haegong; but he was too young that his mother conducted as regent to the king. However, as the Heavenly Emperor's prophecy, there were several uprisings arose, thus the kingdom fell into chaos, and another royal blood, Yang-sang Kim claimed the throne and killed King Haegong. Moreover, the Heavenly Emperor cut off the way to ascend to heaven that after Pyohoon, there was not any saint born in the Silla Kingdom.[375]

In the example story, Pyohoon could meet the Heavenly Emperor because he gained the higher stage of enlightenment, the *nirvana* enlightenment. When an ordinary person gets enlightenment and learns the way to ascend to heaven, there is no guarantee that the person can meet the Heavenly Emperor. In other Korean literature, it is illustrated he or she can meet messengers of the Heavenly Emperor but not the Heavenly Emperor himself. In the story, Pyohoon visiting heaven and encountering the Heavenly Emperor allude to Pyohoon's high stage of spiritual advancement. As aforementioned in chapter 2, Pyohoon was one of the ten disciples of Uisang, and it is recorded in the *Samgook Yusa* that Pyohoon "stayed in the Boolgooksa Buddhist temple and always went back and forth to the heavenly palace"; moreover, Pyohoon's teacher, Uisang, usually stayed in another temple, the Hwangboksa, and "when he and his disciples practiced meditation by walking around a

---

[375] Part of the summary from the Pyohoon story; Ilyeon, *Samgook Yusa*, 167–8.

Buddha stupa in the temple, Uisang never walked on stairways but on airways that they never built stairways for the stupa; then his disciples followed him walking on airways, about four feet behind their teacher."[376] It seems that Uisang and his disciples walking on airways was thought of nothing special. The record also mentions that Uisang's ten disciples all had individual talents, and Pyohoon's talent was the ability to visit the heavenly palace.[377]

In the Pyohoon story section, there is another story about a Buddhist monk, Choongdamsa, who was famous for composing *hyangga*, "Chankiparangga" (the song for praising Mr. Kipa). In Korean classical literature, there is still no consensus about who was the figure called Kipa that Choongdamsa lauded so highly. There are several points of view on who may be Mr. Kipa, but I agree with Joo-dong Yang's view that Kipa was probably Pyohoon;[378] that is the reason Ilyeon recorded their stories in the same section. In the story's section, King Gyungdeok asked Choongdamsa, "I have heard your composition of the *hyangga*, in which the meaning of praising Mr. Kipa was very sublime. Was it true?"; when Choongdamsa answered yes, the king seemed to express enviousness and appeared to recognize who he was referring to about Kipa.[379] The reason for my supposition for the king's opinion is that what the king

---

[376] Ilyeon, "Uisang-yi Hwaumjong-eul Jeonhada," *Samgook Yusa*, 466.

[377] Ibid.

[378] Jong-woo Kim, *Hyangga Moonhark Yeongoo* (Seoul: Yiwoo Choolpansa, 1978), 433.

[379] Ilyeon, "The Pyohoon Story," 165.

requests Choongdamsa right after their conversation, which starts with, "If that is the case, compose 'Anminga' (the song for comforting the people) for me."[380] The king was looking for a Buddhist monk who had a dignified appearance, and it happened to be Choongdamsa; and when he made tea for the king, it had a special fragrance. Thus, the king thought of him as someone special.[381] It seemed Choongdamsa was chosen by the king because of his special attributes in several ways (i.e., his respectful appearance, literariness, and other special talents); the Buddhist monk, Choongdamsa, who eulogizes highly in his *hyangga*, would probably be not anyone else but a respectful Buddhist master. Hence the king requested Choongdamsa, if he composed a famous *hyangga*, "Chankiparangga" to praise [a highly enlightened Buddhist master], someone [like Pyohoon], then, for him, the king who governs the people, compose the song which could comfort the people. Based on the record and the context of their conversation, Mr. Kipa seems to be Pyohoon, and that is probably why Ilyeon recorded their stories in the same section.

Ilyeon described Pyohoon ascended to heaven and met the Heavenly Emperor, so we could deem that he must have obtained a higher stage of enlightenment or the *nirvana* enlightenment. At the end of the story, Ilyeon mentioned that since the way to heaven was cut off, "no saint was born in Silla afterward."[382] Ilyeon considered Pyohoon as a saint;

---

[380] Ibid., 166.
[381] Ibid., 164–5.
[382] Ibid., 168.

thus, it is possible to suppose that Pyohoon acquired the *nirvana* enlightenment, and that the person Choongdamsa admired was Pyohoon is all the more a greater possibility.

There are other sources that mention meeting the Heavenly Emperor, that is, Jiddu Krishnamurti's spiritual flight in encountering the King of the World when he was fifteen years old in Himalayan mountain.[383] In Greek myth, Prometheus was known to ascend to Mount Olympus, where the gods reside, to meet Zeus, the king of the gods.[384] However, depending upon the interpretation of texts, some go up to the heavenly realm and encounter the god, as in the Pyohoon story, and others said to go up to the high mountains and meet the gods there, as in Jiddu Krishnamurti's spiritual flight to Himalayan mountain and Prometheus's ascent to Mount Olympus to meet Zeus. Therefore, I would like to examine what could be considered as the heavenly realm.

According to Greek myth, Zeus, the king of the gods, with the appearance of mankind, has been known to stay on top

---

[383] Jiddu Krishnamurti (1895–1986) entered the Theosophy Society, which was active in India during the nineteenth to the twentieth centuries, at the age of thirteen to fourteen, with his father; then he experienced his first spiritual initiation when he reached fifteen years old (1910 CE) and was able to enter their brotherhood; thus, he wrote to his guardian, Anne Besant, about his experience of meeting the masters of the Theosophy Society by his consciousness. Krishnamurti mentioned he was led to Maitreya by other masters, and finally the next day, he had met the King of the World. Mary Lutyens, *Krishnamurti*, trans. Shi-hwa Rhu (Seoul: Jeongshin Saegaesa, 1985).

[384] *New Larousse Encyclopedia of Mythology*, trans. Richard Aldington and Delano Ames (New York: Crescent Books, 1986), 93.

of Mount Olympus, or in the highest mansion, which could be considered as the heavenly realm; and so other Olympian gods have been known to dwell there.[385] Henry More, the seventeenth-century Platonic philosopher, mentioned that there were different regions of aerial realm: the Ethereal region was the highest, and the Aerial region was in between the Ethereal and the Terrestrial regions; the Aerial region was also divided in three regions that the highest Aerial region was known as "the third region of the air," where angelic figures (i.e., *genii* and *daemons*) were known to reside.[386] More contended these angelic figures sometimes descended to the lower Aerial region to have communion with mankind.[387] He mentioned that the highest region, which was the Ethereal region, could only be occupied by the most purified spirits like gods, and the next highest region was the third region of the Aerial, where angelic figures resided; however, in the lower Aerial region, the deceased souls

---

[385] Hesiod, *Theogony and Works and Days*, trans. M. L. West, Oxford World's Classics (Oxford: Oxford University Press, 2008), 37; *New Larousse Encyclopedia*, 97.

[386] Henry More, "Immortality of the Soul," the third book, axiom 28 and chapter 3, sections 5–7, in *A Collection of Several Philosophical Writings*, 2d ed. (London: James Flejher, 1662), eBook. "The third region of the air" was the hypothesis of Facius Cardanus, who was the father of Hieronymus Cardanus, in which Facius Cardanus contended angels occupied "the third region of the air," and they have no interest in coming down to the lower Aerial region to hurt human beings. However, More disagreed with his view although he agreed with the existence of "the third region of the air" as the highest in the Aerial region.

[387] Henry More, chapter 3, section 7.

reside, but it depends on the souls' purity and power, they were thought to be residing in different levels of the Aerial region.[388]

In the Pyohoon story, Ilyeon specifically mentioned Pyohoon "ascended" to heaven and met the Heavenly Emperor. Although Ilyeon's description of Pyohoon encountering the Heavenly Emperor was very terse, based on the context of the story, and the record, which referred Pyohoon as a saint, we can discern Pyohoon gained the utmost purity or near the highest purity, like the *nirvana* enlightenment, that he could have made spiritual flight in the state of meditation and met the Heavenly Emperor. Based on Henry More's distinction of the different regions, Pyohoon could be considered to reside in the third region of the Aerial, so it could have enabled him to visit the Heavenly Emperor, who probably stayed in the Ethereal region, easily. As Ilyeon expressed Pyohoon's skill was being able to visit the heavenly palace, it could be alluding to his proximity to reach heaven easily due to his spiritual advancement and purity and residing near there. Therefore, Pyohoon was able to carry out the role of intermediary between the Heavenly Emperor and King Gyungdeok. Such as in the Pyohoon story, when one obtains the *nirvana* enlightenment, one can reach a high level of purity that one can ascend to a higher realm, that is, the third region of the Aerial or the Ethereal region, heaven; thus, one can communicate with either angelic figures or gods, respectively, and play the role of messenger or prophet between gods and mankind.

---

[388] Ibid., chapter 3, sections 1 and 3. Henry More's point of view about the deceased souls staying in the Aerial region was said to be similar to the viewpoints of the ancient philosophers and natural theologists.

4.2 Gaining Spiritual Power Is Possible by Having the Union with the Universal Self or a God

"Katha Upanishad" mentions that when one is able to recognize the Light (the Self, *Atman*) is in the state of union with the Universal Self (*Brahman*), then one can be discerned to have acquired enlightenment.[389] Thus, it suggests that it is already in the union with the Self and the Universal Self; and if one realizes such a state, then one can be deemed to have gained enlightenment. As aforementioned in the Nohill and Daldal story, I deem Daldal achieved enlightenment by having the union with his Self and the Universal Self or with emptiness. According to the story, Daldal asked Nohill to help him also to obtain enlightenment; hence, Nohill told Daldal to take a bath in the leftover bathwater, from which Daldal gained enlightenment with the help of Nohill. The bathwater was supposed to contain gold, which signified wisdom infused from Avalokitesvara, so Daldal's bath in the water also connotes his gaining wisdom, which was enlightenment. However, he took the bath alone, which signified he had the union with his Self and the Universal Self or nothingness; in other words, enlightenment Daldal obtained might have been that he was able to see his Light (the Self) being in the union with the Universal Self based on Nohill's teaching. But this level of enlightenment might not have been as fully matured a stage of enlightenment as Nohill's, who had the direct union with the goddess Avalokitesvara, and she alluded he gained the *nirvana* enlightenment by handing over the lotus seat and told him to

---

[389] Paramananda, "Katha Upanishad," part 5, XII, 54.

sit there. Therefore, the story clearly distinguishes two different types of enlightenment: Nohill gained the *nirvana* enlightenment and Daldal enlightenment.

As aforementioned in chapter 3, I deem Nohill and Princess Bari might have awakened their *kundalini* and had the union with Avalokitesvara and the god Musang, respectively, in their *sahasrara chakra* (the crown of the head) or in *anahata chakra* (the heart). Based on other sources (i.e., Gopi Krishna's enlightenment experience and Jiddu Krishnamurti's enlightenment experience), having the *kundalini* awakened enabled them to experience a much higher level of spiritual awakening.[390] In the experience of Gopi Krishna, after he had awakened the *kundalini*, said he, he was able to see the Light (the Self) and was able to have the union with It,[391] which seemed to suggest the *kundalini* awakening was the condition for being able to see the Light (the Self) and be in the state of the union with the Self and the Universal Self. In Jiddu Krishnamurti, after he had awakened his *kundalini*, his consciousness made flight and expanded and thus had the union with nature; this was the same with Gopi Krishna.[392]

However, Daldal's enlightenment experience is difficult to perceive as he had his *kundalini* awakened based on the context of the story's ending, which suggested Amita Buddha, who supposed to symbolize Daldal, gilding was not finished

---

[390] Gopi Krishna, *Kundalini*; Lutyens, *Krishnamurti*.
[391] Gopi Krishna, op. cit.
[392] Ibid.; Lutyens, op. cit.

perfectly because there were not enough of gold paint left to finish it. Daldal seemed to have gained enlightenment with the help of Nohill, who could have awakened his *kundalini*; thus, he was able to see the Light (the Self) and was able to have the union with It, just like Gopi Krishna mentioned about his experience in above. Therefore, Nohill could have instructed Daldal how to see the Light (the Self) and achieve the union with It, based on his experience. In this way, Daldal might have achieved his enlightenment with the teaching of Nohill, but his enlightenment might not have been fully matured because he had not awakened his *kundalini*.

Next, I will examine the nature of Jiddu Krishnamurti's mystical experience in the union with his consciousness and the Universal Self or nature. When Krishnamurti was twenty-seven years old (1922), he went to Ojai, California, and stayed there for a while and experienced his *kundalini* being awakened; during those days, he experienced changes in his physical condition.[393] In one afternoon, he had an unusual mystical experience, during which his consciousness expanded and united with his surrounding nature, whether they were people, plants, or even wind: that day, he had some pain around his neck, so he was resting in the bed and felt his consciousness left his body, yet somehow he was aware of his surroundings; around his house was a road construction man repairing the road with the pickaxe; somehow Chrishnamurti's consciousness expanded and united with the man that he felt like the construction man as well as the road he was repairing, and the pickaxe itself, even

---

[393] Lutyens, *Krishnamurti*.

the tree near the man, and wind blowing around the tree as well as blades of grass near there—he felt identical to them.[394] Since his consciousness united with his surroundings or nature or the Universal Self, he felt identical to them. As he mentioned, "I was in everything; no, rather everything was in me";[395] he was alluding to everything (nature, the Universal Self, *Brahman*), and his consciousness (the Self, *Atman*) was not separated but identical. In other words, his Self and the Universal Self were in the state of union, and he expressed the state in a very plain and easily understandable language.

It seems that there are two types of the union with one's Self and the Universal Self: the first one is like Gopi Krishna's experience of seeing the Light (the Self) being in union with the Universal Self within *anahata chakra* (the heart) after his *kundalini* had awakened; the second one is like Jiddu Krishnamurti's experience of consciousness taking flight and expanding as it united with nature surrounding him after the *kundalini* had awakened. Gopi Krishana also expressed this experience, but for the sake of simply explaining two different types of union taking place, I did not include his experience as an example in this situation. Therefore, for the mystics who had their *kundalini* awakened, both types of union, within oneself and outside of oneself, seem to be a possibility.

In 1930, Jiddu Krishnamurti left the Theosophy Society and sought after his freedom from any kind of spiritual organization,

---

[394] Ibid., 209.
[395] Ibid.

and eventually he became to be known as the spiritual teacher of the world by seeking his own way of truth; during this period, he was most attracted by the educational field; thus, he established several schools in India and in England, but he always wanted to build more schools in India because she needed more.[396] However, due to financial reasons, his friends had to remind him that his wish to establish more schools was not feasible; nevertheless, said Lutyens, he always ended up building more schools because financially it became possible, and students and teachers were gathered as if they were attracted by some kind of force, so the schools received other people's attention.[397]

I deem this kind of miraculous attraction occurred due to Jiddu Krishnamurti's spiritual achievement, that is, his consciousness having the union with the Universal Self; thus, he can materialize what is in his mind in actual forms. There are some stories with similar allusions in the *Samgook Yusa*. Ilyeon recorded the stories of some Buddhist monks who seemed to have awakened their *kundalini* through long years of meditation practices, expanded their consciousnesses, and achieved the union with the Universal Self that Buddhist temples with such monks residing were known for miraculous events: one example is the Samso-Guaneum story. Thus, I will probe into the story and analyze how its miraculous events were possible, and whether the head monk of the temple had any common element to Jiddu Krishnamurti's mystical experience which illustrated to have the union with the Universal Self.

---

[396] Ibid., 364–5.

[397] Ibid., 365.

During the Silla Kingdom period, there was a Buddhist temple called Joongsengsa (the temple for mankind), and it was famous for having miraculous efficacy due to having a famous Bodhisattva effigy. The effigy was made by a well-known Chinese court painter named Seung-yo Jang, who was famous for Buddhist and Daoist portraits during the Wu Emperor of the Yang Kingdom. He got into some complicated misunderstanding when he drew a portrait of the Wu Emperor's favorite concubine, so he moved to Silla and made the Bodhisattva effigy in the Joongsengsa; then the effigy became famous for its efficacy. Thus the temple became widely known for granting good luck.

One of the story among several happened around March 992 CE was that the head of the temple, Sung-tae, was worried because there were not much grains growing outside the temple, so he could not maintain the temple; and it even got to the point which he could not afford to burn incenses for the temple. Thus he went forward to the Bodhisattva effigy and told It that he wanted to leave the temple because he could not maintain it. That night, Sung-tae dreamed of some Great Saint came to him and told him He would bring donations for the temple, so Sung-tae should remain there. Then about thirteen days later, two men from the boundary of Kimhae city came and said that a monk came to get donations for the temple, thus they brought them. To this, the head monk told them they did not send anyone to collect donations; yet he led them to the Bodhisattva effigy in the main hall. Then they were shocked and said that the monk who came to collect donations was him. They bowed to the effigy out of respect.

Ever since this event, the temple has had donations every year.[398]

In the story, we can perceive it was not the Bodhisattva effigy, which had the miraculous efficacy, but the maker of the effigy, Seung-yo Jang, and the head monk of the temple, Sung-tae, were enlightened figures who could enact such efficacy due to their spiritual achievement. The court painter, Seung-yo Jang, was known to have wondrous talent in drawing portraits.[399] When he painted the Wu Emperor's favorite concubine portrait, he did not even paint her like an actual figure, he even drew the part hidden by mistake of his brush, which caused him to be doubted by the emperor; thus, he had to vindicate his innocence by drawing the eleven-headed Avalokitesvara, which the emperor had seen in his dream.[400] From this incident, it is possible to perceive Seung-yo Jang painted portraits not only

---

[398] Part of the summary from the Samso-Guaneum story; Ilyeon, *Samgook Yusa*, 326–30.

[399] Ibid., 326–7.

[400] Ibid., 327.

with his eyes but with spiritual eyes; hence, the Bodhisattva effigy he made in the Joongsengsa probably was imbued with his spiritual power that it could have some kind of special aura around it.

In the story, there are other events that illustrate wondrous efficacy offerings happening in the Joongsengsa ever since Seung-yo Jang made the Bodhisattva effigy. Nevertheless, it is more appropriate to view the Joongsengsa as having been occupied by monks who were highly enlightened, perhaps ones who had gotten the *nirvana* enlightenment. It appears that one of them happened to be Sung-tae, who was the head of the temple and probably acquired the *nirvana* enlightenment and achieved the union with his consciousness and the Universal Self. Therefore, when Sung-tae told in front of the Bodhisattva effigy he would leave the temple because he could not maintain it, it was the Great Saint who told him to stay there in his dream; the Great Saint he saw in his dream could be *Dharma* World (the Universal Self), the Bodhisattva, the spirit of enlightened Seung-yo Jang, or all of the above. In other words, Sung-tae could have achieved the union with any of the above elements; therefore, what Sung-tae wished, to be able to maintain the temple, was also their wishes (viz., their wishes are identical to Sung-tae's because Sung-tae obtained the union with them). This is like Jiddu Krishnamurti could achieve the union with his surroundings in nature, whether they were animate or inanimate; in the same way, Sung-tae perhaps was also able to do that. Thus, Sung-tae could feel identical with the Universal Self, Seung-yo Jang's spirit, or the Bodhisattva effigy, which could have been displaying some wondrous aura. As his name, Sung-tae (the essence of bigness) signifies, the essence is his Self, and the bigness, the Universal Self; hence, the allusion is he being the essence of the Universal Self, which could be referring to his state in the union with his Self and the Universal Self. Therefore, he probably was a greatly enlightened monk, but he did not reveal his spiritual achievement in public, and he rather wished to make the Bodhisattva effigy continuously famous for its efficacy so that the Joongsengsa could carry on its reputation for granting good luck to the people.

There is another story which illustrates one having the union with one's consciousness and the Universal Self. An example is the Wolmyung story in the *Samgook Yusa*.

> Wolmyung stayed in the Sacheonwangsa (the temple of four directions' heavenly emperors) and was very good at playing the flute. One day he was passing a big road in front of the temple by playing the flute; the moon stopped from passing to listen to his flute playing. So people called the road, Wolmyungli, and Wolmyung became famous for the event.[401]

The reason I deem Wolmyung (the bright moon) achieved the union with his consciousness and the Universal Self is based on an allusion that was expressed when "he was passing a big road in front of the temple by playing the flute; the moon stopped from passing to listen to his flute playing."

---

[401] Ilyeon, "The Wolmyung Story," *Samgook Yusa*, 532.

This expression connotes Wolmyung being in equal status as the moon because the sound of Wolmyung's flute playing could even influence the moon's passing. Chang-won Kim mentions that stories under the theme of Gamtong, in book 5 of the *Samgook Yusa*, like the Wolmyung story, recorded about transcendental experiences and differed from other Gameung (response from a deity) stories because Gamtong's transcendental experience arises from *banya* (*prajna,* wisdom); in other words, one has transcendental experience because one gained enlightenment.[402] Therefore, he says that the transcendental experiences are "the crystallization of their enlightenment," and enlightenment is "what causes mysticism and miracles."[403] Furthermore, he perceives that examining the Gamtong theme of the stories, such as the Wolmyung story, they are about "analyzing the contents of enlightenment."[404] Based on his contention, I can discern the allusion of Wolmyung's flute playing was in such a state that even the moon stopped from passing to listen to his flute playing, which signifies his state of enlightenment was at such a high level to cause the miracle.

In the following, I will analyze Wolmyung's mystical experience in a more realistic interpretation. The allusion of the above quoted example is that the sound of his flute playing

---

[402] Chang-won Kim, "*Samgook Yusa* 'Gamtong'-ui Hyangga illki: Hergoojeok Saegae-ui Jinsil," *Gookjae Ermoon* (Gookjae Ermoonharkhui) 31, 2004: 63–64. Kim perceives *banya* (wisdom) is the result obtained from enlightenment, but it also exists within ourselves as faith.

[403] Ibid., 64.

[404] Ibid.

was so delightful that the listeners' minds were all allured to him; thus, the environment surrounding them, even the moon, seemed to be stopped to listen to his flute playing. In other words, the sound of his flute playing was probably so mysterious that it might have reached the moment of transcending spatial and time elements to create an optical illusion; hence, the moon even appeared to be stopped from moving. Wolmyung's soul was meditative, so he could have entered the unity with the flute sound, which caused the listeners to fall into the same unity with the sound; therefore, things surrounding them at that moment seemed to be stopped completely. The other reason I perceive Wolmyung achieved the union with the Universal Self is that his name *Wolmyung* signifies "the bright moon"; thus, Ilyeon identified him as the bright moon (viz., he is the bright moon). Wolmyung must have possessed a special power, so he recorded him as Wolmyung, the bright moon. Wolmyung was also famous for his talent in composing *hyangga,* as aforementioned in chapter 1, about "Jaemang Maega," the *hyangga* he composed upon his sister's memorial ritual. Ilyeon recorded that his *hyangga* were known to have "affected gods in heaven and earth as well as ghosts."[405] These were referring to Wolmyung's spiritual power having reached such a high level that he could even influence the gods and the ghosts, and his mysterious sound of the flute playing could even stop the moon's passing. In these, Ilyeon was expressing the metaphor of how Wolmyung achieved a high level of enlightenment and his union with the Universal Self.

---

[405] Ilyeon, "The Wolmyung Story," 532.

Hae-choon Rhu says that Wolmyung "was an Esoteric Buddhist monk, who had some magical power, which enabled him to hold supernatural power to communicate with nature and believed in Esoteric Buddhism."[406] Then he agrees with Seung-chan Kim's perspective and says that the Esoteric Buddhist monks usually "accept magical power and effectuate the role of praying to gods and ghosts; thus the monks believe in the Esoteric Buddhism can relate with any sects of Buddhism as well as folk religions."[407] Based on these points of view, I can discern that Wolmyung seemed to be an Esoteric Buddhist monk who obtained the *nirvana* enlightenment and achieved the union with his Self and the Universal Self, thus gained spiritual power. Wolmyung's distinction is very similar to aforementioned other mystics (i.e., Pyohoon, Jinjeong, Eckhart, Ruysbroeck, Gopi Krishna, and Giddu Krishnamurti), who transcended the boundary of their religions and achieved the union with their Self and the Universal Self or gods to gain a higher spiritual power.

Wolmyung's talent in playing the flute is like being in a meditative state that he is completely stopped from any action, yet the flute is playing itself only based on his consciousness. This kind of state can only be explained by borrowing the aforementioned example of Giddu Krishnamurti's expression of being in the union with nature, that is, he identified with the road construction man, tree, blades of grass, passing wind,

---

[406] Hae-choon Rhu, "Wolmyungsa-ui Hyangga," 427.

[407] Seung-chan Kim, *Hangook Sanggo Moonharklon* (Seoul: Saemoonsa, 1987), 157. As quoted by Hae-choon Rhu, op. cit., 427.

etc.;[408] hence, Wolmyung's flute playing with his consciousness is like "I am the flute, and the flute is me," "I am the bright moon, and the bright moon is me." Since Wolmyung's consciousness is in deep meditation while playing the flute, his consciousness and the flute playing is united into one; the passing moon also united with his consciousness when Wolmyung was in the union with the flute playing. Therefore, he was also in the union with the moon; consequently, the moon appeared to stop from passing at that moment. Mystics who have acquired the union between their Self and the Universal Self can achieve the union with anything existing in the Universe, as Giddu Krishnamurti indicates in above; moreover, he exclaimed his mystical experience as "I am in everything; no, rather everything is in me."[409] This is only possible because their consciousnesses reached the level that can have the union with anything existing in the Universe; it is also because within themselves, they hold the Universe.

Another good example text that conveys having the union with his Self and nature or the Universal Self is a poem written by a Confucian scholar in the Joseon Dynasty, Soon Song.

> Built a cottage by administering [cultivating] for ten years.
> One-half of it is fresh wind, the other half the bright moon.

---

[408] Lutyens, *Krishnamurti*, 209.
[409] Ibid.

There is no space to bring in the mountain and river, I would leave them in nature.[410]

This is composed in the form of regulated *sijo*, in three lines, yet the poet alluded to his state of being in the union with nature in a very laconic expression. He said that he cultivated for ten years and gained enlightenment, which he connoted as "a cottage." This is a humble expression of the Confucian scholar seeking enlightenment, deemed an ideal virtue of being poor, symbolizing his pure nature. The main reason the *sijo* signifies his enlightenment, his state of union with nature, is the allusion of the second line, in which he said that one-half of the cottage is fresh wind, which signifies his pure consciousness, the other half the bright moon, which he refers to his wisdom attained. As aforementioned in the Wolmyung story, the bright moon symbolizes the state of enlightenment, which is also wisdom obtained. Therefore, Song was connoting that he had gained the pure consciousness and wisdom, which is the effect of enlightenment. However, in the poetry, Song can be deemed to acquire the *nirvana* enlightenment because he expressed that he had gotten the pure consciousness that can only be obtained in the *nirvana* enlightenment or the introvertive mystical experience. Nevertheless, from the third line of the poem it is a little ambiguous that the interpretation could be different. Song mentioned that there was no space to bring the mountain and the river into the cottage, thus, he would leave them in nature and enjoy them. I perceive this expression is again his allusion

---

[410] Soon Song, *Yuckdae Sijo Jeonseo*, ed. Jae-wan Shim (Seoul: Sejong Moonhwasa, 1972), 639 (1803).

of humbleness, just like "a cottage" he selected to signify his enlightenment. Hence, in the last line, two interpretations are possible: one is that he had already gained his enlightenment, which he was seeking; thus, why would he seek after something else (viz., socially or politically)? The other is that he had already achieved the union with nature or the Universal Self, so why would he make a distinction between him and nature when he holds nature already, just like Krishnamurti's awakening, "I am in everything; no, rather everything is in me"?[411] What is so remarkable about Song's and Krishnamurti's implicit expressions for such greatness of their enlightenment perhaps had to do with their power gained yet not wielding it. In the next part, I will discuss the third necessity of gaining enlightenment, which is related to transporting the deceased souls to a higher realm.

4.3 Offering Salvation Is Possible by Transporting the Deceased Souls to a Higher Realm

For the Jinjeong story, Ilyeon titled it "Jinjeong's Filial Piety and Good Deeds Are Equally Beautiful" (Hyoseon Ssangmi); in the story, he mentioned about Jinjeong's filial piety effectuated on his deceased mother, but he was silent about what kind of good deeds Jinjeong offered to others. It seems rather odd that Ilyeon mentioned whatever Jinjeong effected on behalf of others as "good deeds" because he often stressed in the *Samgook Yusa* that an ideal Mahayana Buddhist monk's behavior represents an ideal Bodhisattva, which he espoused to carry out to mankind. Hence, it is possible to presume what Jinjeong did for others was

---

[411] Lutyens, op. cit., 209.

probably something that had taken extraordinary effort. I deem it must be related to transporting the deceased souls to higher places in the other world, thus offering them salvation, just like what he did for his deceased mother.

Among Korean literature scholars, there are two different points of view on transporting the deceased souls to the earthly paradise in Western Pure Land (Seobang Jeongto) and the heavenly paradise, Dosolcheon, which are expressed in "Jaemang Maega," and the Jinjeong story, respectively. One point of view is that regardless of how the deceased souls lived while alive, if the one who performs the deceased souls' transporting ritual has spiritual power, the deceased souls can be transported to the earthly paradise or heaven. The other viewpoint is that no matter who conducts it, if the deceased souls did not live virtuously while alive, it would be impossible to transport them to Western Pure Land or Dosolcheon. As aforementioned in chapter 1, the former view is contended by Ho-gyung Sung, and the latter by Seon-gyung Choi. I am in agreement with the latter perspective that the one who carries out the transporting rituals has to be equipped with spiritual efficacy as well as the deceased soul has had to live virtuously while alive in order to receive the ritual performer's efficacy to be transported to Western Pure Land or heaven, Dosolcheon. In "Jaemang Maega," the background story does not mention much about the ritual receiver, Wolmyung's deceased sister; thus, it is difficult to argue about her quality of character. However, in the Jinjeong story, there are some information about what Jinjeong's mother was like. She was a devout Buddhist based on the following: (1)

she donated the last valuable in the house, a broken three-foot metal rice cooker, to a Buddhist temple construction; (2) she let Jinjeong know that obtaining enlightenment is the best way to carry out his filial piety to her; and (3) there were only a few days' worth of rice left in the house, yet she cooked all of them at once and gave them to Jinjeong and let him leave the house hurriedly to become a Buddhist monk under Uisang's teaching, regardless of how she could survive without her son's support.[412] Then three years later, she passed away; when Jinjeong heard the news, he fell into seven days of meditation.[413] As I mentioned in chapter 3, when Jinjeong was in deep meditation, he probably tried to transport his mother to the heavenly realm, but there must have been some obstacle for her to enter; thus, Jinjeong woke up from the meditation and told something to Uisang; then Uisang gathered his three thousand disciples, went to Choodong, and gave them lectures for ninety days on *Hwaum Daejeon*; when the ninety days of lectures were over, Jinjeong's deceased mother appeared in Jinjeong's dream and told him that she was born again in heaven.[414] Based on the story, Jinjeong's deceased mother's obstacle might have been either her wisdom or virtue accumulation needed to enter the heavenly realm, no matter how poor and honestly she lived while alive. It seemed that Uisang's ninety days of lectures on *Hwaum Daejeon* resolved her obstacle and transported her soul to heaven.

---

[412] Ilyeon, "The Jinjeong Story," 572-3.
[413] Ibid., 573.
[414] Ibid., 573–4.

As aforementioned in chapter 1, Wonhyo distinguished the difficulty in entering between the earthly paradise in Western Pure Land (Seobang Jeongto) and the heavenly paradise, Dosolcheon; in order to enter the heavenly realm, one had to cultivate one's whole life in religious austerity and had to follow more strict precepts.[415] For Jinjeong's deceased mother, a Buddhist laity, to ascend to the heavenly realm has special significance. It perhaps had to do with what Uisang and his disciples pursued as well as Ilyeon. There was the possibility that Ilyeon identified himself with Jinjeong and his mother with Jinjeong's mother,[416] although Ilyeon's mother survived until over ninety years old; thus, Ilyeon retired from the position of the Most Reverend Buddhist Priest in the Goryeo Dynasty and moved to his hometown Buddhist temple, the Yingarksa, where he could support his mother in his late seventies.[417] Based on his filial piety, he probably wished his mother to enter the heavenly realm, like Jinjeong's mother. However, I would like to examine how Jinjeong's deceased mother was able to enter the heavenly realm as a Buddhist laity based on other scholars' theory.

According to the seventeenth-century Platonic philosopher Henry More, ascending to the heavenly realm, the Ethereal region, directly from the Terrestrial region, right after one's death rarely happened; however, he contended that it might be possible if the deceased soul was very noble and heroic.[418]

---

[415] Wonhyo's "Yooshim Anlarkdo," as quoted by Seung-chan Kim, "Wangseng Sasang," 4.

[416] Gang-ok Lee, "Choolga Deukdodam," 200.

[417] Ilyeon, *Samgook Yusa*, 10-11.

[418] More, "Immortality of the Soul," chapter 1, section 5.

Furthermore, More mentioned that only angelical figures can ascend to the highest Aerial region, and the purest soul, like gods, can only ascend to the Ethereal region or the heavenly realm.[419] The reason for his theory was that right after death, the souls are still not completely released from the vital union with matter that exists in the world because the Aerial region where the deceased souls reside are full of good and bad souls.[420] Nevertheless, he argued that it was the human soul that was capable of reaching its purity and thus able to ascend to the Ethereal region, the heavenly realm.[421] This was because the purity of the deceased soul was attracted to "Divine Intellectual Objects"; and More asserted that his opinion on the nature of the deceased soul was similar to Plato's and Aristotle's opinions.[422] Based on More's opinion about the nature of the deceased soul, there are three parties that contributed to Jinjeong mother's ascent to the heavenly realm: (1) Jinjeong's seven-day meditation, which enabled him to find out what was his mother's obstacle, and he probably tried to resolve the obstacle by effecting painstaking memorial rituals for her. (2) Uisang's ninety days of lectures on *Hwaum Daejeon* probably enabled her to purify her soul even more; thus, she could ascend to the heavenly realm. (3) Jinjeong's mother's purity of her soul, stemming from a lifelong faith in Buddhism, contributed to her ascension to heaven. Although Jinjeong's deceased mother's soul might not have been completely released from all matters in the universe right after

---

[419] Ibid., chapter 1, sections 3, 4.

[420] Ibid., and axiom 27.

[421] Ibid., chapter 1, section 4.

[422] Ibid., chapter 1, section 2.

her death, it was her soul's purity that attracted to divine and intellectual objects; in this instance, it might have been Uisang's ninety days lectures, which helped her to gain more wisdom and enabled her to release the matter attached to her soul even more to achieve the utmost purity. Hence, it was possible for her to ascend further up to the heavenly realm. Therefore, for Jinjeong's deceased mother's soul to enter the heavenly realm, all three parties—Jinjeong's seven-day meditation, Uisang's ninety days lectures, and Jinjeong's deceased mother's soul's purity—were needed. The combined efforts enabled Jinjeong's mother to ascend to heaven.

Then there is another opinion why Ilyeon titled the Jinjeong story as "Jinjeong's Filial Piety and Good Deeds Are Equally Beautiful" (Hyoseon Ssangmi). There are Korean scholars who perceive "Hyoseon Ssangmi" represented one of the contemporary Buddhist movements of Hwaumjong, which was started by Uisang. "Hyoseon Ssangmi" literally means "filial piety and good deeds are equally beautiful," but it figuratively means "it is better to become a Buddhist monk and to get enlightened than just support parents for their physical needs, and when they are deceased, the enlightened son can transport his parents' souls to the heavenly realm; thereby, this is considered the higher stage of carrying out filial piety to parents." And Korean scholars contend that this kind of thinking arose among Buddhist monks as a countermeasure to Confucian criticism of how Buddhist monks abandon their parents and do not fulfill their duty of filial piety.[423] Gang-ok Lee avers

---

[423] Doo-jin Kim, "Silla Uisang-gye Hwaumjong-ui Hyoseon

when he analyzes stories of Jinjeong, Shinhyo, and Jinpyo, which carry the theme of "Hyoseon Ssangmi," he can understand the real meaning of Buddhist priesthood and duties of filial piety Ilyeon pursued; then he further claims that "he who is resolute to become a Buddhist monk, he can leave the house leaving behind his parents. However, there are two duties he must fulfill for his parents after he gets enlightened. The first is to transport his deceased parents' souls to the heavenly realm. The next is if his parents are still alive, help them also to get enlightened. Ilyeon seemed to perceive the second choice as the most ideal situation."[424] Therefore, based on these contentions, the Jinjeong story can be perceived to fit the ideal of the movement "Hyoseon Ssangmi": Jinjeong's mother, a devout Buddhist, followed an ideal of a Bodhisattva, as well as role model in motherhood, which made it possible for her son, Jinjeong, to obtain the *nirvana* enlightenment. Jinjeong's mother did not expect her son to stay home to support her. She encouraged him to become a Buddhist monk and to get enlightened; when he did, he helped her to enter the heavenly realm when she was deceased. Thus, they were in a relationship of mutual help. In this way, Jinjeong's enlightenment story perfectly fit into the ideal of the "Hyoseon Ssangmi" movement.

Based on Jinjeong's filial piety, it is possible to hypothesize, as he effected his deceased mother's soul to be transported to heaven, he probably helped other deceased souls to be

---

Ssangmi-ui Shinang," *Hangookhark Nonchong* (Korean Study Center, Gookmin University) 15 (1992): 20–21. As quoted by Gang-ok Lee, op. cit., 220, footnote 11.

[424] Gang-ok Lee, op. cit., 220–1.

transported to the other world by utilizing his skill in falling into deep meditation; and if he could find out there was any obstacle in transporting the deceased souls, then he could resolve the problem and help them to be transported to the other world. This was possible because he gained the *nirvana* enlightenment.

The next is the Daesung story, which I mentioned in chapter 3 briefly; thus, in this section, more details are explained. The story signifies how a highly enlightened Buddhist monk, Jeomgae, can transport the deceased soul to a higher status in the afterlife.

> Jeomgae, a Buddhist monk, who was famous for being virtuous, wished to hold a Buddhist ritual called, *"yooklunhui"* in the Buddhist temple, Heunglunsa; so he went to the house of Bokan to ask for donation. Bokan donated fifty rolls of hemp cloths. Jeomgae blessed him by chanting. Daesung, who was very poor, worked for Bokan, received a few ridge and furrow of a field for his services, and supported his mother. When Jeomgae was blessing Bokan for his donation, Daesung heard what Jeomgae told Bokan, and that made Daesung ruminate on his situation.
>
> Then Daesung told his mother what he heard about Jeomgae blessing Bokan, and he suggested to his mother about donating the field he received from Bokan to Jeomgae's *yooklunhui* to seek a better life in his afterlife. His mother

fain agreed to his suggestion. Not too long after, Daesung died and reincarnated as the Silla Kingdom's Prime Minister, Moon-lyang Kim's son. When his wife was pregnant with Daesung, she heard a sound coming from the sky, "Daesung from Molyangli is about to be born in your house." When he was born, he held a golden name tag, "Daesung" written on it in his left fist. Hence they searched for Daesung, who used to live in Molyangli and found out that he died the day the prime minister's wife got pregnant. Therefore, they brought Daesung's mother living in Molyangli and lived together in the prime minister's house. When Daesung grew up, he also became the prime minister of the Silla Kingdom and built the Boolgooksa Buddhist temple for his present-life parents and constructed the Seokgoolarm Buddhist stone grotto for his past-life parents.[425]

In the story, the Buddhist monk Jeomgae was known to be virtuous; thus, he probably had gotten the *nirvana* enlightenment, and he was the one who wanted to hold *yooklunhui*[426] in the temple so gathered donations from the people. Daesung heard when Jeomgae told Bokan, "If you donate one thing, you will receive ten thousand times of

---

[425] Summary from the Daesung story; Ilyeon, *Samgook Yusa*, 575–6.

[426] See footnote 252 of chapter 3.

it."[427] It made Daesung ponder over his current situation. He realized he did not do good deeds in his past life, so he was born poor in the present life; thus, he wanted to donate all he possessed so that he could be born under a better situation in his afterlife. After he donated everything he had, he died; then he reincarnated as the Silla Kingdom's prime minister's son. Afterward, he also became the prime minister of the kingdom and constructed well-known Buddhist architecture for his past-life parents and the present-life parents, thereby he became famous for his filial piety to his parents and for loyalty to his country. It was Daesung's wisdom that enabled him to realize his current situation when he heard what Jeomgae told Bokan. Hence, he strived to change his destiny by making a spur for his afterlife; however, Jeomgae was the one who kicked the spur. If Jeomgae were not a greatly enlightened monk, no matter what Daesung donated, he probably would not have received ten thousand times in return. The reason Daesung was able to reincarnate as the prime minister's son was because he met a highly enlightened Buddhist monk, Jeomgae. As the meaning of his name *Jeomgae* suggests, he could make other people's lives improve gradually; in other words, Jeomgae's talent or efficacy was to make his followers improve their lives. Therefore, what Daesung donated to Jeomgae made Daesung's afterlife's status to be elevated greatly.

Based on these stories of greatly enlightened monks, Jinjeong and Jeomgae, we can discern that when one gets greatly enlightened, one can make others enter the heavenly realm

---

[427] Ilyeon, "The Daesung Story," 575.

and make others perform good deeds so that their lives can be promoted in the future or the afterlife, respectively. Next, I will reiterate the main point of how Princess Bari gets to transport the deceased souls to the other world.

In chapters 2 and 3, I examined how Princess Bari obtained the *nirvana* enlightenment. I contended that "Princess Bari" embraces several religious elements that it seems to be influenced by the ideal of *poongrhudo*, which has existed since ancient Korea. It appears that the shamanic song accepted all foreign religious elements, which were transmitted to Korea throughout history. However, the mythical element of Princess Bari getting the sacred marriage with the shaman god Musang, which symbolizes Princess Bari obtaining the *nirvana* enlightenment, illustrates a similar element to the Indian Hindu gods' union, that is, Shiva and Shakti union; moreover, the god Musang with whom the princess has the sacred union holds similar attributes to the Hindu god Shiva. Shiva was known as the lord of the deceased souls and the god of the forest.[428] The god Musang was the gatekeeper of the Seocheon Flower Field, where the water of life and the herbs of life exist; it was also known as the other world, where the deceased souls stay. Therefore, the god Shiva and the god Musang share similar attributes, but their names are different. In this way, I perceive the sacred union between Princess Bari and the god Musang as similar to the union between Shakti and Shiva; and Princess Bari uses her husband's sacred function as Shakti Shiva's function. Therefore, the authority Princess Bari gained to transport the deceased souls

---

[428] Zimmer, *Myths and Symbols*; see chapter 3 of this book.

to the other world was by her marriage to the god Musang, who was the god of the other world.

Nevertheless, the story also suggests she gained the ability to transport the deceased souls after she obtained the *nirvana* enlightenment. Before she gains enlightenment, that is, on the way to the other world to find the water of life, she receives the *rahwa* from Shakyamuni and uses it to make the sea change to land and release the deceased souls trapped in hell to wherever they were destined to go—either to the Lotus World or *Nirvana* or other places in the nether world. However, after she obtained the *nirvana* enlightenment, she can transport the deceased souls to the other world without any other help: for example, she transports the deceased souls who died without children or during childbirth to the Lotus World on the way back to this world from the other world. She already gained the authority by marrying the god Musang, who was the god of the other world, which also signifies she acquired the *nirvana* enlightenment. Hence, she can transport the deceased souls to the other world and bring the deceased souls from the other world to this world and revive them.

Transporting the deceased souls in the Jinjeong story and Daesung story in the *Samgook Yusa* and the shamanic song "Princess Bari" all express that the figures who gained the *nirvana* enlightenment could perform such function; by doing so, they can bring salvation to the deceased souls. This is because in the Jinjeong story, Jinjeong was able to find out what decedent souls went through in their postmortem by falling into deep meditation; thus, he was able to transport the deceased souls to the other world by knowing their obstacles and resolving them, such as his deceased mother's soul's transportation to heaven with the help of his teacher, Uisang. In the Daesung story, he was able to reincarnate to the promoted status because he met Jeomgae, who probably had gotten the *nirvana* enlightenment; thus, he was able to influence Daesung's afterlife. Jeomgae probably was able to communicate with gods, just like Pyohoon, who could visit the heavenly palace and meet the Heavenly Emperor and convey King Gyungdeok's wish to have a male heir; in the same way, Jeomgae might have visited the heavenly realm to request Daesung's promoted reincarnation. Princess Bari also transports the deceased souls to the other world after she acquired the *nirvana* enlightenment. According to Heonseon Kim, Princess Bari is known to transport the deceased souls to the Lotus World, which is known to be one of *Nirvana*.[429] Therefore, all three stories express that figures who obtained the *nirvana* enlightenment could effectuate transporting the deceased souls to a higher realm in their afterlife and thus offer them salvation.

Then why is transporting the deceased souls to a higher realm necessary? That is to prepare for the apocalypse of the world. In Mahayana Buddhism, it is known that the Bodhisattvas' ultimate goal is to lead mankind to salvation; thus, they delay their entering *Nirvana* as much as possible. Why would Bodhisattvas be concerned with others' salvation? Would not mankind reach their salvation when they naturally progressed into their maturity? Bodhisattvas are concerned

---

[429] Heon-seon Kim, "Jeoseung-ul Yeoheng haneun," 166.

lest the world would fall into the apocalypse before mankind reaches their salvation. This is because in this world, nothing exists permanently, and when something begins to exist, it goes through natural progress of prosperity to nonexistence. Therefore, we have to prepare for the stage of nonexistence before it is too late.

The apocalypse of the world is even mentioned in Korean "Changsae Shinhwa" (the myth of the creation of the world). The myth contains several mythical elements: creation of heaven and earth, giants created the world, the origin of water and fire, the creation of human beings, two gods competing with each other to control the world, regulating the sun and the moon, the heaven-and-earth marriage and the birth of a progenitor, etc.[430] Among these mythical elements, the apocalypse is denoted in the section of two gods, Mireuk and Seokga,[431] competing with each other to control the world.

There are several different versions of the Korean myth of the creation of the world. The first version was recorded by

---

[430] Heon-seon Kim, *Hangook-ui Changsae Shinhwa* (Seoul: Gilbut, 1994), 17.

[431] Two gods' names do not necessarily refer to present-day Buddhist gods' names. It is more appropriate to understand them as ancient gods' names, pre-Buddhist gods (i.e., Mithra and Varuna). See Georges Dumezil, *Mitra-Varuna: An Essay on Two Indo-European Representations of Sovereignty*, trans. Derek Coltman (New York: Zone Books, 1988). In the Korean shamanic myth, there are other names (i.e., Daebyul Wang and Sobyul Wang) with similar functions. In the Greek myth, two gods competing with each other to control the world would be Ouranous versus Cronus and Cronus versus Zeus; they are comparable to Mireuk and Seokga.

Jin-tae Sohn in 1923 from a shamaness, Ssang-dol Kim, living in Hamheung City, in the South of Hamgyungdo Province; then, in 1930, he published the first collection of shamanic songs, the *Joseon Shin-Ga-Yoo-Pyeon*, in Japan.[432] According to Ssang-dol Kim's version of "The Myth of the Creation of the World," in the section of the mythical element about two gods, Mireuk and Seokga, competing with each other to control the world, it refers to Mireuk's period as peaceful, but Seokga wants to rule the period; thus, they compete with each other three times, and Mireuk won all three times, but in the third competition, Seokga uses a trick to win; hence, Mireuk ends up leaving the world control to Seokga and tells him that Seokga's period would be the apocalypse.[433] The myth does not mention the reason for the apocalypse but just expresses that "due to time and tide, it becomes the apocalypse."[434] The myth only mentions "due to the period, it becomes the apocalypse"; therefore, it seems to be alluding to a similar point of view with other ancient civilizations' prophecies, which perceived that the world would meet the apocalypse some day.[435] The existence of the apocalypse of the world has been contended by many scholars in a variety of fields (i.e., philosophy, religion, history, literature, etc.) since the ancient period.

---

[432] Heon-seon Kim, *Hangook-ui Changsae Shinhwa*, 227.

[433] Ibid., 233–5.

[434] Ibid., 235.

[435] Mercea Eliade, *Le mythe de l'eternel retour*, trans. Jae-joong Shim (Seoul: Yiharksa, 2003).

John Alexander Stewart indicated an interesting viewpoint about the state of Socrates when he spoke about the eschatology of the world while Socrates was having contentions with his disciples in Plato's dialogues (i.e., Phaedo, Phaedrus, Symposium, the Republic, etc.). Stewart perceived that out of many Plato's dialogues, which illustrated Socrates as a prophet appeared to be one of his genuine characters; therefore, he deemed that Socrates might have a condition such as being possessed by a god; and when Socrates narrated about the eschatology, he acted like a prophet, so others who were listening to him became mesmerized by his speech.[436] For this reason, Stewart said that he had a research interest about Socrates being not only as a dialectician but also as a prophet or a mythologist.[437] Hence, we can perceive even during the ancient Greek period, people already had concerns about the apocalypse of the world.

In this chapter's inquiry of the necessity in gaining enlightenment suggested in the stories, and why we need to gain the *nirvana* enlightenment, thus bring salvation to ourselves and others, Henry More's perspective on why ascending to the heavenly realm is necessary seems to be the most pertinent answer to the inquiry. Thus, I shall introduce his theory and concern to fulfill the purpose of this treatise. Henry More, as aforementioned, perceived the deceased souls' residences were usually the Aerial and the Ethereal regions: the Aerial region was said to be occupied by various decedent souls, and the higher Aerial region was occupied by angelic souls; whereas the

---

[436] Stewart, *The Myths of Plato*.
[437] Ibid.

Ethereal region, which was the heavenly realm, was occupied by only gods who had perfect purity of the soul.[438] More's main concern was with those souls residing in the Terrestrial and the Aerial regions when the "Conflagration of the World" and the "Extinction of the Sun" would occur; thus, he examined several different opinions on how to overcome such ordeals and how the deceased souls can ascend to the Ethereal region or the heavenly realm because the Ethereal region was said to be unharmed by those calamities; then, among different opinions, More perceived Plutarch's suggestion as a better option than others.[439] According to him, Plutarch contended that the deceased soul residing in the Aerial region, just like other ancient philosophers' view, if the souls lived virtuously and heroically while alive, they would move on to the Ethereal region; but if they lived in a vice, thus heavy with evil deeds, they would return to the Terrestrial region to reincarnate, to which Plutarch perceived it as confinement in prison, while More called it "the death of the soul."[440] Therefore, Plutarch viewed that the soul favored by God—by performing heroic deeds, cultivating one's virtue, and having disciplinary life while alive—would make the soul eventually ascend to the Ethereal region; to his view, More argued that Plutarch's suggestions were just one of better options among several others' points of view, but it was not the best.[441] In fact, More did not have the best answer to resolve the issue at the hand although he explicitly

---

[438] More, op. cit., axiom 28 and chapter 3, sections 1–3.

[439] Ibid., chapter 17, sections 3, 15.

[440] Ibid., chapter 17, sections 15–16.

[441] Ibid., chapter 17, section 17.

was concerned about what could happen to the souls that had not entered the Ethereal region: "If the Conflagration of the World occurs, men's immortality would be lost. The souls in the Terrestrial and the Aerial regions would be affected by it; but the Ethereal region would be unharmed."[442] More's concern about the "Conflagration of the World" was not anything new but had been the concern ever since ancient civilizations, as aforementioned.[443] It had been known that the world would be destroyed by either water or fire ever since ancient periods; and what More and others were more concerned about was the destruction of the world by fire; however, More's perspective was not as severe as the other philosophers' view, which insisted that the Conflagration would happen worldwide, whereas More argued that it would only occur in the Earth, intermittently in different periods and different places, based on other ancient religious beliefs and poets' views.[444] Afterward, More introduced several hypotheses of other scholars' viewpoints on what could happen to the souls residing in the Terrestrial and the Aerial regions when the Conflagration of the Earth would occur; out of those hypotheses, More was most critical of the stoical point of view, which perceived the souls would revive after the Conflagration of the World.[445] Stoics asserted that one way of recovering the world's order repeatedly was by the

---

[442] Ibid., chapter 18, sections 1, 15.

[443] Ancient Egypt, Greece, Rome, Iran, India, etc.—all prophesied that the apocalypse of the world would occur. Refer to Mercea Eliade, *l'eternel retour*. Also the Korean myth of "The Creation of the World" mentioned it. Heon-seon Kim, *Hangook-ui Changsae Shinhwa*, 235.

[444] More, op. cit., chapter 18, sections 2–5.

[445] Ibid., chapter 18, sections 7–13.

Conflagration of the World: when this occurs, all matters burnt down, yet immortal elements revive again and thus begin a new world; in this way, the world returns to life forever.[446] However, More viewed Stoic's hypothesis as unreasonable because the souls surviving the Conflagration of the World seemed impossible.[447]

More deemed those vicious souls and demons in the Terrestrial region would be destroyed by the Conflagration, but he was primarily concerned that those pious and virtuous souls residing in the Terrestrial and the Aerial regions would be harmed by it unless divinities in the Ethereal region offered some miraculous help; one possible suggestion was that those pious souls residing in the Aerial region would be flown into the Ethereal region to preserve their souls.[448] Furthermore, More mentioned about the "Extinction of the Sun," which could affect the immortalities of the deceased souls in the Aerial region by referring to Descartes's contention that long after in the future, "the Sun may be so inextricably enveloped by the Macula that he is never free from, that he may quite lose his light"; upon his view, More perceived the problem would prevent reproduction in the earth that could cause famine as well as sickness; thereby, it would make the earth desolate.[449] More further claimed that even the deceased souls in the Aerial region would be deficient of the sunlight that they would feel like staying in cold and dark places like in underground prisons, but the condition of

---

[446] Sung-sook Kim, *Marcus Aurelius Antonius*

[447] More, "Immortality of the Soul," chapter 18, section 13.

[448] Ibid., chapter 18, section 15.

[449] Ibid., chapter 19, sections 1–2.

the Ethereal region would not be affected by the diminished sunlight because of their highest location, which would enable them to move from one point of planet to another point easily with their light beings, so they could get light from another planet easily.[450] More seemed to be referring that if the sun lost its light, there could be another star that the Ethereal beings could get light from by moving from one galaxy to another where they could find the substitute light of the sun. This is possible because they are located in the highest point of the world where the fate of one planet, like Earth, would not affect their existence. However, the Terrestrial and the Aerial regions' denizen souls are bound by their locations; thus, any calamities occurring in those regions would affect the resident souls. This notion of the Ethereal region or the heavenly realm being free from any catastrophe of the world was also mentioned in the ancient Korean Buddhist text.[451] The ancient Indians also believed in entering *Nirvana* permanently to be free from any apocalypse, which could occur in the future since the world repeats an endless cycle of the creation and destruction.[452] Therefore, mankind following their religious cultivation methods to obtain enlightenment or the *nirvana* enlightenment to enter *Nirvana* or to reach the heavenly realm as their ultimate goal has existed in both Eastern and Western cultures; the *Samgook Yusa* stories and "Princess Bari" as well as mystical experiences of Western mystics, I examined, well reflected the same goal.

---

[450] Ibid., chapter 19, sections 2, 5.

[451] Hae-choon Rhu, "Wolmyungsa-ui Hyangga," 431.

[452] Eliade, *l'eternel retour*.

However, as More contended, entering the Ethereal region or the heavenly realm for most of the deceased souls would be impossible unless they become perfectly pure or become a divinity, and there is an imminent concern for those pious and virtuous decedent souls residing in the Aerial region if the Conflagration of the Earth occurs.[453] Then how can we delay the Conflagration of the Earth until more souls progress to their enlightenment, thus we can all ascend to the Ethereal region or the heavenly realm?

The knowledge of the world's apocalypse, that is, the Conflagration of the Earth and the Extinction of the Sun, has existed since ancient civilizations, but when the apocalypse would occur has not been known precisely. This probably has to do with how we treat our environment and what kind of relationship we have with gods in the Ethereal region or the heavenly realm. Based on the enlightenment stories I have examined in this research, we can deem there are figures who can effectuate the intermediary role between the heavenly gods and mankind. They can convey each other's messages, like Pyohoon, who carried out the intermediary role between the Heavenly Emperor and King Gyungdeok in the Pyohoon story. Greek texts also illustrate figures who effected the intermediary role between the heavenly god Zeus and mankind (i.e., Eros, Prometheus, and perhaps Atlas). Eros appears in "Symposium," and Diotima calls him "a great spirit" (*daemon*) who conducts the intermediary role between gods and mankind, and she also calls him "the power, which interprets and conveys to the gods

---

[453] More, "Immortality of the Soul."

the prayers and sacrifices of men, and to men the commands and rewards of the gods"; thus, he brings about harmony between them.[454] In other words, Eros is one of the *daemons* who strengthens the relationship between gods and mankind, and mankind to mankind with love. Thus, he makes mortals have offspring, enabling them to become immortals through their descendants. *Daemons* are another type of angelic souls residing in the highest Aerial region, or known to reside in the third Aerial region, which is right below the Ethereal region or the heavenly realm.[455] There is also another type of *daemon* that Greek mythology mentions as a Titan, Atlas, who has been known to uphold the world with his shoulder. Atlas was the son of Iapetus, who was also father to Prometheus.[456] They were Titans. Atlas joined the revolt of Titan against gods in Olympus and ended up getting punishment from Zeus to uphold forever the firmament of the heavens on his shoulders.[457] Hence the allusion of Atlas upholding the heavens forever with his shoulder appears to be similar to what More contended that the Ethereal region or the heavenly realm would not be affected by the apocalypse of the world. In other words, it signifies the heavens or the Ethereal region will be preserved forever. Even an ancient Korean Buddhist text mentions the heavenly realm, Dosolcheon, where Mireuk Bodhisattva resides, would not be affected by calamities arising from flood, fire, war, hunger,

---

[454] Plato, "Symposium," in *Six Great Dialogues*, trans. Benjamin Jowett (Mineola, New York: Dover Publications, Inc., 2007), 166.

[455] More, op. cit., chapter 3, sections 4–5.

[456] *New Larousse Encyclopedia of Mythology*, 93.

[457] Ibid.

poison, etc.[458] Hence, the signification of More mentioning the Ethereal region or the heavenly realm would not be affected by any disaster of the world is similar in both Eastern and Western texts. Furthermore, in the other section of the Greek text also mentions that Atlas is upholding the world with his shoulders;[459] thus, he could be perceived as upholding the heavenly realm, the Ethereal region, and the earthly realm, the Terrestrial region. Moreover, the connotation of Atlas's punishment was that he was the one who had strength to uphold the world and the heavens, which might be alluding to him being a half-god and half-man, who could have carried out the intermediary role between gods and mankind. If he did not possess such strength, Zeus might not have assigned him such punishment. Zeus probably utilized his strength as the punishment. Based on the context of the story, it is possible to presume Atlas might have achieved the union with his Self and the Universal Self; this is because the allusion of upholding the world with his shoulders has to do with his spiritual power, that is, the efficacy of him obtaining a higher state of enlightenment, or the *nirvana* enlightenment. This allusion is somewhat similar to Wolmyung in the *Samgook Yusa* story, whose flute playing sound even stopped the moon from passing, which connotes Wolmyung's spiritual power could even affect the moon's movement. This also symbolizes Wolmyung achieved the union with his Self and the Universal Self; thus, he could affect the moon's movement, as aforementioned in comparing the experience of Jiddu Krishnamurti's union with the Universal

---

[458] Hae-choon Rhu, op. cit., 431.

[459] *New Larousse Encyclopedia of Mythology*, 177.

Self. In the same perspective, Atlas could be seen as the figure who had achieved the higher state of enlightenment; thus, he obtained extraordinary spiritual power to carry out the intermediary role between gods and mankind and to uphold the universe and the heavenly realm on his shoulder. According to More, the heavenly realm can only be resided by the gods who achieved the utmost purity of the soul, and Atlas was assigned to uphold the firmament of the heavens with his shoulder, which alludes to him holding with his pure spiritual power because the heavens can only be occupied by the purest souls; hence, it is inconceivable to perceive Atlas holding the heavenly realm physically, and the same logic applies for him upholding the earthly realm. This is just a metaphor of him upholding the world with his spiritual power.

Another figure, similar to Atlas, who might have achieved a higher state of enlightenment, the *nirvana* enlightenment, thus could be perceived as a half-god and half-man and effectuated an intermediary role between Zeus and mankind: Prometheus. His name means "wisdom to see into the future."[460] Prometheus did not join the other Titans' revolt against the Olympian gods, so he could visit them at his will; then one day he stole fire from the Olympians for mankind, thus he ended up punished by Zeus for thirty years being chained at the top of Caucasus Mountain and his liver pecked by an eagle, but he was released from the punishment by Hercules with Zeus's permission.[461] Right after he was released, he went down to Hades for a while and later

---

[460] Ibid., 93.
[461] Ibid., 93, 95.

got substituted with an immortal, Chiron, in the heavens; thus, Prometheus could ascend to the heavens and became a god; then the source says that "Athenians, who saw in Prometheus the benefactor of mankind and the father of all the arts and sciences, raised an altar to him in the gardens of the Academy."[462] Prometheus enabled mankind to start a civilization, and later he became a god; thus, he was worshiped as the founder of the civilization.

However, before Prometheus became a god, he could be deemed a half-god and half-man, a *daemon*, who conducted an intermediary role between Zeus and mankind, just like how Pyohoon, Jeomgae, and Wolmyung appear in the stories of the *Samgook Yusa*. As Pyohoon ascended to the heavenly palace to convey King Gyungdeok's wish to have a male heir to the Heavenly Emperor, Prometheus also visited the heavenly palace to meet Zeus and carried out a mediating role between the gods and mankind. In the Pyohoon story, Ilyeon referred to Pyohoon as a saint;[463] thus, he could be seen as a half-god and half-man, or he could even be perceived as a god. According to Eliade, in Eastern religions, there are beliefs that a mankind can become a god by practicing various religious cultivation methods, which can be understood as the creation of a new transcendental mankind.[464] This is the point Gopi Krishna stressed in his book, the *Kundalini*, by meditation method, he had awakened the *kundalini* and activated the function of seven *chakras*; thus, he

---

[462] Ibid., 95.

[463] Ilyeon, "The Pyohoon Story," *Samgook Yusa*, 168.

[464] Eliade, *l'eternel retour*.

says that mankind can accomplish transcendental consciousness; consequently, mankind can become a completely transcendental figure.[465] Even the enlightenment stories in the *Samgook Yusa* and "Princess Bari," all make the same references to mankind utilizing some kind of cultivation methods, that is, the Mahayana Buddhism cultivation method, Hinayana Buddhism cultivation method, Hindu Brahmin cultivation method, or *poongrhudo* method, etc.; thereby, they gain enlightenment or the *nirvana* enlightenment, and they effectuate some efficacies (i.e., carry out the intermediary role between gods and mankind, possess spiritual power to help others, and gain the ability to transport the deceased souls to the other world).

Thereon the figures who gained the higher state of enlightenment can help mankind in various ways and make them possible to exist in this world. Eros strengthens the relationship between gods and mankind and also between mankind by love; furthermore, he enables mankind to continue and preserve their races. Atlas makes the whole world operate normally by upholding the world with his shoulders, thus making it possible for mankind and other beings to exist in this world. Prometheus, by bringing fire to mankind, enabled them to start their civilization. Pyohoon carried out the intermediary role between the Heavenly Emperor and King Gyungdeok, as well as the role of a foreseer. Jeomgae brought about reincarnating Daesung to a higher status in his afterlife; thus, he enabled Daesung to build the famous Buddhist architecture for his past-life and present-life parents. Hence, he enabled Daesung

---

[465] Gopi Krishna, *Kundalini*.

to conduct loyalty to his country as well as filial piety to his parents. Jinjeong and Princess Bari can transport the deceased souls to a higher realm of the other world. All these figures' achievements were possible because they have gotten the higher state of enlightenment; hence, they became like a half-god and half-man, transcendental beings.

Walter T. Stace mentioned that Western religions (i.e., Christianity) emphasized that people who gained mystical abilities, so to speak, who obtained enlightenment should share their abilities with other people in society; however, Eastern religions (i.e., Hinduism, Buddhism, etc.) do not emphasize the notion of sharing their mystical abilities with society.[466] Nevertheless, he perceived Mahayana Buddhism as the exception; especially, Bodhisattvas in Mahayana Buddhism took mankind's salvation as their highest goal, therefore Stace considered their pursuit as similar to the Western religions' pursuit.[467] His criticism on the Eastern religions is reasonable. Even the compiler and commentator of the *Samgook Yusa*, Ilyeon, censured his followers about what Stace was criticizing; hence, Ilyeon sometimes covertly and at other moments overtly emphasized what was an ideal of the Mahayana Buddhism monk's behavior as representing an ideal Bodhisattva in the book. However, what mystics contribute to society overtly does not necessarily represent whether they share what they have obtained; whether mystics have shared their abilities overtly or not, they became enlightened because they have contributed to

---

[466] Stace, *Teachings of the Mystics*, 26.
[467] Ibid.

society and could have continuously been making some kind of benefits to the community covertly based on their given function and destiny in society. They were given enlightenment because their abilities were needed for society. Their mystical abilities could be used in more advanced levels of society. These mystics, the enlightened beings (i.e., Atlas and Wolmyung), were related with the world's operation, and Eros strengthened people's relationship with gods and among people. Prometheus and Pyohoon, who were foreseers and intermediaries between gods and mankind, thus could foretell some catastrophes that would occur in the future. There are also Jinjeong, Jeomgae, and Princess Bari, who transport the deceased souls to a higher realm of the other world (i.e., *Nirvana*, the Lotus World, or the heavens). As Henry More was concerned about the immortality of pious and virtuous souls residing in the Aerial region, if the Conflagration of the Earth would occur, who could delay such an apocalypse from happening until more virtuous souls ascend to the Ethereal region or the heavenly realm? It might be figures like Atlas and Wolmyung, who had spiritual power to uphold the world or control the stars' movement, respectively; Prometheus and Pyohoon, who were foreseers and intermediaries between the gods and mankind—they could lead mankind to safety and offer advice about what to do if such a cataclysm arises; then Jinjeong, Jeomgae, and Princess Bari, specialists of the other world, could help the deceased souls to ascend to a higher realm and thus bring about salvation for those souls. We need more of these types of enlightened people. As we can see in the actual ritual practices of "Princess Bari," one princess obtained the *nirvana* enlightenment and gained the ability to go back and forth between this world to the other world; there have been numerous shamanesses who have been borrowing her ability in the shamanic rituals. Therefore, when one person gains the higher state of enlightenment, many people can share it and benefit from it.

Mystics who have gotten the higher state of enlightenment, the *nirvana* enlightenment, signify that they have reached the union with their Self and the Universal Self; therefore, their consciousnesses have expanded beyond ordinary mankind, and their states of being could be extraordinary, universal, or transcendent of a country, culture, language, period, religion, etc. Likewise, if more people obtain the higher state of enlightenment, the *nirvana* enlightenment, they can achieve the union with their Self and the Universal Self. Thus, they could gain extraordinary spiritual power, enabling them to uphold the world or delay calamities from happening in the future; in this way, they would make it possible for more virtuous souls to ascend to the heavenly realm and hence could offer them immortality or salvation. This could be the ultimate goal of the ones who have achieved the higher state of enlightenment or the *nirvana* enlightenment.

CHAPTER 5

CONCLUSION

In the treatise, I examined seven stories recorded in the *Samgook Yusa* and an orally transmitted shamanic song "Princess Bari" in the aspect of their enlightenment experiences. Then I compared the enlightenment stories in the *Samgook Yusa* with other countries' mystical experience texts, and "Princess Bari" to the *Cinderella*, which is known as the story of obtaining wisdom in the West. Therefore, I could probe into the Korean enlightenment stories' unique and universal elements compared to other countries' enlightenment experiences sources.

In chapter 1, I analyzed the previous research on the topic related to the enlightenment experience in the Korean literature articles and other countries' scholars' research on the actual mystical experiences survey done in India and China. Based on their research results, I realized examining enlightenment-related literature could provide some positive insight on the topic; thus, I decided to examine recorded stories in the *Samgook Yusa* and an orally transmitted shamanic song "Princess Bari" to find out how enlightenment experiences are expressed differently between different genre stories. Moreover, comparing these sources also provided information on how men's and women's enlightenment experiences are similar or dissimilar. In the Korean text, there are many sources referring to men's enlightenment experiences, but women's enlightenment experience sources are rare, and they usually appear in the stories as helpers of men's enlightenment. In this regard, "Princess Bari" provides quite valuable information on how a woman gains enlightenment. Based on the examination of both sources, and other countries' texts, the enlightenment experiences seem to transcend culture, religion, period, country, language, gender, etc., although more cross-culture and cross-genre research are needed.

In chapter 2, I analyzed the meaning of enlightenment, in two aspects: enlightenment, that is, attaining wisdom, and the *nirvana* enlightenment, a higher stage of enlightenment. The *nirvana* enlightenment is fully matured, an advanced stage of enlightenment, in which the mystic can enter *Nirvana* at will. The meaning of the *nirvana* enlightenment can be used in two different ways: (1) The mystic completely cuts loose from the ties of the world; thus, he or she gets to join into *Nirvana* or the heavenly realm permanently, which means not fated to be reincarnated to this world. (2) It is possible to enter the *nirvana* enlightenment while alive for a few minutes, hours, or days by completely cutting off from sensory cognizances and being united within oneself. This experience is called the introvertive mystical experience by Western philosophers of mysticism.[468] The enlightenment stories I examined in the treatise, mostly are referring to the *nirvana* enlightenment experience while alive. There are a few stories that indicate wisdom obtaining stage

---

[468] Stace, *Teachings of the Mystics*, 17–22, 83.

of enlightenment that is called by Western philosophers as the extrovertive mystical experience.[469]

In the chapter, I compared Jitong's and Eckhart's extrovertive mystical experiences and found similar elements between their experiences. Then I also compared Eckhart's extrovertive mystical experience, in which he expressed the One as the principal essence of nature, with the second-century Stoic, Aurelius's expression about Oneness: they seem to be referring to a similar entity of the One or the Oneness. Afterward, in analyzing the *nirvana* enlightenment, I first conveyed different views of contention between the Perennialist and Constructivist: the Perennialist asserts that mystics' experiences transcend the period, country, language, religion, culture, etc., and contends for the common-core theory; the Constructivist argues mystics' experiences are all different and asserts for the diverse theory. For the sources examining the *nirvana* enlightenment, or the introvertive mystical experience, I compared Eckhart's and Ruysbroeck's mystical experience sources to "Katha Upanishad" and found out they were expressing the same *nirvana* enlightenment experience or the introvertive mystical experience. Thereafter, I compared Jinjeong's seven days of meditation with the above sources and realized that they were referring to the same experience. Based on these examinations, Rudolf Otto's contention that Eckhart's mystical experiences were similar to Plotinus of Greece, Shankara of India, and mystics of Mahayana Buddhism is convincing. Furthermore, I analyzed Princess Bari's *nirvana* enlightenment and compared it

---

[469] Ibid., 15–17.

to Jinjeong's *nirvana* enlightenment and discovered some similar elements with the aforementioned Upanishad; therefore, their *nirvana* enlightenments are deemed to have some similarities.

In chapter 3, I inquired into the enlightenment methodologies represented in the Nohill and Daldal story, the Jitong story in the *Samgook Yusa*, and "Princess Bari." In the Nohill and Daldal story, Nohill symbolized the Mahayana Buddhism (the Greater Vehicle Buddhism) cultivation method and Daldal, the Hinayana Buddhism (the Lesser Vehicle Buddhism) cultivation method. Nohill obtained the *nirvana* enlightenment by helping a woman who was an avatar of Avalokitesvara and thus received the Bodhisattva's response; whereas Daldal only cared for his enlightenment and thus could not receive Avalokitesvara's response, but with the help from Nohill, he also gained enlightenment. Nevertheless, the story said that Daldal's enlightenment was not as perfect as Nohill's. Based on these distinctions, Ilyeon covertly expressed what is the Mahayana Buddhist monk's proper behavior as he represents an ideal Bodhisattva, which he deemed to be following in Mahayana Buddhism. The Jitong story illustrated how Jitong gained enlightenment after he received the Buddhist monk's precepts from Bohyun Bodhisattva. However, the story was not about which cultivation method he followed; it rather connoted that his sacredness and earnestness were united in one mind, which affected the Bodhisattva's response; thus, he acquired enlightenment. As aforementioned, his experience was a worldly common extrovertive mystical experience, which does not pertain to just one type of religious follower but commonly exists among different religions' followers because his mystical experience arose from a concentrated mind based on his sacredness and earnestness, and that is a common nature exists among mankind.

The Princess Bari story also illustrated she gained the *nirvana* enlightenment by having the union with the god Musang in the other world. This is a shamanic song but contains several religious elements (i.e., Buddhism, Confucianism, immortality, Hinduism, and the ancient Mesopotamian purification ceremony), as well as heroism that seemed to be influenced by *poongrhudo*, which has existed since ancient Korea. *Poongrhudo* was tolerant of different religions transmitted to Korea and accepted their differences for the sake of social harmony and peaceful life. However, the way Princess Bari obtains the *nirvana* enlightenment by having the sacred marriage to the shaman god Musang, which is an element similar to how Nohill gains his *nirvana* enlightenment by having the union with Avalokitesvara. Moreover, their union with the god and the goddess, respectively, could have occurred in their *sahasrara chakra*, just like the union of Shiva and Shakti. Furthermore, Princess Bari's union with the god Musang has some similarity with Cinderella marrying the prince at the end. Nevertheless, the difference between them is that Cinderella alludes to gaining wisdom, which is the earlier stage of enlightenment, although the Jitong story mentions his wisdom is good enough to enter *Nirvana*, so there seems to be an exception; then Princess Bari signifies to gain the *nirvana* enlightenment in the other world. The Princess Bari story alludes to her being born with wisdom from the onset because she was the seventh princess, and the number seven symbolizes wisdom.[470] Moreover, she travels to the other world to look for the water of life for her dying parents, and she ends up gaining the *nirvana* enlightenment by having the union with the god Musang. The *Cinderella* ends the story when she marries the prince, which alludes to her gaining wisdom or enlightenment, but Princess Bari returns to this world and resuscitates her parents after she acquired the *nirvana* enlightenment; thus, the story includes the offering of the efficacy of her gained spiritual power. When we perceive only the attribute of how Princess Bari gains the *nirvana* enlightenment, by having the sacred union with the god, this is similar to how Nohill obtains the *nirvana* enlightenment by having the union with Avalokitesvara, and how Cinderella acquires her enlightenment by marrying the prince. Hence, the way they gain enlightenment, having the union with the deity, is similar; therefore, their enlightenment experiences transcend language, country, period, religion, culture, etc., although more cross-culture and cross-genre comparative research are needed.

In chapter 4, I explored the necessity of gaining enlightenment suggested in the stories of the *Samgook Yusa* and "Princess Bari" in three aspects: (1) Communicating with a god is possible. (2) Gaining spiritual power is possible by having the union with one's Self and the Universal Self or a god. (3) Offering salvation is possible by transporting the deceased souls to a higher realm. In the Pyohoon story, Pyohoon is able to ascend to heaven and meet the Heavenly Emperor to convey King Gyungdeok's wish to have a male heir to

---

[470] See footnote 6.

his throne, and this was possible because he had gained such qualification by obtaining the high stage of enlightenment, the *nirvana* enlightenment. This supposition is possible because Ilyeon referred to him as a saint at the end of the story. Thus, Pyohoon can be deemed a highly enlightened, a half-god and half-man figure. According to Henry More, only a figure who obtained perfect purity can ascend to the Ethereal region or the heavenly realm, and angelic figures usually reside in the highest point of the Aerial region.[471] Pyohoon was connoted a saint by Ilyeon; thus, he probably resided the highest point of the Aerial region and had visited the heavenly realm at his will until the Heavenly Emperor forbade him to visit. Until then, he was able to effectuate an intermediary role between the Heavenly Emperor and King Gyungdeok because he had gained the *nirvana* enlightenment and reached sainthood.

The Samso-Guaneum story and the Wolmyung story are about Buddhist monks who have gained the union with their Self and the Universal Self. The head monk of the Joongsengsa temple, Sung-tae, in the Samso-Guaneum story had significant spiritual power, yet he had hidden his power and made the Bodhisattva effigy famous for granting good fortunes for the people, so the temple continued with its fame for offering good luck to people. Wolmyung in the Wolmyung story had obtained a high level of enlightenment that he was known for the wonderful flute-playing sound that could even stop the moon

---

[471] More, op. cit., axiom 28, chapter 3, sections 1, 9 and chapter 9, section 8.

from passing. The allusion was that his spiritual power reached such a high level that it could even affect an astrological body.

The Jinjeong story and Daesung story illustrate highly enlightened Buddhist monks, Jinjeong and Jeomgae, could understand the nature of the other world by entering deep meditation; thus, they were able to transport the deceased souls: Jinjeong's mother to heaven and Daesung reincarnated to a promoted social status, respectively. Jinjeong was able to transport his deceased mother's soul to heaven with his teacher's, Uisang's, help. However, based on More's theory on the nature of the deceased souls, it seemed that Jinjeong's decedent mother's purity of soul was what attracted to Uisang's ninety days of lectures on *Hwaum Daejeon*, which enabled her to gain wisdom and thus purified her soul even more to enter the heavenly realm. Therefore, Jinjeong, Uisang, and Jinjeong's mother—all three efforts were equally important in his deceased mother's ascension to heaven. Then Daesung's reincarnation as Silla's prime minister's son with the help of a well-known Buddhist monk, Jeomgae, made him famous for building reputable Buddhist temple, the Boolgooksa, for his present-life parents and the Buddhist stone grotto, the Seokgoolarm, for his past-life parents. Therefore, Daesung became famous for constructing well-known Buddhist architecture and for fulfilling his duty of filial piety to his parents. These were possible because Daesung met a greatly enlightened Buddhist monk, Jeomgae.

The story of the shamanic song "Princess Bari" expresses that she gained the *nirvana* enlightenment by having the union with the god Musang in the other world. Before she gained enlightenment, she was able to release the deceased souls trapped in hell by shaking an implement, the *rahwa*, given by Shakyamuni; but after she obtained the *nirvana* enlightenment, she could transport decedent souls to the other world by herself. Therefore, both sources in the *Samgook Yusa* and "Princess Bari" indicate figures who have acquired the *nirvana* enlightenment can effectuate transporting the deceased souls to the other world; hence, they can offer them salvation.

There is another source that stresses the necessity of transporting the deceased souls to the heavenly realm. Henry More, who was a seventeenth-century Platonic philosopher, mentioned there were three regions in this world: the Terrestrial, the Aerial, and the Ethereal regions; he perceived, like other ancient philosophers' view, the deceased souls' residence was the Aerial region, except gods, who achieved perfect purity and who could reside in the Ethereal region, and angelic figures reside in the highest Aerial region.[472] More's main concern with the salvation of the deceased souls had to do with the world's apocalypse (i.e., the Conflagration of the Earth and Extinction of the Sun); he perceived only the Ethereal region, the heavenly realm, would be unharmed from such apocalypse, but all other souls dwelling in the Terrestrial and the Aerial regions would be lost forever unless supernatural power in the heavenly realm offer some kind of help.[473] Therefore, transporting decedent souls to the heavenly realm or the Ethereal region could offer salvation to those decedent souls residing elsewhere. However, as More

---

[472] Ibid.
[473] Ibid., chapter 18, sections 5, 15.

mentioned, decedent souls ascending to the Ethereal region, the heavenly realm, was impossible unless they became perfectly pure like gods or were very noble and heroic. Then the only way more decedent souls can gain time to enter the heavenly realm would be to delay the apocalypse of the world.

How can we delay the apocalypse of the world? The existence of the apocalypse of the world in the future has been known ever since ancient civilizations of the world. Even the Korean myth of the creation of the world, "Changsae Shinhwa," mentions the apocalypse would occur due to time and tide. Thus, all ancient sources indicate the apocalypse would occur sometime in the future but could not predict exactly when it would occur. Perhaps it has to do with how we treat our environment and what kind of relationship we have with gods or supernatural power. Based on the enlightenment stories I inquired into, there are some possibilities for how to delay the apocalypse. For example, in the Wolmyung story, the allusion of—his flute playing even made the passing moon stop to listen to his flute playing—it could be that his flute playing talent reached a certain level that it could even influence the moon's movement. In other words, this is just a metaphor for Wolmyung's high spiritual power that could even affect an astronomical body. Another allusion is to Atlas, mentioned in Greek myth. Atlas was fated to uphold the world and the firmament of the heavens with his shoulders.[474] So to speak, Atlas upholding the firmament of the heavens with his shoulders only makes sense if we understand it in the form of spiritual

---

[474] *New Larousse Encyclopedia of Mythology*, 93.

power. As More mentioned, only perfectly pure souls like gods can stay in the Ethereal region or the heavenly realm. Thus, Atlas upholding the heavens in his physical form is not conceivable. Therefore, this allusion is another metaphor that illustrates Atlas was a highly enlightened figure with extraordinary spiritual power enough to hold an astronomical body. Based on these stories, we can perceive it is possible to affect an astronomical body with spiritual power. Therefore, if more people gain the high-level enlightenment, the *nirvana* enlightenment, more people can uphold the world with their spiritual power that it would be possible to delay the apocalypse of the world in various ways.

The Pyohoon story conveys how the highly enlightened monk Pyohoon carried out an intermediary role between the Heavenly Emperor and King Gyungdeok; hence, he enabled them to communicate with each other. In the same way, Prometheus in Greek myth also effected an intermediary role between Zeus and mankind. He even brought fire from the Olympian gods to his people and thus enabled them to start their civilization.[475] Moreover, Prometheus, as a foreseer, let his son Deucalion and his wife, Pyrrha, prepare for the Flood and made them possible to survive it, and later they became the progenitors of mankind.[476] These highly enlightened figures like Pyohoon and Prometheus allowed mankind to have a relationship with gods or supernatural power in the heavenly realm. Pyohoon was referred to as a saint in the text; hence, it makes it possible

---

[475] Ibid.

[476] Ibid., 93–94.

to suppose he had acquired the *nirvana* enlightenment. Prometheus was known for his wisdom and being a progenitor of civilization; thus, it enables us to hypothesize him as the one who acquired a high stage of enlightenment, just like his brother Atlas. These highly enlightened figures (i.e., Wolmyung, Atlas, Pyohoon, and Prometheus) could provide the means to delay the apocalypse of the world by utilizing their wisdom and spiritual power.

While researching the enlightenment stories in the *Samgook Yusa* to prepare for this treatise, I have been overwhelmingly surprised by how Buddhist practical aspects coincided with the *Upanishads'* theoretical aspects, and the theory of the Western mysticism (i.e., the extrovertive mystical experience and the introvertive mystical experience), as well as how they accorded with Rudolf Otto's contention of Eckhart's mystical experiences were similar to Plotinus of Greece, Shankara of India, and mystics of Mahayana Buddhism. Moreover, uncovering the enlightenment stories recorded in the *Samgook Yusa*, which were compiled and commentated by Ilyeon, the way he alluded deep meanings, layered in multifarious form with such terse expressions was amazing. The more I probed into the enlightenment stories, the more details could be discovered, like finding hidden messages written on blank wax papers; by shining candlelight on them, one can encounter the hidden messages.

I have also been astonished by how different religious elements are well syncretised in the shamanic song "Princess Bari"; they are well harmonized and balanced, becoming natural parts of the shamanic song. Such a mixture of different religious elements in the song was possible because Koreans accepted *poongrhudo*, which tolerated other religions for social harmony and peaceful life. The Princess Bari story I probed in the treatise well reflected their wish for a happy life in this world and their desire for immortality in the other world. Likewise, the shamanic song "Princess Bari" illustrates their unconscious value, paralleling the ideal of *poongrhudo*. Moreover, the song voices brilliantly how the Goddess of Necromancer gained the *nirvana* enlightenment and the legitimacy to transport decedent souls to the other world.

BIBLIOGRAPHY

Anthony, Francis-Vincent, Chris A. M. Hermans, and Carl Sterkens. "Comparative Study of Mystical Experience Among Christian, Muslim, and Hindu Students in Tamil Nadu, India." *Journal for the Scientific Study of Religion* 49, no. 2 (June 2010): 264–77.

Bari Gongjoo Jeonjib (The complete collection of "Princess Bari") 2 vols. Ed. Jin-young Kim and Tae-hwan Hong. Seoul: Minsokwon, 1997.

Baring, Anne and Jules Cashford. *The Myth of the Goddess: Evolution of an Image*. London: Arkana, Penguin Books, 1993.

Bayley, Harold. *The Lost Language of Symbolism*. 1912. Reprint, London: Forgotten Books, 2015.

Chen, Zhuo, Ralph W. Hood Jr., Wen Qi, and D. J. Watson. "Common Core Thesis and Qualitative and Quantitative Analysis of Mysticism in Chinese Buddhist Monks and Nuns." *Journal for the Scientific Study of Religion* 50, no. 4 (December 2011): 654–70.

Cho, Dong-il. *Samgook Sidae Seolhwa-ui Theut Pullyi*. Seoul: Jibmoondang, 1990.

Cho, Hyun-seol. "Baridaeki-wa Moo-ui Yunli." *Gookmoonhark Yeongoo* (Gookmoonharkhui) 37 (2018).

Cho, Pyung-hwan. "Mita Sasang-gua Hyangga." *Gyeorae Ermoonhark* (Geongookdae Guger Gookmoonhark Yeongoohui) 19 (1995).

Choi, Seon-gyung. "Women's Images Denoted in the *Samgook Yusa*." *Hangook Gojeon Yeosung Moonhark Yeongoo* (Hangook Gojeon Yeosung Moonharkhui) 16 (2008).

Cox, Marian Roalfe. *Three Hundred and Forty-Five Variants of Cinderella, Catskin, and Capo'Rushes: Abstracted and Tabulated, with a Discussion of Medieval Analogies and Notes*. 1893. Reprint, London: Forgotten Books, 2014. E-book.

Dumezil, Georges. *Mitra-Varuna: An Essay on Two Indo-European Representations of Sovereignty*. Trans. Derek Coltman. New York: Zone Books, 1988.

Dundes, Alan. "Structural Typology in North American Indian Folktales." In *The Study of Folklore*, 206–65. Englewood Cliffs: Prentice Hall, 1965.

Eliade, Mercea. "Shamanism: An Overview." *Encyclopedia of Religion* 13 (1987): 201–8.

———. *Shamanism: Archaic Technique of Ecstasy*. Trans. William R. Trask. 2d ed. Princeton: Bollingen Paperback Printing, 1974.

Forman, Robert K. C. "Paramartha and Modern Constructivists on Mysticism: Epistemological Monomorphism Versus Duomorphism." *Philosophy East and West* 39, no. 4 (October 1989).

Gellman, Jerome. "Mysticism." *The Stanford Encyclopedia of Philosophy* (Summer 2019 Edition). Edward N. Zalta, ed. https://plato.stanford.edu/archives/sum2019/entries/mysticism/.

Go, Woon-ki. *Ilyeon*. Seoul: Hankilsa, 1997.

Gooksa Pyunchan Wewonhui, comp. "Eumsa, Seungsang, Geotchirae-deungui Biruhan Poongsok-eul Cheoljeohe Geumji shikida." *Joseon Wangjo Sillok*. Sejong 76. 19th year. February 14, 1437. The Fourth Article.

———. "Moogyuck-ui Poongsok-gua Eumsa-reul Geumhada." *Joseon Wangjo Sillok*. Sungjong 88. 9th year. January 20, 1478. The Sixth Article.

Guthrie, W. K. C. *Orpheus and Greek Religion*. London: Methuen, 1935.

Hesiod. *Theogony and Works and Days*. Trans. M. L. West. Oxford World's Classics. Oxford: Oxford University Press, 2008.

Hong, Sung-arm. "Poongrhudo-ui Yinyum-gua Moonharkae-ui Sooyong Yangsang." *Hanminjok Moonhwa Yeongoo* (Hanminjok Moonhwaharkhui) 1 (1996).

Ilyeon, comp. *Samgook Yusa*. Trans. Won-joong Kim. Seoul: Eulyu Moonhwasa, 2003.

Jang, Young-lan. "Hangook Shinhwasok-ui Yeosung-ui Juchae Uishik-gua Mosung Shinhwa-ui   J e o n b o k j e o k Kijae." *Hangook Yeosung Cheolhark* (Hangook Yeosung Cheolharkhui) 8 (2007).

Jung, C. G. *The Redbook*. Ed. Sonu Shamdasani. New York: W. W. Norton and Company, 2009.

Katz, Steven T. "Language Epistemology and Mysticism." In *Mysticism and Philosophical Analysis.* Ed. Steven T. Katz, 22–74. New York: Oxford University Press, 1978.

Kim, Bu-shik. *Samgook Saki.* Comm. by Jong-sung Kim. Seoul: Janglark, 2004.

Kim, Chang-won. "*Samgook Yusa* Gamtong-ui Hyangga Ilki: Hergoojeok Saegae-ui Jinshil." *Gookjae Ermoon* (Gookjae Ermoonharkhui) 31 (2004).

Kim, Doo-jin. "Silla Uisang-gae Hwaumjong-ui 'Hyoseon Ssangmi-ui Shinang.'" *Hangookhark Nonchong* (Korean Study Center, Gookmin University) 15 (1992).

Kim, Heon-seon. *Hangook-ui Changsae Shinhwa.* Seoul: Gilbut, 1994.

———. "Bari Gongjoo-ui Yeosung Shinhwajeok Sunggyuck Yeongoo." *Jonggyo-wa Moonhwa* (Seoul University) 1 (2004).

———. "Jeoseung-eul Yeohenghaneun Yeoshin-ui Bigyo Yeongoo: Bari Gongjoo, Cheon Choong-hee, and Inanna." *Bigyo Minsokhark* (Bigyo Minsokharkhui) 33 (2007).

Kim, Hwa-gyung. *Saegae Shinhwa Sokui Yeosungdeul.* Seoul: Dowon Media, 2003.

Kim, Hwan-hee. "Shamanist Myth of 'Princess Bari' and Its Western Counterparts: Comparative Study of the Tales of the Water of Life." *Comparative Korean Studies* 10, no. 1 (2002).

Kim, Jong-ui. *Minsok Harksool Jaryo Chongseo Moosok 8.* Seoul: Doseo Choolpan Woori Madang Ter, 2005.

Kim, Jong-woo. *Hyangga Moonhark Yeongoo*. Seoul: Yiwoo Choolpansa, 1978.

Kim, Moon-tae. "Samgook Yusa Sojae Daebijeok Inmool-ui Deukdo Yangsang." *Gojeon Moonhark Yeongoo* (Hangook Gojeon Moonharkhui) 41 (2012).

Kim, Seok-su. "Cheolharkjeok Guanjeom-aeseo Bon Hangookyin-ui Joogeumguan: Seoyang Cheolhark-ui Joogeumguan-gua Guanlyeonhayeo." *Hangookyin-ui Joogeum-gua Salm*. Seoul: Cheolhark-gua Hyunsilsa, 2001.

Kim, Seung-chan. "Silla Jeongto Wangseng Sasang-gua Hyangga." *Inmoon Nonchong* (Busan University) 28, no. 1 (1985).

———. *Hangook Sanggo Moonharklon*. Seoul: Saemoonsa, 1987.

Kim, Tae-gon. "Hangook Moosok-ui Naesaeguan." *Hangook Jonggyosa Yeongoo* (Hangook Jonggyosa Harkhui) 1 (1972).

Kramer, Samuel Noah. *Sumerian Mythology: A Study of Spiritual and Literary Achievement in the Third Millennium B.C.* Rev. ed. Philadelphia: University of Pennsylvania Press, 1972.

———, ed. *Mythologies of the Ancient World*. Garden City, NY: Anchor Books, Doubleday and Company, Inc., 1961.

Krishna, Gopi. *Kundalini*. Trans. Ki-cheon Yu. Seoul: Goryowon Media, 1991.

Lee, Dae-hyung. "Samgook Yusa-ae Natanan Mosung-ui Hyungsanghwa." *Hangook Gojeon Yeosung Moonhark Yeongoo*. (Hangook Gojeon Yeosung Moonharkhui) 14 (2007).

Lee, Gang-ok. "*Samgook Yusa* Choolga Deukdodam mit Choolga Sungbooldam-ui Chosesok Jihyang Yangsang." *Gojeon Moonhark Yeongoo* (Hangook Gojeon Moonharkhui) 30 (2006).

Lee, Ki-baek. *Silla Sidae-ui Gookga Boolgyo-wa Yoogyo*. Seoul: Hangook Yeongoowon, 1978.

Lutyens, Mary. *Krishnamurti*. Trans. Shi-hwa Rhu. Seoul: Jeongshin Saegaesa, 1985.

Marlow, A. N. "Hinduism and Buddhism in Greek Philosophy." *Philosophy East and West* 4, no. 1 (April 1954).

More, Henry. "Immortality of the Soul." The Third Book. In *A Collection of Several Philosophical Writings*. 2d ed. London: James Flejher, 1662. E-book.

New Larousse Encyclopedia of Mythology. Trans. Richard Aldington and Delano Ames. New York, NY: Crescent Books, 1986.

Otto, Rudolf. *Mysticism East and West: A Comparative Analysis of the Nature of Mysticism*. Trans. Bertha L. Bracey and Richenda C. Payne. Eugene, OR: Wipf and Stock Publishers, 2016.

Owen, Stephen, trans. and ed. *Anthology of Chinese Culture: Beginnings to 1911*. New York: W. W. Norton and Company, 1996.

Plato. "Phaedrus." In *Six Great Dialogues*. Trans. Benjamin Jowett, 93–139. Mineola, NY: Dover Publications, Inc., 2007.

———. "Symposium." In *Six Great Dialogues*. Trans. Benjamin Jowett, 141–82. Mineola, NY: Dover Publications, Inc., 2007.

———. "The Republic." In *Six Great Dialogues*. Trans. Benjamin Jowett, 183–460. Mineola, NY: Dover Publications, Inc., 2007.

Rhu, Hae-choon. "Wolmyungsa-ui Hyangga Moonhark-gua Geu Baegyung Seolhwa-ui Yeongoo." *Ermoon Nonchong* (Gyungbook Ermoonharkhui) 31, no. 1 (1997).

Ruysbroeck, Jan van. *The Adornment of the Spiritual Marriage*. Trans. C. A. Wynschenck, DOM. London: J. M. Dent and Sons, Ltd., 1916.

Seo, Cheol-won, "Hyangga geurigo *Samgook Yusa*-reul Tonghae Bon Sillayin-ui Naesae Guannyum." *Hangook Shiga Yeongoo* (Hangook Shigaharkhui) 37 (2014).

Seo, Dae-seok. "Bari Gongjoo Yeongoo." *Hangook Mooga-ui Yeongoo*. Seoul: Moonhark Sasangsa, 1997.

Seo, Gyung-hee. "Samgook Yusa-ae Natanan Hwaumseon-ui Moonharkjeok Hyungsanghwa." Ph D diss. Seogang University, 2004.

Sohn, Jin-tae. *Joseon Shin-Ga-Yoo-Pyeon*. Japan, 1930.

Song, Soon. *Yuckdae Sijo Jeonseo*. Ed. Jae-wan Shim. Seoul: Sejong Moonhwasa, 1972.

Stace, Walter T., ed. *The Teachings of the Mystics: Selections from the Great Mystics and Mystical Writings of the World*. New York, NY: A Mentor Book, 1960.

Stewart, John Alexander, MA, trans. *The Myths of Plato*. 1905. Reprint, London: Forgotten Books, 2013. E-book.

Sung, Ho-gyung. "Jaemang Maega-ui Shi Saegae." *Googer Gookmoonhark* (Googer Gookmoonharkhui) no. 143 (2006).

Suzuki, D. T. "The Basis of Buddhist Philosophy." In *Understanding Mysticism*. Ed. Richard Woods, 126–45. Garden City, NY: Image Books, 1980.

The Dhammapada. Trans. S. Radhakrishnan. Oxford: Oxford University Press, 1951.

The Upanishads. Trans. Swami Paramananda. San Bernardino, CA: Pantianos Classics, 2017.

Underhill, Evelyn. "The Essentials of Mysticism." In *Understanding Mysticism*. Ed. Richard Woods, 26–41. Garden City, NY: Image Books, 1980.

Webster's New Universal Unabridged Dictionary. 2d ed. New York, NY: Barnes and Noble Books, 2003.

Yu, Dong-shik. *Poongrhudo-wa Hangook-ui Jonggyo Sasang*. Seoul: Yeonsae University Press, 1997.

Yu, Seon-young. "Bari Gongjoo-reul Tonghaeseo Bon Hangookyin-ui Joogeumguan." *Hangook-ui Minsok-gua Moonhwa* (Minsokhark Yeongoo, Gyunghee University) 13 (December 2008).

Zimmer, Heinrich. *Myths and Symbols in Indian Arts and Civilization*. Ed. Joseph Campbell. Princeton, NJ: Princeton University Press, 2017.

Printed in the USA
CPSIA information can be obtained
at www.ICGtesting.com
JSHW020205180823
46668JS00017B/13